Charles Allen

Charles Allen was born in India, where six generations of his family served under the British Raj. He established his reputation with his celebrated oral histories, broadcast on BBC Radio and published as *Plain Tales from the Raj*, *Tales from the Dark Continent* and *Tales from the South China Seas*. *Soldier Sahibs: The Men Who Made the North-West Frontier*, was described as 'magnificent' (*Sunday Times*), 'a considerable achievement' (*The Spectator*) and 'marvellous' (*Daily Telegraph*). Charles Allen lives in Somerset.

THE BUDDHA
AND THE SAHIBS

*The men who discovered
India's lost religion*

Charles Allen

JOHN MURRAY

© Charles Allen 2002

First published in Great Britain in 2002 by John Murray (Publishers)
A division of Hodder Headline

Paperback edition 2003

The right of Charles Allen to be identified as the Author of the Work
has been asserted by him in accordance with the Copyright, Designs
and Patents Act 1988.

4

A CIP catalogue record for this title is available from the British Library

ISBN-13 978-0-7195-5428-5
ISBN-10 0-7195-5428-4

Typeset in Monotype Bembo by Servis Filmsetting Ltd, Manchester

Printed and bound by Clays Ltd, St Ives plc

Hodder Headline policy is to use papers that are natural, renewable and
recyclable products and made from wood grown in sustainable forests.
The logging and manufacturing processes are expected to conform to
the environmental regulations of the country of origin.

John Murray (Publishers)
338 Euston Road
London NW1 3BH

Naught but the Topes themselves remain to mock
Time's ceaseless efforts; yet they proudly stand
Silent and lasting upon their parent rock,
And still as cities under magic's wand;
Till curious Saxons, from a distant land,
Unlocked the treasures of two thousand years.

The Bhilsa Topes (Anon.), 1854

Contents

Illustrations

Line drawings in the text

List of illustrations

The author and publishers would like to thank the following for permission to reproduce illustrations: Plate 1, Oriental and India Office Collection at the British Library (hereafter OIOC) WD 14; 3, Mackenzie Collection, OIOC WD 698/24; 4, Royal Asiatic Society (hereafter RAS) 029.004; 5, OIOC MSS Eur. D. 95/224; 6, Ras 07.006; 7, V&A Picture Library Ct. No. 156844; 8, OIOC WD 4283; 9, Patrick Conner and Martyn Gregory Art Gallery; 10, OIOC WD 3478; 11, OIOC WD 4190; 12, OIOC WD 4027; 15, National Portrait Gallery, London, 1707; 16, RAS 022.020; 17, Royal Geographical Society T00617 X; 19, RAS 040.520; 20, Royal Engineers Library & Museum, Chatham; 21, OIOC Album WD 546/1b; 22, OIOC Add. Or. 4617; 23, OIOC 1000/2773; 25 and 26, Theosophical Society of India; 27, Foreign and Commonwealth Office Library; 28, OIOC SW 196/ Vol 26.1; 29 and 30, OIOC Photos 1007/4 D.739–740; 31, OIOC Photo 10/6/41. Plate 13 is taken from *Moore's Views of Rangoon*, 1825 and plate 18 from James Fergusson, *Illustrations of Rock-Cut Temples of India*, 1845.

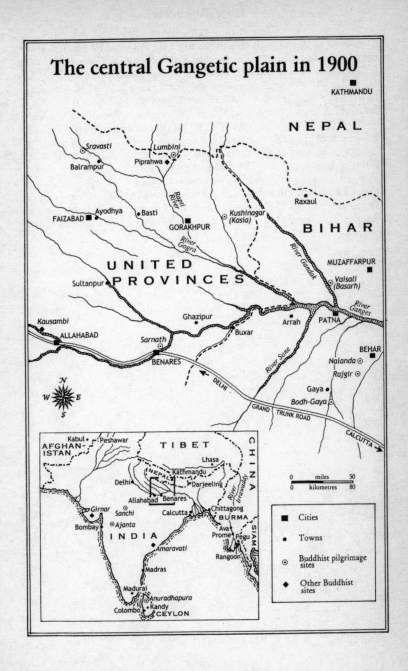

The central Gangetic plain in 1900

KATHMANDU

NEPAL

Sravasti
Lumbini
Balrampur
Piprahwa
Raxaul

BIHAR

Basti
Kushinagar
(Kasia)
FAIZABAD
Ayodhya
GORAKHPUR
Rapti River
River Gogra
MUZAFFARPUR

UNITED
PROVINCES
Sultanpur
Vaisali
(Basarh)
River Gandak
River Ganges

Kausambi
Ghazipur
Arrah
PATNA
ALLAHABAD
Buxar
BEHAR
Sarnath
River Sone
Nalanda
Rajgir
BENARES
Gaya
DELHI
Bodh-Gaya
GRAND TRUNK ROAD
CALCUTTA

N
W E
S

AFGHAN-
ISTAN
Kabul
Peshawar
TIBET
CHINA
Lhasa
Kathmandu
NEPAL
Delhi
Darjeeling
River Irrawaddy
Allahabad
Benares
Girnar
Sanchi
Chittagong
BURMA
Bombay
Ajanta
Calcutta
Ava
Prome
Pegu
INDIA
Amaravati
SIAM
Rangoon
Madras
Madurai
Anuradhapura
Kandy
Colombo
CEYLON

0   miles   50
0   kilometres   80

■ Cities

● Towns

⊙ Buddhist pilgrimage
   sites

◆ Other Buddhist
   sites

Prologue

The Orientalists

O N A warm afternoon in February 1997 I sat drinking tea on the lawn of the Director's bungalow beside the Archaeological Museum of Taxila in north Pakistan, surrounded by the ruins of five ancient cities. Taxila was a satrapy of the Achaeminid empire of the Persians in the sixth and fifth centuries before the Christian Era (BCE). Here in 326 BCE Alexander the Great met the exiled Sandrokottos, who then returned to India to overthrow a royal dynasty and establish his own at the great city of Pataliputra beside the Ganges. One generation later the young prince Ashoka Maurya ruled over Taxila as a viceroy to his father, King Bindusara, son of Sandrokottos, before returning to Pataliputra to establish himself as the first emperor of India and the first to propagate the teachings of Buddhism, the *Dharma*.

After the collapse of the Mauryas successive waves of invaders from Central Asia descended on Taxila, among them the Kushans who took control of the new trade route that linked China to the West and became wealthy on the proceeds. Under their great king Kanishka, who ruled in the second quarter of the second century of the Christian Era (CE), Buddhism had prospered. The Chinese Buddhist pilgrim Fa Hian visited Gandhara in the year 400 CE and found the Dharma to be 'very flourishing' here and throughout northern India. However, by the time a second Chinese monk, Sunyun, arrived in India a hundred and twenty years later the scene had changed dramatically: Gandhara had been overrun by the *Huna* or White Huns, and Buddhists were actively persecuted under the warlord Mihirakula: 'The disposition of this king was cruel and vindictive and he practised the most barbarous atrocities. He did not believe in the Dharma and liked to worship demons.' When a third Chinese pilgrim, Huan Tsang, reached Gandhara in 629 CE he was shocked to find Buddhism in decline and what he termed the 'heretical faith' of Hinduism in the ascendant.

Three and a half centuries later the Hindu rulers of Gandhara were overthrown by the armies of the *Turuskas*, the Turks who fought under the green banners of Islam. Under Mahmud, the Lion of Ghazni, the elimination of idolatry began in earnest. It continued in northern India, on and off, for the next seven centuries, only ending with the death of Emperor Aurangzeb in 1707. In Afghanistan it has continued up to the present day, most memorably with the dynamiting of the Buddhist colossi at Bamian by the Taliban in March 2001. It is no accident that the chief victims of the Taliban, and of the *mujahidin* before them, were the Hazara peoples of central and western Afghanistan, whose ancestors long adhered to Buddhism before finally converting to the minority Shia sect. Indeed, many of the rock-caves in which Osama bin Laden and his fellow bigots have sought refuge during the recent war against terrorism were originally excavated by Buddhists for their *viharas* or monastic retreats.

In India the obliteration of the past ended with the arrival of the British, who for all their sins never built their churches on the sites of Hindu temples, or converted Buddhist images into Christian ones (although there were instances of Moslem mausolea being turned into government offices, and of Public Works Department engineers recycling bricks from ancient ruins to provide foundations for their roads and railways). It was in British India, too, that the process of destruction was reversed and the recovery of the past begun – thanks to men like John Marshall, who in 1903 at the age of twenty-six went out to India to take up the post of Director-General of the Archaeological Survey of India. It was Marshall who in 1924 announced to the world the discovery 'of the remains of a long forgotten civilisation': the ancient Indus Valley Civilisation of Mohenjo-daro and Harappa, which had flourished for more than twelve hundred years in the third and second millennia BCE. But it was also Marshall who over a period of a quarter of a century uncovered the later Gandhara civilisation, site by site. It was Marshall who built the excellent little museum at Taxila, and it was in his garden that I sat in the February sunshine drinking my tea from a porcelain teaset that was once his. Hovering at my elbow with Sir John Marshall's teapot was the elderly caretaker of the bungalow. He claimed that in his youth, as part of the Marshall household staff at Taxila, he had served Sir John as he served me now. Unlikely, but just possible, for Marshall left Taxila in 1937.

Later that same day in 1997 I met the present director of the Taxila museum, a dedicated young man who was having desperate problems trying to keep the site open without funds. In the evening he invited me to join him and his staff as they sat down together at *Iftar*, the light snack of dates and fruit that marks the breaking of the day's fast during the month of Ramadan. Traditionally a moment of celebration, that day it was a depressing affair. The staff had not been paid for several months, and they had just heard that a sports stadium for the nearby military cantonment was to be built over Taxila's oldest city, only partially excavated by Marshall. Neglect of the infidel past was also the order of the day elsewhere in Pakistan. In Peshawar the stairs and corridors of the fine late-Victorian Museum were thick with dust, and rainwater dripped into buckets through leaks in the roof. The museum's magnificent collection of Gandharan statuary could only be seen with the aid of a torch. Tucked away on the lower shelf of a display cabinet, unlabelled, was what had once been the prize exhibit: a richly decorated copper casket containing a crystal reliquary and three fragments of bone, recovered by John Marshall during his excavations at the site of what had been one of the wonders of Asia, King Kanishka's Great Tower.

A few days later I stood on the plain of Hadda, outside Jalalabad in Afghanistan, where the Chinese pilgrims mentioned earlier had prostrated themselves before relics of the Buddha. In the 1830s this plain was described as being dotted as far as the eye could see with what were then called *topes*, dome-shaped monuments containing relics of Buddhist saints, better known today as *stupas*. Now, in 1997, the remaining stupas were few and far between. My guide, a *mujahidin*-turned-Taliban, explained that this had been the scene of fierce fighting between the Afghans and Russian tanks and artillery. I asked after the whereabouts of a *vihara* excavated by the French in the 1970s, said to be the finest Buddhist site yet found in Afghanistan. Gone, said my guide. The local commander, taking exception to the many idols it contained, had ordered it to be destroyed. It was the same story elsewhere: King Kanishka's summer capital had been levelled flat by Russian bulldozers and was now under the tarmac of Bagram, the largest airfield in Asia; in Kabul the wealth of Buddhist statuary in the National Museum had been defaced (and was later pulverised, on Mullah Omar's orders, in the wake of the dynamiting at Bamian).

John Marshall was the first modern archaeologist to work in Asia – modern in the sense that he was qualified, and a full-time professional. But others had preceded him, amateurs whose chief qualification was a fascination with local culture and an interest in the past. They termed themselves 'Orientalists', a word coined originally to describe a person from lands east of Europe, which towards the end of the eighteenth century acquired the additional meaning of 'someone versed in oriental languages and literature'. Two centuries later, in the last quarter of the twentieth century, 'Orientalist' and the attendant term 'Orientalism' ('Oriental scholarship: knowledge of Eastern languages') gained a further meaning when in 1978 the American academic Edward Said published *Orientalism*, and sent a shock-wave through academic circles in Europe and America that continues to reverberate to this day.

Professor Said's central assertion was that Orientalism was an instrument of Western imperialism, in the form of 'an accepted grid for filtering through the Orient into Western consciousness' whereby, in setting out to 'discover' the cultures of Asia, Orientalists reshaped an Orient to suit their own Occidental prejudices. 'The Oriental', Said wrote, 'is depicted as something one judges (as in a court of law), something one studies and depicts (as in a curriculum), something one disciplines (as in a school or prison), something one illustrates (as in a zoological manual). The point is that in each of these cases the Oriental is contained and represented by dominating frameworks.'

The back-pedalling that took place in Departments of Oriental

Studies in the 1980s as Western academics sought to correct their political positions in the light of these fulminations was something wondrous to behold. Today the term Orientalism carries heavy pejorative overtones, while the Orientalist is judged in much the same terms as those Orientals whom he himself, according to Said, once sought to judge, study, depict, discipline, illustrate, contain and represent.

What Professor Said and his many supporters have consistently failed to ask is where we would be *without* the Orientalists. They – the 'sahibs' of my title – were products of the Enlightenment that transformed European thinking in the late eighteenth century, modern men who saw the world differently from their predecessors. As Orientalists they initiated the recovery of South Asia's lost past. The European discovery of Buddhism and the subsequent resurgence of Buddhism in South Asia arose directly out of their activities. They also established the methodology upon which the subcontinent's own historians, archaeologists, philologists and students continue to base their studies. What Said and his supporters seem to find so objectionable about this process is that these young men (few women, alas, apart from those two remarkable middle-aged Victorian travellers and proto-feminists, Madame Blavatsky and Alexandra David-Neel) were Westerners,who brought their own baggage with them. They were also mostly Britons, and so it was mostly British ideas that they drew upon.

When first confronted by the Himalayan mountain barrier, one early British Orientalist, Brian Hodgson, spoke of it despairingly as 'a mighty maze without a plan'. The same could be said for the state of knowledge, two centuries ago, about India's past – except that here was a maze that was for the most part buried out of sight. Working to uncover this hidden maze without the historical and cultural signposts that we now take for granted, its excavators had little option but to turn for reference to what they already knew and understood. In doing so, the first Orientalists drew many conclusions that now seem laughable, such as that the historical Buddha was African in origin, or that the British Isles were an integral part of Hindu cosmography. Even the greatest of the first generation of Orientalists, Sir William Jones, died believing that history began with Adam and Eve and the Flood, unable to

conceive that India could have a past pre-dating the great lawgiv-
ers of the Old Testament.

But men like 'Oriental' Jones brought far more to India than cultural baggage. For some, their Orientalism became a passion that
overrode other considerations. They became captivated by one or
other of India's many mysteries and surrendered to its charms,
whether it was architecture, botany, zoology, or some altogether
more rarefied subject such as Rajput genealogy or Indo-Scythian
coinage. And, as the following chapters relate, few survived India's
fatal embrace to go home to die in Cheltenham. In the light of Said's
charges, it is particularly ironic that the Orientalism which initiated,
supported and ultimately defended Indian studies in its early days
should then have become a victim of the Anglicisation championed
by Thomas Babington Macaulay and his friends in the mid 1830s
and the reforms intended to reshape India on British lines. Always
thereafter on the defensive, and with precious little government
support or encouragement, the heirs of Sir William Jones struggled
on to uncover further, and preserve, what was to them an alien
culture – until, at last, a champion appeared on the Indian scene
who was determined to ensure that India's historical and religious
heritage should be universally recognised for what it was worth. A
further irony Edward Said's many supporters would not appreciate is
that this champion was the man whom Indian nationalists most love
to hate: Lord Curzon, Viceroy of India from 1899 to 1904, the man
who once declared that 'the sacredness of India haunts me like a
passion'. Modern India owes a huge debt to this preserver of its
national treasures – as it does to those Orientalists for whom Said
and a number of nationalist historians have so little time.

Jones and the first generation of Orientalists focused their attentions chiefly on Moslem and Brahmin culture for the simple
reason that Islam and Hinduism, along with Islamic and Hindu
institutions, dominated the landscape. With the exception of small
pockets of Jainism in western and central India and patches of
Christianity in south India and Goa, no other religions were in
evidence. The land which had nurtured the historical Buddha and
given rise to the early Buddhist civilisations had been so thoroughly cleansed that the first Orientalists could see no trace of
Buddhism on Indian soil.

Nationalist Indian historians are happy to heap blame for the destruction of Hindu temples on the waves of Muslim iconoclasts who wreaked havoc on their country from the time of Muhammad ibn Qasim onwards. They have less to say about the destructive role of Brahmin zealots in the overthrow of Buddhist *viharas* and the absorption of Buddhist beliefs and iconography into reformed Hinduism – just as they remain largely silent about the impact on the rest of Asia of what was India's greatest export: the civilising influence of Buddhism. In these same circles the pioneering work of Orientalists such as Jones, Prinsep and Cunningham is often portrayed as part of an anti-Brahmin, pro-Buddhist conspiracy of 'Britishers' against Mother India.

This book, then, is an attempt to set the record straight. It tells how the person of Gautama Buddha, prince of the Sakya clan, and the faith he inspired was 'discovered' in the nineteenth century by a small group of Westerners and restored – not just to India, but to the wider world. It is a tale of chance, inspiration, set-back, scandal, dogged perseverance, and all the other twists and turns one would hope to find in a good story – including a happy ending. It is an extraordinary tale, and a true one. And no less extraordinary are the men who made this discovery possible: the Orientalist sahibs.

I

The Botanising Surgeon

THE STATE of Bihar straddles the central Gangetic flood-plain like a vast pancake. About a third of the state lies between the north bank of the Ganges and the foothills of Nepal, while the remaining two-thirds spread south until they come up against the mountain heartlands of central India. North of the river the plain seems endless, but from the south bank the horizon is broken here and there by what seem at a distance to be scattered heaps of rubble, fly-tipped by some giant dumper-truck. Few of these hills rise more than a thousand feet above the plain, but they provide some much-needed features in the landscape.

For three months of the year Bihar is a sun-baked dust-bowl. Once the scorching winds of the *kharian* have blown themselves out in late May nothing seems to move except the kites turning in the sky. Then the clouds bank and the Rains break, splitting the plain into scores of roaring torrents that wash away roads, bridges, entire villages. The earth softens, the floods drain away almost as quickly as they came, and Bihar breathes again. Within days a great magic takes place as clay comes to life: lime-green shoots carpet the plain, darkening to Devon green as they grow. And then, just as nature seems to have achieved the Middle Way in the climatic bliss of the Cold Weather, the sun swings back into Cancer: the sap sinks, vegetation chars from olive to khaki and dries into the colours of autumn. Rivers that briefly filled water-courses half a mile wide dwindle into pools and then puddles, until by mid April only those fed by the melting snows of the Himalayas continue to flow. The water-table sinks and Bihar steels itself once more for the Hot Weather.

The historical figure that we call the Buddha is said to have prophesied that Bihar would give rise to a great civilisation, but would also be threatened by 'feud, fire and flood'. And so it has proved. This is a region that takes its name from the Sanskrit word *vihara*, meaning 'monastic centre'; for centuries it was a land of monasteries, a beacon of piety, learning and culture. Many of these religious complexes lie unlocated to this day, insignificant bumps in the landscape that after centuries of quarrying have been further pared down by the ploughshares of generations of *ryots*, the peasant farmers of northern India. Of those that have been excavated, all show evidence of their final destruction at the hands of the Afghan and Turkic soldiers of Sultan Muhammad Ghori, his general Bhaktiar Khilji and other Moslem invaders in the last years of the twelfth century. Today the land of monasteries is one of India's most troubled states, bankrupt and wracked by inter-caste rivalry, political thuggery, endemic corruption, and general lawlessness.

The process of reclaiming Bihar's past began some two centuries ago. If one were to look for a specific moment, then the morning of 16 October, at the start of the Cold Weather of 1811, would be as good as any, for it was on that date that a party of travellers left the riverside town of Monghyr, some two hundred and fifty miles upstream from Calcutta, and headed west. We must imagine a Bihar far wilder then than it is today, largely a patchwork of scrub and *sal* forest broken by clearings made up of small fields of new-planted paddy and clusters of mud and thatch huts. These pockets are linked by raised tracks just wide enough for bullock-carts. Trees rather than dwellings dominate this rural landscape – carefully-tended copses of trees, each with their own properties and religious connotations: great groves of banyan (*Ficus benghalensis*) that provide shade in the Hot Weather and shelter in the Rains; the imperishable *pipal* or *bodhi* tree (*Ficus religiosa*) that must never be used for firewood; the medicinal *neem* or margosa (*Azadirachta indica*) that wards off disease and evil spirits (and mosquitoes) and is worshipped by gardeners; the *bel* or wood apple tree (*Aegle marmelos*) and the Ashok tree (*Saraca indica*), both sacred to followers of

Lord Shiva; as well as others of more mundane value such as the bamboo, the banana plantain, and the date palm whose improbably jagged trunk carries the scars of the toddy-tapper's knife.

The Pax Britannica has only recently imposed itself across this land, and travellers still seek safety in numbers. In this instance, we know that the core of the party from Monghyr consists of two elephants, a line of bullock-carts and a crowd of some forty to fifty people, of whom a dozen shoulder muskets and wear the distinctive red jacket of the Bengal Native Infantry. Its leader does not walk; his preferred mode of transport is the *palkee*, or palanquin, a covered litter borne by eight bearers working in two teams. Whenever he wishes for a better view of the countryside, or to make a formal entrance, he calls for the litter to be set down and transfers to one of his elephants. This is not due to laziness; the gentleman has a gammy leg. His appearance is a matter for conjecture. All that posterity has to go on is a brief note left by an only son who was little more than an infant when his aged father died: 'My personal recollection of him is that he was a tall man with a ruddy complexion and very white hair and that he suffered from a wound in one of his legs which he got in his youth when he was a surgeon on board a man-of-war in some engagement in the West Indies.'

What we do know is that the gentleman in the palkee is a *Sahib*. This imported Arabic word has already shifted its meaning from 'companion' to 'master', and since the arrival of the British in Bengal has been acquiring the more specific usage of 'foreign master'. It is unlikely that the ruddy complexion attributed to him is from the sun, since we can be pretty certain that whenever he emerges from his *palkee* he claps on a broad-brimmed hat and calls for a bearer to hoist his parasol. These two symbols of authority mark him out as a civilian and a servant of *Jehan Kampani*, the 'Powerful Company', corrupted by the British into 'John Company' but itself merely the local sobriquet for the trading organisation that likes to be addressed as 'The Honourable the East India Company' (EICo). Although John Company taxes and governs Bengal in the name of the Emperor of Delhi, it has long since ceased to defer to any local authority but its own Governor-General.

The sahib in question is Dr Francis Buchanan. He is approaching fifty, which is elderly by Company standards. By those same standards most of his peers consider him a man passed over, as someone of minor status in society and no fortune to speak of, nor even a wife. Although Dr Buchanan's true calling is botany, we now find him in the role of a jack-of-all-trades, charged by the Governor-General to undertake a statistical survey of the territories under the Bengal Presidency, with a brief to investigate 'the state of agriculture, arts and commerce; the religion, manners and customs; the history, natural and civil, and antiquities'. In fact, he has spent the greater part of his seventeen years in India on journeys like this; over the last four of those years he has encompassed some fifty thousand miles of Bengal and Assam, itemising the contents of every division, sub-division and district of Shahabad, Bhagalpore, Dinagepore, Paraniya, Rungpore – and now of Patna and Bihar. For seven months of the year he has pitched his tents beside a village, a grove or a ruin, sleeping under canvas or the open sky, rarely with a *pukka* or solid roof over his head. For company he has had only 'a learned Brahmin', a scholarly *pandit* drawn from the Hindu priestly caste who can read and translate Sanskrit for him, as well as a pair of clerks who handle his correspondence and half a dozen scouts who act as his eyes and ears. The rest of his camp is made up of servants, palanquin-bearers, *mahouts* (elephant-keepers), bullock-cart drivers, grass-cutters and matchlockmen. This company must satisfy his needs as best it can. This has become his world, quite possibly one that he has come to prefer above any other, for in Calcutta Dr Buchanan has gained the reputation of a sour man with a grievance, someone happiest in his own company. But, by chance, Dr Buchanan has qualifications that will allow him to make a vital connection and so open a window into the past.

Perhaps the least significant of those qualifications is his medical degree, which he obtained at Edinburgh University. Even so, we may safely surmise that while at Edinburgh young Francis Buchanan learned the value of scientific method, as well as being greatly influenced by the botanist Dr John Hope – to the extent that once he had completed his medical studies he returned to his father's estate outside Glasgow to spend his days classifying mosses. Since his father was piling up debts at this time we must assume it was financial necessity that eventually drove the young Dr Buchanan to sea. In 1785, aged twenty-four, he embarked on what is believed to have been the first of three extended voyages to the East that kept him in gainful employment for nine years. Family tradition asserts that he entered the Royal Navy as Assistant Surgeon; but as no such grade existed at that time and there is no record of him ever having served in the Navy, the probability is that he was a Surgeon's Mate and then Surgeon on an East Indiaman.

What is beyond doubt is that on 26 September 1794 Dr Francis Buchanan, aged thirty-three, entered the service of the EICo as an Assistant Surgeon on the Bengal Establishment. To note that the post was less than a gentleman of Dr Buchanan's background and experience might have expected is to miss the point. What has been termed the Age of Rapaciousness in India had been cut short by the reforms of Lord North's India Bill, of Warren Hastings and Lord Cornwallis, but Bengal in 1794 remained a land of opportunity where a young gentleman blessed with patronage and a stout constitution could give the pagoda tree a good hard shake and return home with a modest fortune before acquiring so much as one grey hair upon his head. And, to start with, fortune did indeed seem to smile upon Francis Buchanan, for in Calcutta he immediately fell in with another Scot who had studied medicine and botany under John Hope at Edinburgh. This was Dr William Roxburgh, the EICo's chief botanist in the East and Superintendent of its Calcutta Botanic Garden. Dr Roxburgh's star was then very much in the ascendant: he was about to publish his three-volume *Plants of the Coast of Coromandel* – which became the corner-stone of the scientific classification of Indian flora – and he had the ear of the authorities. Through Roxburgh's patronage, Dr Buchanan was soon offered a plum: the post of surgeon on an EICo embassy to the hitherto closed Court of Ava, the central core of the land that we today call Burma – or, at a pinch, Myanmar.

The eastern territories of Bengal bordered on a region inhabited by a number of tribes of whom one, the Burma, had long been dominant. For centuries their power had been concentrated along the low-lying regions of the Irrawaddy–Sittang delta and the coastal strip known as Arakan; then, in the fifteenth century, it had shifted some five hundred miles upriver to a bend in the Irrawaddy named Inwa, which the British simplified into Ava. In its search for new trading opportunities the EICo had regularly despatched embassies to the Court of Ava, but few had been allowed upriver beyond the port of Pegu; and of those that did succeed in reaching Ava, all had been treated with polite indifference. The kings of Ava were simply not interested. However, in the late autumn of 1794 a clash occurred on the Bengal–Ava border when several thousand Burmese troops entered Chittagong in hot pursuit of some rebels. It provoked the Governor-General in Calcutta to send an envoy to the Court of Ava, Captain Michael Symes of HM 76th Regiment of Foot, who was charged with establishing diplomatic relations and, if possible, setting up trading links. Besides Dr Buchanan, Captain Symes was accompanied by his Assistant, a Mr Wood, a learned Hindu from the Brahmin caste to act as his *munshi* or interpreter-cum-scribe, and an escort of fourteen sepoys.

Politically, the mission was a failure. In December 1795 a disgruntled Symes returned to Calcutta to complain that he had been treated with 'insufferable arrogance'. Yet he and his compatriots had at least managed to see the King of Ava. After many delays they had been allowed to proceed upriver and, after further delays, had finally been granted an audience. On the afternoon of the appointed day the three Britons had made their way in a grand procession of elephants to the king's palace where, after kicking their heels until late into the night, they had at last been ushered, shoeless, into the hall of audience. 'We had been seated little more than quarter of an hour,' wrote Symes in his account of the mission, 'when the folding doors that concealed the seat opened with a loud noise, and discovered his majesty ascending a flight of steps that led up to the throne.' To the astonishment of his foreign guests, the king was seen to be so weighed down by his royal regalia that he had to lean on a balustrade to support himself: 'If what we were told was true, that he carried on his dress fifteen *viss*, upwards of fifty pounds *avoirdupois* of gold, his difficulty of ascent was not surprising . . . His crown was a high conical cap, richly studded with precious stones. His fingers were covered with rings, and in his dress he bore the appearance of a man cased in golden armour, whilst a gilded, or probably golden, wing on each shoulder did not add much lightness to his figure.'

The king had been pleased to accept a gift of Benares silks, and Symes's hopes had risen; but just when it seemed that his audience was about to get under way, the gilded monarch had struggled to his feet, to withdraw as silently and awkwardly as he had arrived. It was the British emissary's first and last glimpse of the ruler of Ava, and the EICo had to settle for a token treaty allowing a British Resident to be based several hundred miles away at the river port of Yangon, Anglicised by the British into Rangoon.

But if Captain Symes felt he had wasted his time, his surgeon took away a very different view, because it was here in the Kingdom of Ava that Francis Buchanan first came in to his own – not as a medical man, but as a naturalist and master intelligence-gatherer. In Ava he discovered in himself an appetite for information, as well as a capacity for both amassing and classifying that information. The land of the Burmas, still *terra incognita* as far as the British were concerned, had been set before him as on a plate – and he fell upon it with the appetite of a starving man. Much of his information he gathered at first hand, by personal observation or by collecting it himself, but he also relied heavily on raw data brought to him by others, either paid informants or members of his own native-born staff. As a result, he returned to Calcutta with notebooks, journals, folders and boxes stuffed with statistics, notes and specimens. From the EICo's point of view, the most valuable were the series of maps of the country that Buchanan had been able to compile by the ingenious method of questioning dozens of local informants and then comparing and cross-referencing their answers. What counted for Dr Roxburgh was his protégé's magnificent haul of botanical specimens, drawings, and accompanying notes. These were speedily despatched to the EICo's Court of Directors in London, on whose board sat Sir Joseph Banks. The grand old man of English botany appears to have been sufficiently impressed to present them before the Royal Society, of which he was President, but without troubling to acknowledge their source, so giving the impression that they were his own work. Their collector had to content himself with knowing that the Burmese *launzen* tree had been named the type of the genus *Buchanania*.

What failed to excite any interest at all was the information Buchanan had brought back regarding the religion of the Burmese.

While waiting to be granted their audience with the king of Ava, the three Britons had been taken out to view the new capital being built outside the existing city. Here a large golden-roofed temple had been constructed (see illustration below) to house what was said to be a most famous statue, fourteen feet high and cast in solid bronze, that had been seized from a temple on the coast at Arakan and dragged in triumph over the mountains as war booty. Captain Symes was not impressed by the sight of what he termed 'this brazen representation of the divinity', and the 'tumultuous enthusiasm' of the crowds that followed them into the temple had sickened him: 'We soon turned from these wretched fanatics, and the object of their stupid adoration.'

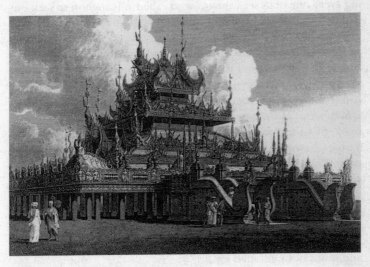

In his *Account of an Embassy to the Kingdom of Ava*, published in London in 1800, Symes later wrote that 'The Birmans are Hindoos: not votaries of Brahma, but sectaries of Boodh.' His book contained an entire chapter devoted to the 'heterodox religion and philosophy' of this sect and drew heavily on an unacknowledged source – his surgeon, Dr Francis Buchanan. However, Dr Buchanan's information was itself second-hand, for it had come from an Italian missionary named Padre Vincentius Sangermano.

The Church of Rome had fared rather better in Ava than John Company. Over the years various Catholic missionary orders had lobbied for the right to set up missions in the country, and in 1783

Father Sangermano of the Barnabite Order had been allowed to proceed to Ava, arriving just in time to witness the last stages of a bloody power struggle that ended with a new king on the throne and his conquest of the coastal region. Despite his reputation for violence, King Bodawpaya treated Father Sangermano kindly and allowed him to build a small church and a college for missionaries at Rangoon. Although he won few converts, the Italian father was befriended by the regional governor and soon became a popular local figure. The EICo was quick to recognise the value of the missionary's privileged position, and orders were set down requiring every one of its sea captains who called at Rangoon to seek out Father Sangermano and afford him every facility. By the spring of 1795 he had been settled in the country for more than a decade, and was on hand to welcome Symes and his party to Rangoon.

The Barnabite father had made a special study of the religion of the Burmese, the better to refute its doctrines with his own. He had even gone to the trouble of making Latin translations of a number of Burmese religious texts: a history, a cosmography, a book of ordinations relating to the laws of their religion, and a paper drawn up by a senior prelate in response to a series of questions. Being a man of generous disposition, Sangermano presented copies of his translations to Captain Symes, who in turn passed them on to Dr Buchanan, as the better Latin scholar. This was just as well, for otherwise Buchanan would not have had access to them: although Father Sangermano retired to Rome in 1808, he died before he could complete his *Description of the Burmese Empire* and it was not published until 1883.

After his return to Calcutta, Dr Buchanan's newly-revealed talent for intelligence-gathering led to a series of postings in outlying districts of Bengal where he was given free rein to enquire into the natural resources of the area and how they might best be exploited commercially. This was lonely work, but it allowed him to divide his evenings between his botanical studies and the translation of Sangermano's papers. Buchanan's own paper *On the Religion and Literature of the Burmas* was completed towards the end of 1797, and on Roxburgh's advice was shown to the Governor-General, Sir John Shore. It appeared in print in Calcutta two years later, the first serious account in English of the Buddhist religion.

In the same year in which Buchanan's paper was published, Tipu Sultan of Mysore died at the storming and capture of his stronghold of Seringapatam by the EICo's Madras Army. Huge swathes of conquered territories in south India were now added to the Madras Presidency. While the members of the Court of Directors of the EICo in London wrung their hands and wrote angry letters protesting at the actions being taken on their behalf, in India Sir John Shore's successor, the ambitious Marquess Wellesley, pressed on with his plans to replace the near anarchy that had prevailed over much of the region with an effective system of government. One of Wellesley's first acts was to approve the appointment of an official to tour the newly-conquered territories and report back on what he found. Again, it was Dr Roxburgh who came forward to propose the man for the job. 'Dr Buchanan', he wrote, 'is the best Botanist I know of in India and in every other respect the best qualified to furnish you with an account of the Vegetable Products of these countries. He is also a good Zoologist; in short in every way qualified for the research.' The outcome was that Buchanan spent the next three years in the newly-created post of 'statistical surveyor', leading small parties through the ravaged south Indian countryside to gather information on every subject that might be of possible benefit to the EICo, from the best methods of cultivating peppers to the ramifications of the Hindu caste system, as well as other more abstruse matters, of interest only to antiquarians or members of learned societies.

This survey produced a voluminous report running into three volumes that was forwarded with the Governor-General's plaudits to the EICo's Court of Directors in Leadenhall Street, who ordered its immediate publication. Dr Buchanan, in the meantime, had returned to Bengal – where he was almost immediately attached to another foreign embassy: in February 1802 he was directed to take up his surgeon's bag and accompany a Captain Knox on a mission to the Court of Nepal in Kathmandu, where he was provided with a second but very different view of the religion he had first encountered in Ava.

In April 1802 Knox's mission trekked over the foothills of the Himalayas to reach the valley of Kathmandu. 'We are in sight of Catmandu,' wrote Buchanan, 'in a bare ugly valley resembling many of those in Scotland before the introduction of fences.' Ten days later he was writing from inside the confines of the newly-established British Residency, deliberately sited by the Nepalese on a notoriously blighted and spirit-ridden spot just outside the city walls: 'I have much professional duty,' he now wrote, 'the country being most unhealthy and wish for nothing more than to be out of it again as soon as possible.'

These remarks are drawn from a bundle of correspondence between Dr Buchanan and Dr Roxburgh, now in the archives of the Royal Botanic Garden at Kew. The content is almost entirely confined to matters botanical, with very few observations as personal as those quoted above. It may be that Buchanan kept his letters short and to the point because he knew the Nepalese authorities were intercepting the embassy's mail; but, given that Dr Roxburgh was now his closest friend, they convey the impression of a pretty cold fish. For their part, the Nepalese authorities made no secret of their distrust of the British; the embassy had been forced on them, and they were determined to avoid further entanglement with this most dangerous power. They placed severe restrictions on the movements of the embassy's members, so that for the twelve months Captain Knox and Dr Buchanan remained in Nepal they were virtual prisoners in the grounds of the British Residency.

Despite these constraints Dr Buchanan did everything he could to gather information about the country by proxy, relying heavily on the initiative of his *munshi*, a high-caste Bengali named Ramajai Batacharji, described as 'an intelligent brahman from Calcutta, whom I employed to obtain information, so far as I prudently could, without alarming a jealous government, or giving offence to the Resident, under whose authority I was acting'. As this note suggests, Dr Buchanan found Captain Knox's restrictions on his fact-finding activities almost as hard to bear as those placed on them by the Nepalese. Tensions between the two men grew to such a pitch that Buchanan eventually applied to Calcutta for a transfer: 'I have grown heartily tired of my situation,' he wrote to Roxburgh at the end of the year. But already it had become obvious to Lord Wellesley that the Nepalese were determined to avoid any sort of political entanglement with the EICo, and in March 1803 Captain Knox and his party were recalled.

As in Ava a decade earlier, the failure of the Nepal mission was offset to some degree by the amount of intelligence gathered. Captain Knox was able to produce a valuable report on the political situation in Kathmandu, while Dr Buchanan presented himself to Dr Roxburgh at the Calcutta Botanic Gardens with a magnificent collection of some 1,500 plant specimens and numerous drawings – as well as the raw material for what he intended should be the first detailed account of the Kingdom of Nepal.

Once again Dr Buchanan had cause to be thankful for the patronage of his good friend Dr Roxburgh, for he was now invited by Lord Wellesley to become his personal physician, and at the same time to take charge of his Institution for Promoting the Natural History of India. This was one of a number of bodies for the advancement of science and learning that Lord Wellesley was in the process of setting up – in defiance of orders – as part of his grand plan for an *Imperium Britannicum* in the East. The Institution consisted of a menagerie and aviary at Barrackpore, just a few miles upriver from Calcutta, where the Governor-General had his weekend retreat. Dr Buchanan became its first Supervisor, with instructions to make a 'correct account of all the most remarkable quadrupeds and birds in the provinces subject to the British Government in India'. It was a non-salaried post, but since Buchanan's medical duties were now minimal he was able to devote himself almost wholly to natural history studies. To assist him, every civil and military officer in the service of the Company was sent a direct order from the Governor-General that any interesting zoological specimen encountered in the course of his duties was to be sent forthwith, dead or alive, to Barrackpore. This ensured that Dr Buchanan and his staff were kept fully occupied: as each specimen was received it was examined and described by the doctor and then drawn twice by his team of native artists, a copy for the Company and one for the Governor-General's private collection.

We may assume that the years 1804 and 1805 were happy ones for Francis Buchanan, spent doing what he most enjoyed, in good company and comfortable surroundings. The publication in London of his Mysore Survey by order of the EICo's Court of Directors had made his reputation. He now had the support of the two greatest naturalists of the age, Sir Joseph Banks in London and

Dr William Roxburgh in Calcutta – to say nothing of the ear of the Governor-General. Many years later, Lord Wellesley wrote warmly of the 'intimate acquaintance and friendship which was established between us', and of Buchanan's 'independence, and frankness'. He also remarked on 'the manly spirit of truth and honour which animated [his] intercourse with all persons of power', which suggests that Buchanan was not one to mince his words. But then, Lord Wellesley was hardly diplomatic himself; as Governor-General of India he pursued courses of action that took no account of the EICo's mounting financial burdens, determined both to make his own mark and to advance Britain from a trading organisation led by 'men of mere facts, figures and money-bags' into an imperial power governed by proconsuls. By the spring of 1805 the Court of Directors was facing bankruptcy and had had enough: Lord Wellesley was recalled.

Dr Buchanan accompanied his august but now politically isolated 'patient' back to London, where he began at once to lobby for the post he most coveted: that of Superintendent of the Calcutta Botanic Garden. Dr Roxburgh was now in his late fifties, his health had begun to deteriorate, and he had himself made it known that he wished his protégé to succeed him. Buchanan presented to the EICo's Court of Directors his private collection of natural history drawings made in Barrackpore, together with his herbarium of Nepalese plants and his Nepal journal. He joined the Royal Society and solicited the support of its President, Sir Joseph Banks. These efforts paid off, and late in 1806 he once more set sail for India, posted as full Surgeon and secure in the knowledge that he had been nominated Roxburgh's successor. The job, he believed, was his.

He arrived back in Calcutta to find that Dr Roxburgh had undergone a change of heart. Despite his poor health, he now intended to stay on as Superintendent and keep his chair warm for his assistant, his son William. In the meantime, it had been arranged that Dr Buchanan should conduct another of the statistical surveys he was so very good at, this time of the country under the immediate authority of the Bengal Presidency. There was nothing Buchanan could do but bite his tongue and take what was offered.

So it came about that in October 1807 an understandably bitter man began what was to prove the most comprehensive survey ever carried out by a single officer of the EICo. It was to keep him occupied until the Hot Weather of 1814 – and in November 1811 it found him heading south from Patna with his little band of retainers towards the town of Gaya and, just beyond, a huddle of stone temples that went by the name of Bodh-Gaya. There, at last, the knowledge Dr Francis Buchanan had gained in Burma and Nepal came into its own.

2

Tales from the East

A GREAT MANY of the young men who took John Company's rupee in the eighteenth century were from the same genteel background as Dr Francis Buchanan. Even though only a minority went out to India with bachelors' degrees, these young gentlemen-traders were products of an age in which sons of the gentry received a solid grounding in the Classics, mathematics and philosophy. Even the silliest of the young gentlemen who stepped through the portals of East India House in Leadenhall Street, aged sixteen or seventeen, a cane in one hand and a hat in the other, could parse a Latin sentence and read out a passage of Homer in the original. When in 1806 the East India College for the training of the EICo's administrators-to-be came to be set up, no candidate was deemed qualified for admission 'unless he be able to render into English some portion of the works of the following Greek authors – Homer, Herodotus, Xenophon, Thucydides, Sophocles and Euripides; nor unless he can render into English some portion of the following Latin authors – Livy, Terence, Cicero, Tacitus, Vergil and Horace.'

It was from these and other Classical sources that John Company's young servants gained their first impressions of the Orient and of Eastern philosophy. They took on board the Greek predilection for attributing every sort of ancient wisdom to the Egyptians. They were familiar with Pythagoras's theory of the transmigration of the soul from body to body. They knew their

Pindar, who in his poetry dwelt on metempsychosis – the notion of the future existence of the soul after death, and how man might develop into something godlike through the constant practise of righteousness. They might even have read Plato's *Phaedrus*, in which he wrote, of souls travelling in cycles of necessity, that 'each soul returning to the election of a second life, shall receive one agreeable to his desire'. They certainly knew all about the Persian Empire of Darius and Xerxes, the land-bridge that had linked the Mediterranean world with India. And from Herodotus they learned the Greek version of Indian history, which was that the god Dionysus had gone to India from Greece, conquered the people, founded cities, introduced laws, and taught the Indians to sow the land and cultivate vines.

Much of this would have seemed pretty dull stuff to young minds. But there was one name from the ancient world that never failed to fire the imagination: Alexander the Great, the man who opened the road to India and briefly linked East and West. Alexander's extraordinary progress across Asia to the plains of the Punjab was well documented, as was his legacy. One of his Macedonian viceroys was the general Seleucus Nikator, ruler of Bactria, who after Alexander's death set out to extend his dominions east of the Indus, turning to diplomacy when warfare failed. In the year 303 BCE Seleucus sent an ambassador named Megasthenes to the court of his Indian opponent, Emperor Sandrokottos. When Megasthenes returned after an absence of some ten years he had a great deal to tell of his residence in the city on the banks of the River Ganges, where Sandrokottos had his court. 'The greatest city in India is that which is called Palimbothra,' wrote Megasthenes, 'in the dominions of the Prasians, where the streams of the Erannoboas and the Ganges unite, the Ganges being the greatest of all rivers, and the Erannoboas being perhaps the third largest.' The city of Palimbothra was eighty stadia in length and fifteen in breadth, laid out in the shape of a parallelogram and girded by a wooden palisade and ditch. As for its ruler, Sandrokottos had been born humble but had been prompted to seize the throne by a dream in which he was licked clean by a lion, the Indian and Persian symbol of kingship. He had gone on to overthrow the foreign oppressors of his people, but after his victory had 'forfeited by his tyranny all title to the name of liberator, for he oppressed with servitude the very people whom he had emancipated from foreign thralldom'.

Megasthenes's *Indica* was lost, but fragments survived at second hand in the writings of Arrian, Strabo, Justin and other historians of the Roman period to become the Western world's main source of information on India and Indian culture for more than a thousand years. From Megasthenes by way of Strabo, it was known that two kinds of philosophers were to be found in India, 'one called *Brachmanes* and the other *Sarmanes*'. Asked to explain the difference between the two sects, one of the Brachmanes had explained to Megasthenes that his own was of 'fairer repute' than the other, suggesting a degree of rivalry between the two. Perhaps not altogether unsurprisingly, Megasthenes ended by having few kind words to say for the Sarmanes, whose main characteristics were asceticism, frugal habits, begging for alms, and admitting women to their numbers while at the same time abstaining from 'the delights of love'.

The more serious-minded among the young Britons who took berth aboard the Indiamen that yearly sailed from England in the early summer would have had no difficulty in identifying Megasthenes's Brachmanes as Brahmans (today usually written in English as 'Brahmins'), the hereditary priests who dominated the Hindu caste structure. But the identity of his Sarmanes would certainly have left even the most scholarly of our young men puzzling. Today we know that the word comes from the Sanskrit *Shramana* – the root word for an ascetic that, exported along the Silk Road to China, became the *Shaman* of Siberia. The true identity of these Sarmanes, however, remained mysterious until very late in the eighteenth century.

When those young hopefuls stepped ashore as 'griffins' or newcomers on the coasts of Malabar, Coromandel or Bengal, they entered a country without a past. They knew about the Mughals, whose emperors had dominated India for four centuries but who were now in terminal decline; they knew that various dynasties of Afghans, Turks and Persians had ruled over different parts of India before the Mughals, and that these Moors or Mohammedans were not to be confused with the bulk of the population, made up of heathen Gentoos or Hindus. But what had gone before the arrival of the Mohammedans was entirely a matter for conjecture – except for that single glimpse of India late in the third century BCE provided by Megasthenes after his sojourn at the court of King Sandrokcottos at Palimbothra. Centuries of fire and sword had almost totally severed India's links with its pre-Islamic past. Within Hindu society the Brahmins remained the official custodians of learning, but that learning – like much of Hindu society itself – had become fragmented, ossified and introverted. During centuries of persecution and decline the Brahmins had gradually turned in upon themselves, and what scholarship they retained was for themselves only. Their sacred texts and the language of those texts were not to be shared with those of lower caste – and especially not with those whom they regarded as far beyond the pale, unclean foreigners from over the black water whose very shadows polluted.

The same phenomenon that had broken India's ties with its past had also severed its ancient links with the Mediterranean world, ending the exchange of ideas that had gone hand in hand with trade at the time when Gandhara was the central market-place and cross-roads of Asia. Silk Road traffic had carried Christianity deep into China in one direction, Buddhism to the shores of the Mediterranean in the other. Towards the end of the second century CE Clement of Alexandria, a Greek Father of the early Christian Church, had questioned a group of Indian traders at the port of Alexandria. They had identified themselves as *Sarmanae* – *Shramana* Latinised – and described themselves as followers of a teacher 'whom by excessive reverence they have exalted into a god'. They worshipped 'a kind of pyramid beneath which they think the bones of some divinity lie buried' and they lived in religious communities they called *Vehar*, explained by Bishop Clement as '*templum dei primarii Buddoe quem Indos ut Deum venerari*: the temple of the primary god Buddo whom the Indians worshipped as a god'. Bishop Clement and his disciple Origen were familiar to eighteenth-century British students of Church history as vigorous defenders of orthodoxy against the heresies that threatened to split the early Christian Church. One such was the teaching of the Egyptian gnostic Basilides, who promoted the quintessentially Buddhist belief that enlightenment could only be achieved through personal initiation from a spiritual teacher – the guru (in Sanskrit; in Tibetan, *lama*) – and that the soul was affected through its transmigration by accumulated thoughts and deeds. In attacking gnosticism in his *Stromata*, Bishop Clement of Alexandria condemned the heresy that 'the soul has previously sinned in another life, and endures its punishment here'. Students of Buddhism will recognise this as the doctrine of *karma*.

The degree to which Buddhist philosophy, ritual and iconography influenced the early Christian Church is a fascinating subject, but lies outside the scope of this book. One example of the Church's borrowing from Buddhism deserves to be mentioned, however, if only because it became one of the most popular religious romances of medieval Europe. The tale of the two Christian saints Barlaam and Josaphat tells of an Indian prince, Josaphat, whose father tries unsuccessfully to protect him from the outside world. He becomes so distressed by the suffering he sees that he seeks out a holy man, Barlaam, and finally renounces the world to become a saintly ascetic. The legend of Barlaam and Josaphat became so widely accepted that their names were entered in the Church's Roll of Saints and their own day, 27 November, was assigned to them. Josaphat makes his first public appearance in the West in *Lives of the Saints*, written in Latin by a Byzantine hagiographer named Simeon Metaphrastes – but Metaphrastes was drawing on a Greek version of the story translated from his native Georgian by a monk of Mount Athos named Euthymus. This Georgian text had, in its turn, come to Macedonia from Jerusalem, where it had been translated from the Arabic by Greek Orthodox monks. It is, of course, the story of what Buddhists would term the Great Renunciation. Its original source was probably *Buddhacarita*, a popular Sanskrit biography of Gautama Buddha that most probably travelled westwards to Damascus by way of the Manichaean Church, the most inclusive and pervasive of the Christian heresies. As it moved westward, so the original Sanskrit *Bodhisattva*, or 'awakened one', metamorphised by stages into 'Budhasaf' (Arabic), 'Iodasaph' (Georgian), 'Ioasaph' (Greek) and finally 'Josaphat' (Latin).

The Arab–Islamic barrier remained all but impenetrable for a thousand years. When the Western world eventually resumed contact with the Eastern it was only able do so because the eruption of the Mongols had weakened the Islamic Khanates of central Asia, the area known to the West as Tartary. A series of papal emissaries sent to the court of the Great Khan of the Mongols reopened the old land routes and returned with confused tales of Nestorian Christians vying with idolators for the ear of the Great Khan at Karakoram. Hard on the heels of the emissaries went enterprising traders, most notably the Polos of Venice: in 1265 Niccolo and Maffeo, and a decade later their young nephew Marco, who spent seventeen of his twenty-four years abroad in the territories of Kublai Khan. However garbled and adulterated, Marco Polo's account of these years opened a window on the East that gave medieval Europe its first clear view not of Tartary and Cathay alone but of many of the lands that bordered them.

As a faithful son of the Church, Marco Polo held the view that anyone who was not Christian, Jew or Saracen (then the standard European term for Muslim, soon to be replaced by Moor) was an idolater, and that there was little to choose between one form of idolatry and another. His years of service at the court of Kublai Khan allowed him to observe at close quarters the Tibetan lamas whose teachings had by then been adopted by the Mongols as their state religion. The only thing about these lamas that impressed him was their fearsome reputation as sorcerers, although he noted that Kublai Khan revered a prophet named Sakyamuni Burkhan, whom he regarded as on a par with Moses, Jesus Christ and Mohammed.

When the Polos were finally permitted to return home they did so by sea, making a slow progress through China and south-east Asia that brought them across the Bay of Bengal to the island of Ceylon, and then to India. One reason why the authenticity of Marco Polo's *Description of the World* continues to be questioned is its many discrepancies, for which the fact that scores of different versions in at least a dozen languages were in circulation before the end of the fourteenth century is only a partial explanation. A case in point is Marco Polo's account of Ceylon, which consists of two contradictory reports. One is entirely fantastical: he tells us this is an enormous island that was once larger still, but has been so buffeted by Westerlies that it has shrunk to its present size; now it is 'completely flat so that it can only be sighted by sailors when they are very close to it'. These remarks were clearly based on hearsay, perhaps sailors' tales noted down in passing as his vessel swept past the island and on to the country of Malabar, the 'most beautiful place in India', where the Venetian stayed long enough to consider himself fully qualified to give 'a true account of the country'. And indeed, among such Arabian Nights delights as the ingenious means by which diamonds are gathered in the gorges of Motupalli (by throwing down sticky pieces of meat, which are then picked up by white eagles), we are given a well-informed treatise on the religious practices of south India in which Polo remarks on the high moral standards of the Brahmins. And then, at the close of this same chapter, his tone changes. 'So much for the ways of these idolaters,' he concludes. 'But we must not forget an astounding thing which happened in Ceylon.'

Then we are back again in Ceylon, but this time it is a real island, with a high mountain at its centre whose summit can only be reached with the help of fixed iron chains. 'It is thought that Adam, the first man, is buried up there,' writes Marco Polo. 'This is what the Saracens believe, though the idolaters say it is Sakyamuni Burkhan's tomb' – the same prophet whose name was so revered by Kublai Khan. The word 'burkhan', we are told, means 'holy', but no explanation is forthcoming for 'Sakyamuni' other than that he was 'the first man in whose name an idol was made'. The 'astounding thing' that happened in Ceylon turns out to be the life and death of this Sakyamuni Burkhan, the 'holiest man who had ever existed and the first man to be venerated as a saint'. There then follows a detailed account of his life and subsequent deification (here taken from Teresa Waugh's recent translation from the Italian):

He was the son of a rich and powerful king and he led such a good life that he turned away from the things of the world and refused to be king. When the king saw that his son was not interested in worldly things and did not want to be king, he was furious and offered him many bribes. He was even prepared to abdicate all power in his son's favour, leaving him to reign as he wanted. The son replied that he wanted nothing. When the father was finally convinced he was ready to die of sorrow, which was not altogether surprising as he had only one son and no one else to succeed him. He decided to do one thing which he was sure would turn the son's mind towards worldly things and persuade him to accept the kingdom and the crown. He housed his son in a beautiful palace with 30,000 beautiful serving maids. No other man was allowed inside the palace. The young girls put him to bed, prepared his meals and always kept him company. They sang and danced for him and, in accordance with the king's orders, did everything possible to please him. But it was impossible to seduce the young man. On the contrary, he seemed determined to become more chaste every day, and led a very austere life.

It should be said that the young prince had been so carefully brought up that he had never been outside the palace, had never seen a dead body or met anyone who was not completely healthy. His father would not allow him to see an old or unhappy man. But one day the young man went out riding and came across a dead body. He had never seen such a thing and was amazed. He asked his attendants what it was and they told him it was a body.

'What,' exclaimed the prince, 'do all men die?'

They told him that of course they did.

The young man said no more, but rode on deep in thought. After a little while he met a toothless old man who could no longer walk. The king's son asked who this was and why he was unable to walk. He was told that the man has lost his teeth because of old age and that old age prevented him from walking. The young man was deeply moved and he returned to his palace saying that he no longer wished to remain in so sad a world, but wanted to go and find his creator who would never die. So he left his father's palace and went off into the steep mountains, where he lived an abstemious, frugal and chaste life.

Here is the already familiar story of Barlaam and Josaphat – but without Barlaam and with additional detail supplied. When the prince dies a statue is made of him in gold and his subjects worship it as though it is a god. We also learn that this Sakyamuni has already lived through many previous lives: 'It was said that the prince had died eighty-four deaths and that each time he had been reincarnated as a different animal – first an ox, then a horse, then a dog, until finally, the eighty-fourth time, he became a god . . . All this happened in Ceylon.'

Marco Polo concludes his story of Sakyamuni Burkhan by telling us that the idolators believed the mountain tomb on the island to contain his teeth, hair and begging bowl – Kublai Khan had come to hear of these relics, he recalls, and in the year 1284 had sent an embassy to Ceylon; it returned with two large molars, some hair, and a beautiful bowl made of green porphyry. 'The whole of Khan-balik', Polo writes, 'turned out to welcome the relics, which the priests took into their care with much joy and veneration, and there were great celebrations. The priests found in their scriptures that the green porphyry bowl had a magic property. If food for one man were put into it, it would feed five. The great Khan put this to the test and it was proved to be true.'

Whether Marco Polo actually witnessed the magic properties of the green porphyry bowl is unclear, but he was evidently much impressed with the sanctity of its former owner. He concludes his account with the comment that, 'for a certainty, if he had been baptised a Christian he would have been a great saint before God'.

The next manifestations from the West were of a very different order from the papal emissaries and traders who had pioneered the overland routes, and they came by sea. In the year 1498 it was inscribed in the 'great chronicle' of Ceylon, the *Mahavamsa*, how a messenger reported to the king of the island that 'a new people had arrived, white and beautifully made, who wore iron coats and iron caps, and drank blood [wine] and ate stones; who gave a gold coin for a fish, or even a lime; and who had a kind of instrument that could produce thunder and lightning, and balls which, put into these instruments, could fly many miles, and break ramparts, and destroy forts.' A Portuguese fleet had arrived off India's Malabar coast.

The story of the Portuguese irruption into Calicut and Goa, soon afterwards reinforced by the heavy weaponry of the Reformation in the shape of the Jesuits and the Inquisition, is too familiar to bear repeating here. What is not so well-known is the invasion of the island of Ceylon in 1560 by a Portuguese expedition led by the Viceroy of Goa, Dom Constantino de Braganza.

Ceylon was of particular interest to every seafaring nation in Europe and Asia, for it commanded all movements of shipping into and out of the Bay of Bengal and thus the route to the spice islands of the East Indies, the source of the world's most profitable trade goods. It was also the world's chief supplier of cinnamon, the bark of a tree that grew particularly well in the low-lying coastal regions surrounding the mountainous interior. A desire to secure direct access to this precious commodity undoubtedly added impetus to Dom Constantino's expedition, but what actually launched it was religious zeal. The heir to the throne of a petty kingdom on Ceylon had fled to Goa as a refugee, and there converted to Christianity. Gaining the Viceroy's ear, he whispered into it that a number of other Christians on the island were being persecuted by his usurping brother – which was enough to galvanise the Viceroy into landing near Jaffna, at the northern point of the island, with a force of 1,200 armed men.

The Portuguese invasion was Christendom's first direct assault on Asia's oldest-established religion and it left its adherents profoundly shaken. After a brisk engagement, the defenders fled and the Portuguese sacked the city. Temples were generally an easy target, but while looting one particular shrine the troops came up against unexpected resistance from its unarmed guardians, whose grief when finally vanquished convinced the Portuguese that they had captured some rare treasure. A jewelled casket was discovered, which when prised open revealed a human tooth set in gold. Enquiries suggested that this was the most famous relic in all Asia: the tooth of a supposed saint who was worshipped as a god. It was believed not only to cleanse the sins of all who saw it, but to confer the temporal kingship of Asia on whoever owned it. For centuries this devilish object had been kept in a temple at Kandy, a city buried deep in the mountains at the centre of the island: it was in Jaffna by mere chance.

The Portuguese in Goa knew all about sacred relics. The body of their own saintly Francis Xavier had only recently been installed in the Jesuit College of St Paul, to say nothing of fragments of the True Cross and phials containing drops of the *Sangre Réal*. So the

Viceroy was pleased to carry away this most potent symbol of stewardship of the Indies – more pleased still when he received a message brought by a Portuguese sea-captain from Pegu, the renowned city of temples sited on the Irrawaddy–Salween delta on the far side of the Bay of Bengal. It was an offer from a pagan king to buy the tooth for a sum that today would be the equivalent of some ten million pounds sterling. Dom Constantino accepted the offer without hesitation – a mistake, says Faria y Sousa, who chronicled these events in his *Asia Portuguese*: he felt the Viceroy should have held out for more. Before the sale could take place, however, the Archbishop of Goa intervened to threaten the Viceroy with the wrath of the Inquisition should he proceed with it. A special joint meeting of Goa's grand council and ecclesiastical court was convened, at which it was decided not only to reject the offer from Pegu but also to destroy this offence unto God.

On the day determined for the tooth's destruction a great crowd filled the square in front of Goa's cathedral to watch the spectacle of the *auto da fé*. They saw the Archbishop pronounce sentence on the heretical object before he ground it to dust with a mortar and pestle and then poured the powder into a burning brazier. Finally, the ashes and embers were carefully collected and thrown into the sea. It was a public act of faith, a demonstration that not even riches could deflect the Portuguese from their quest to rid Asia of its false gods.

The Portuguese went on to impose a treaty on the King of Kandy that gave them control over the export of the island's cinnamon, which they enforced by building a ring of strongholds along the coast. Under the shadow of their cannon they propagated their faith most zealously, destroying idols and requiring the native population under their control to convert to Christianity. Recusants fled into the hinterland, too wild and too mountainous to allow pursuit. This minimal penetration of the interior was the pattern of the Portuguese in Asia: it fell to the Jesuit missionaries to push inland from the coast and seek to get to grips with Asia's idolatry.

The pioneering missions of Francis Xavier in 1550–51 among the heathens in southern Japan (largely followers of the Rinzai Zen sect of Buddhism, dismissed by Xavier as 'a fraudulent law and an invention of the Devil') and of Matteo Ricci between 1582 and

1610 in China (where the syncretic Buddhism being practised, accommodating Taoist and Confucian elements, led him to believe that it was a form of Pythagoreanism brought from Greece by way of India) are too peripheral to this story to be repeated here; the exploits of the Jesuits and other missionaries in Grand Tartary or Tibet have also been recounted elsewhere. What all the missionary-explorers of the sixteenth and seventeenth centuries remarked upon, with varying degrees of shock and disquiet, was the disturbing similarity between the rites and trappings of the Church of Rome and those practised throughout Tibet and Mongolia. 'They celebrate the Sacrifice of the Mass with Bread and Wine,' wrote the German Jesuit John Grueber, after reaching Lhasa in 1661, 'give extreme Unction, bless married Folks, say Prayers over the Sick, make Nunneries, sing in the Service of the Choir, observe divers Fasts during the year, undergo most severe Penances, and, among the rest, Whippings; consecrate Bishops, and send out Missionaries who live in extreme Poverty, and travel bare-foot through the Deserts as far as China.'

As further and similar accounts from missionaries in China were received at the Society's headquarters in Rome, the Church came to realise the necessity of explaining these horrifying similarities, and disassociating itself from them. It did so by demonising what was first called the religion of 'Menipe' or 'Fo' but soon came to be known as 'Lamaism'. The attack was led by the German Jesuit scholar Athanasius Kircher, who denounced this religion as a perversion of the Church's own sacred rites. 'The Devil', he declared in his *China Illustrata*, published in 1667, 'in way of abuse hath transferred, as he hath done all the other Mysteries of the Christian Religion, the Veneration which is due unto the Pope of Rome, the only Vicar of Christ on Earth, unto the superstitious Worship of barbarous people.' The chief object of this worship and veneration was the person of the Grand or Dalai Lama of Lhasa: 'From him, as from a certain Fountain, floweth the whole form and mode of their Religion, or rather mad and brain-sick idolatry . . . Strangers at their approach fall prostrate with their heads to the ground, and kiss him with incredible Veneration, which is no other than that which is performed upon the Pope of Rome; so that hence the fraud and deceit of the Devil may easily and plainly appear.'

As well as venerating the Grand Lama, these barbarians worshipped numerous idols, 'amongst which, that which they call *Menipe*, hath the preeminence . . . Before this Demon or false God this foolish People commence their sacred Rites, with many unwonted Gesticulations and Dances, often repeating of these words: *O Manipe Mi Hum, O Manipe Mi Hum*, that is, *O Manipe save us*; and these sottish People are wont to set many sorts of viands and meats before the Idol for the propitiating or appeasing of the Deity.' Tucked away in those layers of vituperation is Kircher's observation that the idol Menipe originated in India, which in turn had received its gods from Egypt.

Ironically, this and subsequent attacks on Tibetan Buddhism by the Catholic Church (see illustration above) were eagerly seized upon by European Protestants in their propaganda war against the idolatrous practices of the 'Romanish religion'. Anti-Catholic polemicists of the mid eighteenth century, like the Englishman Thomas Astley, milked for all its worth the 'surprising conformity' between Lamaism and the Church of Rome.

The English were the late-comers on the Asian scene. No

English translation of Marco Polo's *Description* was printed until 1579, and there was little interest in capturing a slice of the spice trade until after the opening of the sea-lanes in the wake of the defeat of the Spanish Armada. But within a decade of that triumph Englishmen could read accounts of the travels of their own countrymen and their tales of the magnificence of the court of the Great Mogul. One of the first came from the merchant-adventurer Ralph Fitch, who embarked on the *Tyger* bound for Tripolis in Syria with a small group of friends in 1584 and returned to London seven years later, having penetrated as far east as Portuguese Malacca. His stolid narrative is the antithesis of Polo's, rarely dwelling on matters outside his commercial interests. But Fitch spent almost two years travelling through Pegu and the 'country of the Langeiannes' (today, Burma and northern Thailand), about whose idolatrous practices he was uncharacteristically forthcoming. He was greatly taken by the large number of what he termed *Varellaes* or *Pagodes*, which he describes as being 'Idole temples . . . round like a sugar Loafe, some as high as a Church, very broad beneath, some a quarter of a mile in compasse. Within they be all Earth done about with Stone. They consume in these *Varellaes* great quantity of Golde; for that they be all gilded aloft: and many of them from the top to the bottom: and every ten or twelve yeeres they must be new gilded, because the rain consumeth off the golde: for they stand open abroad. If they did not consume their golde in these vanities, it would be very plentiful and goode cheape in Pegu.'

The finest of these 'Varellaes' was a vast golden pagoda near the mouth of the River Irrawaddy:

About two dayes journey from Pegu there is a *Varelle* or *Pagode*, which is the pilgrimage of the Pegues. It is called *Dogonne*, and is of a wonderful bignesse, and is all gilded from the foot to the toppe . . . There are houses very faire round about for the *Tallipoies* to preach in, which are full of images both of men and women, which are all gilded ouer with golde. It is the fairest place, as I suppose, that is in the world: it standeth very high, and there are foure wayes to it, in such wise that a man may goe in the shade above two miles in length.

Society in Pegu was dominated by a religious order of what Fitch mistakenly called priests, the *Tallipoies*:

> The *Tallipoies* go very strangely apparelled with one camboline or thinne cloth next to their Body of a brown colour, another of yellow doubled many times upon their Shoulders: and these two be girded to them with a broad Girdle . . . None of them weareth Shoes; with their right Armes bare and a great broad Sombrero or shadow [in fact, a waxed-paper parasol] in their hands to defend them in the Summer from the Sunne, and in the Winter from the Rain . . . And they go with a great Pot made of Wood or fine Earth, and covered, tied with a broad Girdle upon their Shoulder, which commeth under their Arme, wherewith they goe to begge their Victuals which they eate, which is Rice, Fish and Herbs. They demand nothing, but come to the Doore, and the People presently doe give them, some one thing and some another.

As a description of the Buddhist monks or *bhikkhu* of Burma and Thailand – known more popularly today as *pongyi* – this could hardly be bettered.

In 1641 and 1648 Malacca and Muscat, the eastern and western doors of Portugal's trade corridor, fell to the Dutch. In 1656 Columbo was lost and two years later, with the surrender of the Portuguese fort at Jaffna, the Dutch United East India Company became the new rulers of Ceylon's coastal belt as well as the dominant power in the East Indies. The Dutch set about enforcing their monopoly of Ceylon's cinnamon trade with a hard-nosed efficiency that put the Portuguese to shame. Being good Protestants, they took exception to the Roman practices the Portuguese had introduced and now persecuted the island's Catholic converts with almost as much zeal as their predecessors had harried heathens.

But while the Dutch concentrated their efforts on reducing the Portuguese fortresses – at enormous cost in terms of manpower and shipping – the 'Company of Merchants of London Trading into the East Indies' that became the East India Company quietly went about developing its trading links with India, many of them concentrated on Madras and the Coast of Coromandel.

In mid November 1659 a fleet of East Indiamen laden with peppers, cotton small goods and other commodities of the India trade gathered in the roads off Fort St George, Madras, prior to sailing back to England. A sudden storm blew up: a number of vessels were dismasted and blown ashore, while others were forced to cut their anchors and run before the wind. One of the latter was the frigate *Ann*, Master John Loveland, Commander his natural son Robert Knox. They ordered the ships's mast to be axed by the board and steered the *Ann* as best they could for the Bay of Cothiar on the isle of Ceylon, reputed to be the largest and finest natural harbour in the Indies (and better known today as Trincomalee). Here they found safe haven and were warmly received by the local people, who brought them victuals and fresh water. Thinking it safe to go ashore, Robert Knox and his father landed with sixteen members of their crew, only to be seized and made prisoner. After two months of impasse, the remaining members of the crew on board the *Ann* upped anchor and sailed out of the bay.

Knox and his father were separated from the rest of their crew. Soon both were stricken with ague, and within weeks John Loveland had died in his son's arms. Alone and friendless, Robert Knox was forced to dig his father's grave and bury him unaided. After a year he was offered the chance to enter the King of Ceylon's service as a militiaman. He refused, and was then marched deep into the mountainous interior of the country, where he remained in a state of semi-slavery for some thirteen years. In time he earned enough to buy a patch of land and plant an orchard, where he was eventually joined by three members of his crew. Here they lived together 'lovingly and contentedly' but with little hope of securing their liberty. After another two years had passed Knox received a summons to attend the royal court in Kandy, at the very heart of the island. Here he was again offered the chance to join the king's service, and when he again refused was once more banished to a remote part of the country. In 1679, after a number of botched attempts to escape, Knox and his one remaining companion finally succeeded in crossing the island undetected and reaching a Dutch fort on the north coast. After a roundabout passage that took them first to the Dutch East Indies, the two escapees eventually got back to England.

When Robert Knox arrived in London in 1680 he had a wondrous tale to tell, already set down in manuscript. Rushed into print, it was an immediate success, inspiring a generation of writers – most notably, Daniel Defoe and Jonathan Swift – and helping to shape the popular image of oriental rulers as despotic, cruel and debauched. Knox was in no doubt that all his troubles could be attributed to one man alone, the King of Kandy, and he wanted the world to know it. A cache of letters preserved in the Bodleian Library shows Robert Knox to have been the very model of a seventeenth-century sea-dog: rough and tough, ill-tempered and a misogynist. Such was the man chosen by fate to be Buddhism's first messenger to the British Isles.

'The religion of the country is idolatry', is how Knox began the first of his two chapters on the religion of Ceylon. 'There are many both Gods and Devils, which they worship, known by particular names which they call them by.' He had, however, observed two quite distinct forms of idolatry practised on the island. One was no different from what he had seen on the Indian mainland, characterised by a multiplicity of gods for whom he had little time: 'Idols and Images most monstrous to behold, some of Silver, some of Brass and other Metals: and also planted Sticks, and Targets, and most strange kind of Arms, as Bills, Arrows, Spears and Swords.' The second religion revolved around a single, central figure:

There is another great God, whom they call *Buddou*, unto whom the Salvation of Souls belongs. Him they believe once to have come upon the Earth. And when he was here, that he did usually sit under a large shady Tree, called *Bogoha*. Which Trees ever since are accounted Holy, and under which with great Solemnities they do to this day celebrate the Ceremonies of his Worship . . . The Places where he is commemorated are two, not temples but the one a Mountain and the other a Tree . . . The Mountain is at the South end of the Country, called

Hammalella, but by the Christian People, Adam's Peak, the highest in the whole Island; where is the Print of the *Buddou*'s foot, which he left on the top of that Mountain in a Rock, from whence he ascended to Heaven . . . The Tree is at the North end of the King's Dominions at Annarodgburro [Anuradhapura, the 'Buried City of Ceylon', destroyed by Tamil invaders in the ninth century]. This Tree, they say, came flying over from the other Coast, and there planted it self, as it now stands, under which the *Buddou*-God at his being on earth used, as they say, often to sit . . . This tree they call the *Bo-gahah*; we the God tree.

Both the religions of the island had their temples, which Knox (like Ralph Fitch before him) termed pagodas, a term widely believed to be either Chinese or Portuguese in origin but which almost certainly has its roots in the Sanskrit word *bhagavat*, meaning 'sacred'. Inside the pagodas of 'Buddou' only one form of idol was to be found: 'Images of men cross-legged with yellow coats on like the *Gonni*-Priests, their hair frizzled and their hands before them like women. And these they say are the spirits of holy men departed.' The 'Gonni-priests' (see illustration overleaf) lived in what Knox correctly termed *vihars* and were distinguished from the rest of the populace both by their dress – 'a yellow coat gathered together about their wast [waist] and comes over their left shoulder, girt about with a belt of fine pack-thread' – and their abstemious way of life:

Their Heads are shaved, and they go bare-headed and carry in their Hands a round Fan with a wooden Handle, which is to keep the Sun off the Hands [*sic:* heads]. They have great benefit and honour. They enjoy their own Lands without paying scot or lot or any Taxes to the King. They are honoured in such a measure, that the People, where ever they go, bow down to them as they do to their God . . . They are debarred from laying their Hands to any manner of work; and may not marry or touch Women, nor eat but one Meal a day, unless it be Fruit and Rice and Water, that they may eat morning and evening: nor must they drink wine.

Except at festival times the general population of the island showed little interest in religion, but took their cue from the priests by following a clear set of beliefs: 'These people do firmly believe in a resurrection of the Body, and the immortality of Souls and a future State . . . They do believe that those they call Gods are the Spirits of Men that formerly have lived upon the Earth. They hold that in the other Worlds, those that are good Men tho they be poor and mean in this World, yet there they shall become high eminent; and that wicked Men shall be turned into Beasts.' Accompanying these beliefs was a moral code in which pacifism, vegetarianism and charity played important parts:

They reckon the chief points of Goodness to consist in giving to the Priests, in making *Pudgiahs* [*puja*, or worship], sacrifices to their Gods, in forbearing shedding the blood of any creature . . . and in abstaining from eating any flesh at all, because they would not have any hand, or any thing to do in killing any living thing . . . It is accounted religion to be just and sober and chaste and true, and to be endowed with other Virtues, as we do account it. They give to the poor out of a Principle of Charity, which they extend to Foreigners, as well as to their own Country-men. But of every measure of Rice they boyl in their Houses for their Families they will take out a Handful, as much as they can gripe, and keep it by itself . . . and this they give and distribute to such Poor as they please.

What amounted to the first outline of Buddhism and its basic tenets to be set down in the English language made little impression on readers much more interested in Ceylon's commercial potential as a spice island and pearl fishery. As the Dutch strengthened their hold on this and the other spice islands of the Indies, Ceylon and its exotic religions faded into the background. The EICo, meanwhile, redoubled its efforts to outperform its rivals on the Indian mainland. Led by gentlemen risk-takers, it entered into a series of alliances with local rulers that strengthened and extended its trading bases. In 1717 the Company was granted an Imperial *firman* from the Mogul emperor giving it the right to trade in Bengal without payment of duties. Taking full advantage of this commercial coup, within thirty years it had become inextricably enmeshed in the local economy of Bengal, and by 1760 was the ruling power in all but name. India was suddenly a land of opportunity, and from that time onward the lowly starting position of EICo 'writer' or clerk was increasingly sought-after as the younger sons of the gentry of England, Scotland and Ireland jostled among themselves to secure a foothold at the base of the pagoda tree – the pagodas, in this new context, being gold coins rather than gilded temples.

3

Oriental Jones and
the Asiatic Society

IN SEPTEMBER 1783, as the thirty-four-year-old Johann Wolfgang von Goethe prepared to abandon Weimar for the wider horizons of Italy and the Mediterranean, a thirty-seven-year-old Welshman named Jones stepped ashore at Calcutta to begin his own quest for fulfilment. Both men had a passion for neo-Classical scholarship, both were children of the Enlightenment, and Goethe's often-quoted remark on entering Rome – 'Only now do I begin to live' – could just as easily have come from the lips of William Jones, as the frigate *Crocodile* slipped with the tide past Garden Reach and dropped anchor off Fort William. What Goethe went on to achieve in the course of a long and fruitful life is widely known, yet who outside the confines of South Asian and Sanskrit studies knows of the scarcely less extraordinary attainments of Sir William Jones, accomplished in the last ten years and seven months of his life?

The Enlightenment was nicely defined by the philosopher David Hume as 'a sudden and sensible change in the opinions of men . . . by the progress of learning and liberty'. Although usually credited to *un petit troupeau des philosphes*, its roots were set as firmly in early eighteenth-century England and Scotland as anywhere in Europe. Revisionists now present the English Enlightenment as a philosophy tainted by totalitarianism, what Eric Hobsbawm has mocked (in his courageously unfashionable essay *On History*, 1997) as 'a conspiracy of dead white men in periwigs to provide the intellectual foundation for Western imperialism'. The fact is that these 'dwmps' introduced a new intellectual rigour to Western Europe and brought about a change in attitudes that gave impetus as much to republicanism as to imperialism.

William Jones's father was a mathematician of humble origins but exceptional ability who became tutor to the heir of the Earl of Macclesfield. However, Jones *père* died when his son was only three, and the responsibility for bringing up the infant William fell on his widowed mother, who did so in accordance with the libertarian principles of John Locke. The child was reciting Shakespeare and Gay at the age of four, and at thirteen wrote down the whole of *The Tempest* from memory. Soon declared by his Classics master at Harrow School to know more than he, William moved on by his own request to University College, Oxford, which had gained a wide reputation for Oriental scholarship. He had already taught himself Hebrew at school, to which he now added Arabic and Persian. William then turned, like his father before him, to the aristocracy for employment, becoming a tutor to the Spencer heir. The connection opened doors, and in 1768 he was asked to translate a Persian manuscript, a life of Nadir Shah, brought to England by King Christian VII of Denmark. He now became, in a word, an Orientalist, and produced a flood of translations from the Persian and Arabic that helped to create a growing public appetite for things Oriental. Here were texts as worthy of study as anything from Greece or Rome: 'The heroic poem of Ferdusi might be versified as easily as the Iliad, and I see no reason why the Delivery of Persia by Cyrus should not be a subject as interesting to us, as the anger of Achilles, or the wandering of Ulysses.'

In 1771 Jones became a popular figure when he accused France's leading Persian scholar of being a fraud. The French, rivals of the British as much in scholarship as in war, had stolen a march by proclaiming themselves leaders of a *renaissance orientale*. This claim was based largely on the work of the improbably named Abraham-Hyacinthe Anquetil-Duperron, who in 1754 had gone out to the French possessions in India as a common soldier with the intention of studying ancient texts. Evicted with his compatriots from

Pondicherry by the victorious British in 1761, Anquetil-Duperron had returned to Paris with some two hundred manuscripts. His *Zend-Avesta, Ouvrage de Zoroastre* created a sensation in France, but its boastful tone, coupled with his insulting remarks about the low standards of scholarship at Oxford, provoked Jones to a counter-attack. His accusations were largely unjustified, but Jones was nevertheless seen as the champion of British scholarship and became widely lauded as 'Persian Jones' or 'Oriental Jones'. In 1772 he was elected a Fellow of the Royal Society, and a year later was invited to join Samuel Johnson's even more exclusive circle at the Turk's Head in Soho.

Disagreements over young George Spencer's education forced Jones to look for another source of income so he enrolled at the Middle Temple, and was called to the Bar in 1774. The breadth of his learning was by now prodigious: the historian Edward Gibbon spoke of him as 'the only lawyer conversant with the year-books of Westminster, the commentaries of Ulpian, the Attic pleadings of Isaeus, and the sentences of the Arabian and Persian *cadhis*.'

Jones divided his time between the law, Oxford and politics. He published a radical pamphlet, *The Principles of Government*, which went through nine editions, and at one point even went to France, with the intention of moving on from there to republican America. Once in France, however, Jones was shaken by all the revolutionary talk, and returned to England expressing disgust at the notion that 'the will of the rabble is the law'. He tried to gain a seat in Parliament as a member for Oxford and failed; more seriously, he also failed to get the Professorship in Arabic at Oxford he believed to be his by right.

It was in 1778, at this critical juncture in William Jones's life, that he was offered a seat on the bench of the newly-established Supreme Court in Bengal, worth £6,000 a year (at least £140,000 today). For some years he had been paying court to a clergyman's daughter, Anna Maria Shipley, whom he had known since his days as an undergraduate. Hitherto he had been a man without prospects: the Indian judgeship would enable him to make in five or six years what would take him twenty in England – and return 'still a young man with thirty thousand pounds in my pocket'. Like most Whigs, Jones was no friend of the EICo, which he regarded as a corrupt, self-serving body in desperate need of radical reform. But he knew the Governor-General, Warren Hastings, who had spoken kindly of his recently-published *Grammar of the Persian Language*.

Warren Hastings had his dark side; he became increasingly intolerant of criticism, and ruthless in the pursuit of those whom he judged to be his enemies. Yet the fact remains that he brought to Bengal a breadth of vision that set him far apart from his peers. Since his appointment in October 1774 he had halted the worst abuses, such as the notorious *dastuk* system which had given Company officials unlimited scope to make private fortunes by imposing their own trade duties. He had laid the ground for extensive reforms in administration and revenue collection in Bengal, and had established a judicial system of civil and criminal courts that took account of native Indian as well as English law – something Jones heartily approved of.

Far and away more important than all these reforms, however, was Hastings's introduction to the government of India of the revolutionary notion of shared humanity. Nowhere is this philosophy better expressed than in the epitaph he himself wrote for the tombstone of a young civilian administrator, Augustus Cleveland, who died upriver in Bihar of a fever at the age of twenty-nine. Hastings set down that Cleveland was a man who 'without bloodshed or terrors of authority, employing only the means of conciliation, confidence and benevolence, attempted and accomplished the entire subjection of the lawless and savage inhabitants of the jungle territory of Rajmahal . . . and attached them to the British Government by a conquest over their minds, the most permanent as the most rational mode of dominion.'

Hastings abhorred the popular view of his countrymen that the peoples of the subcontinent were 'creatures scarcely elevated above the degree of savage life'. From his own experiences as a servant of the EICo in Bengal he held Indians to be 'gentle, benevolent and more susceptible for kindness shown them than prompt to vengeance for wrongs sustained', with 'as sound integrity, and as honourable feelings, as any of this kingdom'; and they too had 'natural rights'. Proficient in Urdu, Persian and Bengali, Hastings considered a knowledge of Indian culture an absolute prerequisite for a sound administration – a view that would have occurred to none of his predecessors and few of his contemporaries. Again and again in his official correspondence with the less-than-sympathetic Board of Control that had taken over many of the powers of the EICo's Directorate he stressed the need to respect the laws and customs of the Indians, and to encourage 'social communication with people over whom we exercise a dominion'. But no more in this than in other matters was he speaking for his fellow-Britons in India, most of whom preferred to live apart from a people they held in low regard.

One means Hastings saw of lessening this social gulf was through the establishment of a cadre of civil servants familiar with the language and customs of the people they administered, and one of his first acts after settling himself into Government House in Calcutta was to urge the EICo's Directors to see to it that these 'civilians' were given a thorough grounding in oriental languages and history. Out of his own pocket he founded a *Madrasa* or 'school of learning' in Calcutta for the pursuit of Muslim studies, arguing that nothing could 'conciliate the affection of the natives' so well as 'toleration in matters of religion, and an adoption of such original institutes of the country, as do not immediately clash with the laws or interests of the conquerors'. The presence of such a man at the Company's helm in India gave Jones every hope that great things might be achieved there under his aegis.

There were a number of other individuals in Bengal whom Jones could regard as natural allies. The most powerful was the Chief Justice, Sir Elijah Impey, who had shown himself a staunch supporter of Warren Hastings. At their palatial house just off Chowringhee in Calcutta the Impeys had set up a salon – and a menagerie. Their eccentricities included a keen interest in Indian art, of which they were pioneer collectors. At Sir Elijah's side as the Second Judge of the High Court was an old friend of Jones from University College days, Sir Robert Chambers, a former intimate of Dr Johnson and now a keen collector of Sanskrit manuscripts. Two other acquaintances from Oxford were also beginning to make their mark in Bengal, Charles Wilkins and Nathaniel Halhed. Both had studied Persian as undergraduates before going out to India as 'writers' or clerks in the EICo's Bengal Establishment. After learning Bengali at the Writers' Building, the

Company's head office and administrative nerve centre in Calcutta, both had been despatched up-country to learn their trade as 'factors' at one of the EICo's many outlying 'factories' or trading depots.

Halhed, the younger of the two, was the first to distinguish himself, publishing in 1776 his translation from the Persian of an ancient text on Hindu law. Though derived from a second-hand source, this *Code of Gentoo Laws* gave British jurists their first glimpse of what was clearly a very sophisticated system. Halhed next began to compile a Bengali grammar, then found there was no one in Bengal with the necessary skills to turn it into print. He turned for advice to his friend Charles Wilkins, who concluded that the only way to get the grammar printed was to do it themselves. Wilkins found a disused warehouse at Hugli, the former Portuguese settlement upriver from Calcutta, and there set himself up as an amateur printer. It was an extraordinary effort, involving as it did the shaping and casting of founts by hand to produce a Bengali typeface, but in 1778 Wilkins published Halhed's *Grammar of the Bengali Language*. Thus Bengali became the first native Indian language to be made available in printed form. Wilkins followed by casting a fount of Persian types, which was used for many years to print the EICo's Regulations.

Wilkin's achievement had repercussions that went far beyond Bengal: for the first time the authorities were able to promulgate their edicts directly in the languages of those they governed; more significantly, perhaps, those vernacular languages were themselves liberated by becoming widely available in printed form. Hitherto Wilkins and Halhed had faced a wall of hostility whenever they sought to enquire into the sacred texts held by the Brahmins. In Northern India these were all written in Sanskrit, the language of the Gods, so it followed that only those sanctified by the Gods as their intermediaries – the Brahmins – should have access to them. For the Brahmin pandits who served as the Hindu community's scholars and teachers, the preservation of the core teachings of Brahminism was a sacred duty – one that also gave them an absolute monopoly of learning, so that it was very much in their interests to ensure that Sanskrit remained an esoteric, secret language.

All this changed with the establishment of Wilkins's vernacular press and the publication of Halhed's Bengali Grammar, both widely applauded by the native Indian population. The same Brahmins who had refused Wilkins's pleas to be allowed to study Sanskrit now offered to teach it to him – with the result that within a year Wilkins had brought out a Sanskrit Grammar. Another year on and Wilkins reached another milestone by becoming the first man to decipher an ancient Sanskrit inscription. In November 1780, while visiting one of the EICo's trading depots under his charge, at Buddal in Bihar, he noticed what at first glance appeared to be 'the trunk of a coconut tree broken off in the middle' rising out of a weed-filled swamp. More careful examination revealed it to be a 'decapitated monumental pillar', a broken column bearing an inscription 'engrained in the stone'. Using printer's ink and a roller, he made two reversed impressions of the inscription, which he then took back to his house to work on. It was immediately apparent to Wilkins that the characters were different from those of the Sanskrit he had been learning. In the Nagari script he was familiar with (today known as Devanagari), the letters of each word were linked together by overlining, whereas the letters on the pillar at Buddal, although grouped together into words, remained separate. The letters themselves, however, were not dissimilar from the Nagari, and he had soon deciphered what proved to be a royal grant of land. Clearly this must be a form of Sanskrit dating from India's still unknown past.

What was of particular interest to William Jones, however, was Charles Wilkins's current project: he had begun work on the translation of a section of a Sanskrit epic said to be many times longer than Homer's *Iliad*. The epic was the *Mahabharata*, the extract the *Bhagavad Gita* or 'Song of God', a devotional poem of some six hundred verses arranged in eighteen cantos which tells how the Hindu god Krishna, acting as the warrior Arjuna's charioteer, helps Arjuna decide when he has qualms about doing battle with his kinsmen, the Kauravas. But Wilkins, increasingly plagued by ill-health, to say nothing of the demands of his work as a Company official, was making slow progress.

A challenge of a different sort was posed by William Jones's fellow Orientalists on the Continent, particularly the French.

After winning widespread praise for his revelations of Persian religion, Anquetil-Duperron was now working on the many Sanskrit texts he had acquired. The naturalist Le Gentil de la Galaisière, following extensive travels through the French possessions in southeast Asia, announced that the religions of these countries bore such a remarkable similarity as to indicate a common source. And hard on the heels of these two was another Frenchman, the celebrated traveller and savant Pierre Sonnerat, whose *Voyages aux Indes Orientales* argued that India was nothing less than the cradle of humanity. Also breaking new ground was Carsten Niebuhr, the only survivor of a Danish scientific expedition to the Indies, whose *Voyage en Arabie et en autres pays circonvoisins*, published in 1779, supported de la Galaisière's claims that India possessed a culture as ancient and as rich as that of Ancient Egypt. Writing of the monumental Hindu cave-sculptures on Bombay's Elephanta Island, still magnificent despite the damage inflicted by the musketry of the Portuguese, the Dane declared them to be 'far superior to the design and arrangement of Egyptian figures, and besides, very beautiful in relation to their great antiquity . . . to create such effect, far greater knowledge of design and sculpture was necessary than ever was possessed by the Egyptians'.

Galled by this trespassing on what its members liked to consider an exclusively British sphere of interest, the Society of Antiquaries now set about demonstrating their pre-eminence in the field. A long-neglected account of his exploration of the Elephanta caves by a Captain Pyke made some seventy years earlier – and thus before the French had begun *their* enquiries – together with drawings in the Society's possession of statuary from the nearby caves of Salsette, became the central features of the seventh volume of the Society's journal *Archaeologia*.

A series of frustrating setbacks delayed Jones's Indian appointment, and it took the personal intervention of the King to confirm him in the post – and the knighthood that went with it. In March 1783 he was knighted, three weeks later he married his sweetheart by Special Licence, and in mid April Sir William and Lady Jones sailed for India.

It was on board the fast-sailing *Crocodile* that Jones's quite extraordinary ambition first found expression, in a list he made of what might be accomplished in the ten years he proposed to spend on the subcontinent, under the general heading 'Objects of Enquiry during my Residence in India'. The sixteen 'objects' begin with the laws of the Hindus and Mohammedans, end with the constitution of the Marathas, and include 'The poetry, rhetoric and morality of Asia', 'Medicine, chemistry, surgery, and anatomy of the Indians', together with histories of Great Britain and the recent American war. As the voyage progressed, however, so the significance of what lay ahead of him grew – to the exclusion of what now lay behind. As the *Crocodile*'s bow turned away from the east coast of Africa towards India and its sails filled with the south-westerlies, Jones experienced a sort of epiphany: 'It gave me inexpressible pleasure to find myself in the midst of so noble an amphitheatre, almost encircled by the vast regions of Asia, which had ever been esteemed the nurse of sciences, the inventress of delightful and useful arts, the scene of glorious actions, fertile in the productions of human genius, abounding in natural wonders, and infinitely diversified in the forms of religions and government.' How little was known about this ancient world – and 'how important and extensive a field was yet unexplored'.

Jones now began to ask himself hard questions about how such an exploration might be accomplished. After much deliberation he concluded that it could only be done through 'the united efforts of many' – the many being, in this instance, his countrymen in Bengal. Britain had its Royal Society, its Society of Antiquaries and the newly-established Royal Academy; the French had their Académie des Inscriptions et des Belles Lettres; and the Dutch had just set up a Batavian Society, specifically to pursue enquiries pertaining to their territories in the Dutch East Indies. So India too must have its own learned society. It would be based in Bengal, and it would have no rigid rules; in fact, there would be 'but one rule, namely, to have no rules at all'. Its members would 'investigate whatever is rare in the stupendous fabric of nature . . . correct the geography of Asia by new observations and discoveries . . . trace the annals, and even traditions, of those nations, who from time to time have peopled or desolated it . . . bring to light their various forms of government, with their institutions civil and religious' – and much, much more besides.

Thus the Asiatick Society (soon afterwards to become the Asiatic Society, and in 1835 the Asiatic Society of Bengal) was conceived.

Calcutta in 1783 was not yet the 'City of Palaces' its later admirers claimed it to be, but it was the fastest-growing town in Asia, with the wealth of its small European community on conspicuous display. William Jones left no account of his introduction to it, but one of those who did was John Prinsep, who had arrived in Calcutta just weeks after Warren Hastings took up his appointment as Governor-General. In an unpublished memoir he described waking on the deck of the tender that had carried him up the Hugli River with the tide to find himself confronted by a scene 'more like a vision than any reality I could anticipate' (see Plate 12). He continued:

> The first object on my left was a very handsome Fort [Fort William] and large Battery with the Flag up and drums beating. On my right I almost instantly beheld first one then others in quick succession, of elegant classic built houses adorned with luxurious plantations of green trees and lawns equally verdant and apparently close mowed. Inhabitants on their banks were gazing at leisure to see us and were cheered by the boatmen to indicate that we were strangers – 'Taza Belayat Logh' [new British people] as I have since heard was the term by which we were designated.
>
> Next, the Fort opened to our view, reminding me of Valenciennes, regular, majestic and commanding. The stream seemed to widen as we proceeded and straight before us we beheld a stately forest of masts, vessels, an immense city and all the bustle of a commercial business. On the opposite side of the water stood several respectable country houses like those which had first attracted notice.
>
> A few minutes after this magic scene had dazzled our eyes I landed with my baggage at the Custom House and proceeded to the 'Punch-House' in the Bazaar with ten guineas that I had borrowed from my friend to bear my expenses till I should have presented myself to the Fort Major.

John Prinsep had brought with him letters of introduction that immediately opened doors. 'I could not help being surprised at the style of hospitality offered to me,' he wrote, 'for, once respectably introduced, I found myself at home everywhere. No formality, no stiffness or reserve, everybody happy to receive the stranger, and anxious to put himself on a footing of enquiring particulars of news, politics and fashion at home. Those who gave the best answers were considered the best informed . . . Such at that time was the happy footing on which Society subsisted .'

When the Joneses disembarked at the Custom House nine years later they were accorded a far grander reception, including a guard of honour and a salute of guns. Calcutta society was now rather less welcoming, however. The town was still driven by trade, with new warehouses rising every day to cover the fields on the Howra bank across the Hugli, but its real masters were now covenanted men, civil servants who had signed away their rights to trade freely in return for large salaries and pensions. They, together with the officers of the ever-expanding Bengal Army, had begun to reshape Calcutta society as the 'civil and military'. That society did not, of course, include Indians, even though the two cultures met and worked closely together during daylight hours. Virtually every Briton in Calcutta had his *sircar*, an agent who acted as his intermediary and looked after his financial affairs, lending him the large sums required to cover his initial outlay and in later years (if his investment still lived) reaping the rewards. But that was business, and when the sun set the two tribes went their different ways. A raja or nawab might entertain a group of Europeans in his house for a *nautch* at which singers and dancers performed, but his female quarters were out of bounds. He might sit down with Europeans at table, but religious custom made it impossible for him to share their food: the Muslim could not drink wine, touch pork or risk eating meat that had not been killed by the knife, while the largely vegetarian Hindu could not risk defilement by eating with those whom his religion classed as outcastes.

Unwittingly, Calcutta society was beginning to replicate the caste system of the Hindus, with covenanted officials becoming as exclusive as the Brahmins. The four judges who sat on the bench of the Supreme Court might reasonably have expected to be included in the ranks of these 'heaven-born' but, being govern-ment-appointed and not Company men, they were regarded as interlopers, and for all their authority, they too found themselves virtual outcasts, regarded on all sides with suspicion. This isola-tion was reinforced when Sir Elijah Impey, the Chief Justice, was abruptly recalled to England to face impeachment on a charge of judicial murder (later dismissed). His Deputy Sir Robert Chambers was absent up-country, so that within weeks of his arrival Jones was playing a leading role at the Supreme Court – where he made plain his wish that the twenty million British sub-jects in Bengal should receive the full protection of British law, and that 'the natives of these important provinces be indulged in their own prejudices, civil and religious, and suffered to enjoy their own customs unmolested'. This accorded with Hastings's views – but not with those of Calcutta society.

Jones himself was too preoccupied with his work and his studies to be troubled by the opinions of others. In accordance with his ambition to 'know India better than any other European ever knew it' he quickly established a routine whereby he rose an hour before dawn and exercised by walking from his house to the Fort, a distance of about three miles. Here he would climb into his palan-quin to be carried to the Courthouse, 'where cold-bathing, dress-ing and breakfast take up an hour'. Then began the day's work. 'By seven I am ready for my pandit,' Jones wrote to his former pupil, now Earl Spencer. 'At eight come a Persian or Arab [a Muslim scholar probably of Afghan origin] alternately with whom I read till nine; at nine come the attorneys with affidavits; I am then robed and ready for court, where I sit on the bench, one day with another, five hours. At three I dress and dine.' Dinner was an extended affair that lasted until sunset, at which time the Joneses would go out to take the air: 'When the sun is sunk in the Ganges we drive back to the Gardens either in our post-chaise or Anna's phaeton drawn by a pair of beautiful Nepal horses. After tea-time we read; and never sit up, if we can avoid it, after ten . . . We are literally lulled to sleep by Persian nightingales and cease to wonder that the Bulbul with a thousand tales makes such a figure in Oriental poetry.' They had brought out with them on the *Crocodile* a pair of sheep, intended for the table, but these had become pets, along with a variety of other domestic and wild creatures – 'flocks and herds that eat bread out of our hands'. At one point they even acquired an orphaned tiger cub that was so successfully suckled by a she-goat that, as Jones wrote, 'you might see a kid and a tiger playing together at Anna's feet'.

A delightful cameo of the Joneses at home can be found in the journals of Thomas Twining, who arrived in Calcutta in 1790 as a seventeen-year-old 'griffin' armed with a letter of introduction that immediately secured him an invitation to spend the afternoon with the famous 'Oriental Jones':

> Sir William was very cheerful and agreeable. He made some observations on the mysterious word *om* of the Hindoos, and other Indian subjects. While sitting after dinner he suddenly called out with a loud voice 'Othello, Othello'. Waiting for a minute or two and Othello not coming, he repeated his summons, 'Othello, Othello'. His particularly fine voice, his white Indian dress, surmounted by a small black wig, his cheerfulness and great celebrity, rendered this scene extremely interesting. I was surprised that no one, Muslim or Hindoo, answered his summons. At last I saw a black turtle of very large size, crawling slowly towards us from an adjoining room.

As Twining's testimony shows, William Jones had taken to wearing *en déshabille* the toga-like dress of Bengal, which his compatriots called 'Brahmin robes'. This (or its Muslim equivalent, the *pyjama* or 'leg-clothing'), together with such Indian customs as a daily sluice in cold water, 'shampooing' (the kneading of the head and shoulders), and the smoking of the hookah, were just acceptable at the time. What was unacceptable was the adoption of Indian values, hence the dismay of a later visitor to Calcutta, a Mrs Fenton, at finding that a British general, 'believed to be in a sane mind, rather a man of ability', had 'for some years adopted the habits and religion, if religion it may be named, of these people'. This was Charles 'Hindoo' Stuart, a pioneer collector of Indian art, who walked every morning from his house in Wood Street to bathe in the Ganges and was rumoured to 'offer puja [worship] to idols'. Hindoo Stuart was the author of the notorious *Vindication of the Hindoos*, and caused public outrage by a series of letters he wrote to the editor of the Calcutta newspaper *The Telegraph* urging memsahibs to 'throw away their whalebone and their iron' in favour of the sari that so liberally displayed 'those charms that the bounty of heaven hath bestowed'. They might then bathe in these robes, as Indian women did, and so emerge from the water with the drapery clinging to their bodies: 'Had I despotic power, our fair ones should soon follow the example, being fully persuaded it would eminently contribute to keep the bridal torch for ever in a blaze.'

Not that the Joneses were isolated from their own kind, for there existed in Bengal a small coterie of like-minded individuals who took their cue from their patron Warren Hastings. Of these only a few were independent merchants, one of them being John Farquhar, an enthusiastic student of Hindu philosophy (he died a millionaire in 1826, disappointed in his desire to endow a Chair of Atheism at Aberdeen: his offer was indignantly rejected as contrary to that university's charter). Many more were to be found in the ranks of the military, including two senior army commanders, General John Carnac and General Charles Chapman. The majority, however, were civilians in the Anglo-Indian sense – government officials, as senior as Warren Hastings's close ally and consultant on revenue matters, the Persian scholar John Shore, and as junior as Jonathan Duncan, an insignificant junior revenue official when Jones arrived but soon to make his mark as the EICo's Resident in Benares.

Together they made a hard core of enthusiasts who provided William Jones with the base he was looking for. Early in January 1784 letters were sent to a number of people in Calcutta outlining Jones's plans for a society for the encouragement of Oriental studies and inviting them to meet in two weeks' time in the Grand Jury Room of the Supreme Court. The response was disappointing, but on 15 January Jones delivered to the twenty-nine persons present the oration he had drafted on board the 'sweet little *Crocodile*'. The Asiatick Society was to be modelled on the Royal Society, but made up of active members whose only necessary qualification would be 'a love of knowledge and a zeal for the promotion of it'. The object of their enquiries would be 'man and nature; whatever is performed by the one or produced by the other', with an emphasis on combined scholarship – joint investigations, rather in the manner of research groups. They would meet every Thursday at 7 p.m. to hear and discuss members' papers, which would duly be published in an 'Asiatick miscellany'. The question of 'learned natives' having membership was fudged; a paper written by a Muslim scholar from Benares appears in the first volume of *Asiatick Researches*, but no Indian is listed as a member until 1829.

The Governor-General was asked to be the Society's President but declined: Hastings understood what Jones had yet to grasp, that his involvement in the Society would doom it to failure. Only later, after his old friend the parliamentary orator Edmund Burke had threatened to do all in his power to have him recalled if he sided with Hastings, did Jones realise how fragile was Hastings's position in India, and what enmity he had aroused in England. Hastings's wish was that the presidency should go to the man 'whose genius planned the institution', and so William Jones became the Asiatick Society's first President, a position he retained until his death.

In fact, Jones *was* the Asiatick Society in these early years. Although an honorary secretary was appointed, it was Jones who saw to the day-to-day running of the Society's affairs and acted as the editor of its journal, to which he himself contributed twenty-nine papers. It was Jones's phenomenal energy that provided the Society with its momentum: his appeals to potential informants asking for their help, his constant chivvying of members for papers, his correspondence with other scholars in Britain and Europe; above all, his direction and guidance in new areas of research. However, it very soon become clear that he had been hopelessly optimistic in expecting the co-operation of his fellow Britons in Bengal, the majority of whom had better things to do with their leisure hours. To make matters more difficult, Jones soon lost his closest ally, when Charles Wilkins moved to Benares – partly to get away from Calcutta's pestilential night vapours, but also because he had hopes of furthering his Sanskrit studies in the city that had long been regarded as the fount of Hindu learning.

A year after its foundation the Asiatick Society's members still numbered no more than thirty. When Jones stood up to deliver his presidential discourse on the occasion of its second anniversary, he urged those few members present to think of their great rival in Europe and act accordingly, expressing the wish 'that the activity of the French in the same pursuits may not be superior to ours'. Although its numbers grew steadily over the next few years, by 1792 the Asiatick Society still had only a hundred and ten members, and its meetings rarely produced attendance figures in excess of twenty. Jones's original weekly meetings were soon abandoned for monthly ones, which then became irregular gatherings held seven or eight times a year. In October 1789 he wrote to a friend in England describing the travails of what he termed his 'expiring Society'. It was a 'puny rickity child' that was being kept alive by his efforts alone – and 'I cannot alone support it'. One reason for the lack of success was that the printing of the society's journal was repeatedly postponed because a constant backlog of official publications kept the limited capacity of the government's presses at full stretch. The log-jam was eventually broken in 1789, in which year the first two volumes of *Asiatick Researches* were at last printed. The contents were a revelation, arousing unprecedented interest both in British India and in Europe. Now at last the Asiatick Society had become the force for Orientalism that William Jones had intended it to be.

4

Jones and the Language of the Gods

FOR ALL that it is one of the oldest cities in Asia and the holiest of the seven sacred pilgrimage sites of Hinduism, the Benares we see today is a comparatively modern construct. Many of its thousands of temples are replacements of earlier shrines destroyed by Muslim iconoclasts, rebuilt and then destroyed again, in some cases five times over. Every one of the mosques in the city raised by Emperor Shah Jehan and his son Aurangzeb stands on the site of a Hindu temple. The world-famous river frontage tourists marvel at from their river-boats at dawn owes its appearance to the warlords of the Marathas, who in the eighteenth century used some of the spoils gathered from their depredations of central India to pay for the construction of many of Benares's finest temples and ghats.

Benares was ceded to the EICo by the Nawab Wazir of Oude in 1775 and the British soon began to make themselves at home in their customary manner, laying out a Civil Station beyond the boundaries of the 'native' city north of the River Varuna. This was where Charles Wilkins arrived in March 1784 to escape the Calcutta Hot Weather and to further improve his Sanskrit. He soon afterwards received a letter from Sir William Jones, who hoped that he was now 'settled among the venerable scholars and philosophers of that ancient city' and making 'advances every day in the untrodden paths of Hindu learning'. Much as he envied 'the infinite pleasure' his friend must be deriving from a subject 'so new and interesting', life was too short to consider learning Sanskrit himself – and besides, there was so much else waiting to be revealed: 'A version of the *Jog Bashest* [*Yogavasistha*] was brought to me the other day, in which I discovered much of the Platonick metaphysicks and morality; nor can I help believing, that Plato drew many of his notions (through Egypt, where he resided some time) from the sages of Hindustan. My present pursuit is the Indian system of musick.'

Jones was soon allowed to read the manuscript of Wilkins's completed translation of the *Bhagavad Gita*. His reaction is undocumented, but we can safely assume it to have been no less enthusiastic than that of the Governor-General, who declared the work to be 'of a sublimity of conception, reasoning and diction almost unequalled' and its subject 'a single exception, amongst all the religions of mankind, of a theology accurately corresponding with that of the Christian disposition, and most powerfully illustrating its fundamental doctrines'. Indeed, Hastings was happy to place the *Bhagavad Gita* on a level with 'the most admired passages of the Iliad or Odyssey, or the first and sixth books of our own Milton'. It could only have been produced by a great civilisation, and a very old one at that, perhaps 'preceding even the first efforts of civilisation in our own quarter of the globe'. He ordered the manuscript to be sent at once to East India House, where the Board of Control, unable to see quite what this had to do with their new administration, eventually and reluctantly agreed to Hastings's request for its publication.

The obverse of Hastings's enthusiasm for the *Bhagavad Gita* was the distaste he felt for the representations of one Charles Grant, Commercial Resident at Malda, who considered Indians to be 'a race of men lamentably degenerate and base . . . governed by malevolent and licentious passions, strongly exemplifying the effects produced on society by great and general corruption of manners, and sunk in misery by their vices'. Grant believed that they had reached this state because of their enslavement to superstition. The solution he proposed was to make known to these benighted peoples 'the pure and benign principle of our divine religion'. In this respect Charles Grant was as potent an instrument for change as William Jones. Warren Hastings had resisted his petitions for Christian missionaries to be allowed to proselytise in Bengal, as did Lord Cornwallis, his successor as Governor-General, and Grant's early resignation in 1790 seemed to indicate a realisation that his efforts had been in vain. But he resigned only to join forces with the growing band of evangelicals, non-conformists and Utilitarians in England who shared his belief that by 'communicating light, knowledge and improvement, we shall attach the Hindu people to ourselves'.

In 1785 Charles Wilkins was asked by a Mr Wilmot to examine an unusual inscription. It was a rubbing taken of a stone plaque that had been shown to Mr Wilmot by the *mahant* or head priest of a Hindu temple just a few miles south of the pilgrimage town of Gaya in Bihar, at a site he named as '*Bood-dha-gaya*'. Wilkins at once recognised it as being similar to the archaic script he had found on the Buddal pillar five years earlier. The inscription bore a date: 'Friday, the fourth day of the new moon, in the month of *Madhoo*, when in the seventh or mansion of *Ganisa*, and in the year of the Era of *Veekramadeetya* 1005.' According to the Brahmin calendar, it was now the 1,842nd year of the Vikramaditya Era, which meant that the Bood-dha-gaya stone dated from the middle of the tenth century CE.

As well as a date, the stone carried a long message: it had been erected so that learned men should know that it marked the place where, 'in the midst of a wild and dreadful forest, flourishing with trees of sweet-scented flowers, and abounding in fruits and roots, infested with lions and tigers, destitute of human society, and frequented by *Moonees* [ascetics], resided *Bood-dha*, the Author of Happiness . . . He who is omnipresent, and everlastingly to be contemplated, the Supreme Being, the Eternal One, the Divinity worthy to be adored by the most praiseworthy of mankind, appeared here with a portion of his divine nature.' The stone went on to explain that this holy site had been rediscovered by someone named as 'the illustrious Amara', a devotee of the Hindu god Vishnu, who after learning that this was 'the place of the Supreme Being, *Bood-dha*', had caused an image to be carved here and a temple erected as 'the house of *Bood-dha*'.

When Wilkins's several pioneering translations eventually appeared in the first volume of *Asiatick Researches* in 1789, little notice was paid to this identification of Bodh-Gaya as 'the place of the Supreme Being, *Bood-dha*'.

At the start of the Cold Weather of 1785 the Joneses rented a simple *bangla* or country house north of Calcutta at Krishnagar, which William Jones described in a letter to a friend in England as 'a thatched cottage with an upper story and a covered verome or veranda as they call it here all round boarded and ten or twelve feet broad. It stands on a dry plain where many a garden flower grows wild . . . how preferable is this pastoral mansion (though built entirely of vegetable substances without glass, mortar, metal or any mineral except iron nails from its roof to its foundation) to the marble palaces which you have seen in Italy.' This became the Joneses' Indian Arcadia, a retreat to which they retired at the start of every Cold Weather, when the countryside was at its most lush. Here their dreams of a pastoral idyll became a reality, for Anna Maria's delicate constitution always seemed to regain its strength at Krishnagar, allowing Jones to write that, as content as he had been in England, 'I was never happy till I settled in India.'

A second reason for his happiness was that just a few miles away was the town of Navadwip, a celebrated seat of Sanskrit learning known locally as the 'Benares of Bengal'. As soon as he and Anna Maria had settled into their country bungalow Jones approached the Brahmin scholars at Navadwip to ask for their help in learning Sanskrit. What had caused him to change his mind about doing so was that a further deterioration in his health had forced Charles Wilkins to decide upon a return to England. If Jones was to continue his exploration of Sanskrit literature, therefore, he would have to learn the language himself.

Despite the offer of large sums of money the pandits of Krishnagar refused to co-operate, and when Jones continued to press his case they left in a body to attend a far-off festival. But then Jones came to hear of an retired Hindu physician named Ramlochan Cantaberna, who had taught Sanskrit in his younger days. After laying down strict conditions as to the use to which Jones's knowledge of Sanskrit was to be put, Pandit Ramlochan agreed to help. A simple sketch of him by Lady Jones, drawn in Krishnagar, carries a note stating that he belonged to the Vaishya caste of shopkeepers, farmers and craftsmen. How he acquired his knowledge of Sanskrit remains a mystery.

After a long recuperation at Bath following his return to

England in 1786, Charles Wilkins continued to translate and publish various Sanskrit manuscripts he had acquired at Benares, most notably *Hitopadesa*, and later became the EICo's first Librarian at East India House. Further scholarly appointments followed, together with honours from universities and learned societies, culminating in a knighthood in 1833. His fellow-pioneer Nathaniel Halhed, who had returned to England in 1785 to take up a career in politics, did not fare so well: he was elected MP for Lymington, but then became a supporter of the lunatic prophet Richard Brothers, an association that proved fatal to his political advancement. Although Wilkins later found him a post at East India House, Halhed was never able to fulfil the promise of his early years in Bengal.

William Jones, meanwhile, had entered the most fruitful and creative phase of his adult life, and Sanskrit was at its heart. Throughout the autumn of 1785 he worked intensively with Pandit Ramlochan on the grammar, at the same time reading Sanskrit texts with the aid of Persian translations. This deep immersion enabled him to learn the language, by his own account, 'more grammatically and accurately than the indolence of childhood, and the impatience of youth allowed me to learn any other'. He made such rapid progress that by February 1786 he was able to stand up before a meeting of the Asiatick Society and declare the Sanskrit language to be 'of a wonderful structure; more perfect than the Greek, more copious than the Latin, and more exquisitely refined than either'. Furthermore, he had made a remarkable discovery: that Sanskrit had an obvious kinship with Greek and Latin. Not only was there a common vocabulary for many words, most strikingly in numerals and such nouns of common relationship as the word mother (in Sanskrit *mata*, in Latin *mater*, in Greek μητηρ), but all three languages shared the same system of grammar, the conjugation of verbs and nouns being distinguished by the characteristic features of gender, singular and plural, and declension. In sum, Sanskrit bore to Latin and Greek 'a stronger affinity, both in the roots of verbs, and in the forms of grammar, than can possibly have been produced by accident; so strong, indeed, that no philologist could examine all three without believing them to have sprung from some common source.' There was a similar reason for supposing that 'both the Gothick and Celtick, though blended with a different idiom, had the same origin with Sanscrit; and the old Persian might be added to the same family'.

With this statement Jones announced the discovery of the common origin of what came to be known as the Indo-European language pool. His subsequent paper on 'Asiatick Orthography', published in the first volume of *Asiatick Researches*, both initiated the process that brought the science of comparative philology to bear on Sanskrit and laid the foundations of the scientific study of languages.

Jones's central argument was that 'the first race of Persians and Indians, to whom we may add the Romans and Greeks, the Goths and the old Egyptians or the Ethiops, originally spoke the same language and professed the same popular faith'. That common language was, of course, Sanskrit; as to their shared religion, Jones had no difficulty in finding common ground between the gods of the Greeks and the Hindus: 'We must not be surprised at finding all the pagan deities male and female melt into each other'. Thus Ganesha was Janus, Vishnu was Ceres, Shiva was Jupiter, and so on. This was at once extraordinarily perceptive and deeply flawed. Like the botanist Linnaeus, the most advanced natural historian of the age, Jones believed that all humans had a common origin in Adam and Eve and a family tree that could be traced back to Noah and his sons. It followed that Hindu history and theology tied in with the Book of Genesis and at least part of the Old Testament.

The opportunity to confirm this view of a common early history came in the autumn of 1787 when Jones met Warren Hastings's former pandit, Radhakanta Sharman. The old man brought with him what he said was a summary of the Puranic view of Indian history, originally prepared for his patron, and Jones fell upon it with great excitement. It included a series of lists of royal dynasties, the *Rajavamsa*, which enabled him to draw up a comparative chronology of Indian history and world history – albeit one determined by his own Genesis-fixed view. This chronology of Indian royal dynasties started with Raja Abhimanyu in 2029 BCE and ended with Raja Devapala in 23 BCE. Roughly midway between the two dates was a law-giver variously referred to as

'Boodha', 'Boodh', 'Sacya', or the 'lion of Sac' (*Sakya Simha* or 'lion of the Sakyas'), whose birth Jones placed at 1027 BCE.

Invaluable as these lists of kings were, they were not the accurate genealogical trees that a paper he read to the Asiatick Society in June 1790 showed Jones believed them to be. He announced: 'We may safely conclude that the Mosaick and Indian chronicles are perfectly consistent; that *Manu*, son of Brahma, was the *Adima*, or first created mortal, and consequently our Adam; that *Manu*, child of the sun, was preserved with seven others, in a *bahitra* or capacious ark, from our universal deluge, and must therefore be our Noah.' In his enthusiasm for his 'common culture' theory he had cobbled together a comparative table of ancient history that was to dog his fellow Orientalists for the next forty years.

To be fair to Jones, he was not solely to blame. In Benares an enthusiastic young Lieutenant of Engineers named Francis Wilford had determined to take Charles Wilkins's mantle upon himself by becoming the third Englishman to learn Sanskrit. Lieutenant Wilford also worked on the *Rajavamsa*, adding weight to Jones's thesis with his own even wilder speculations. Faced with the same 'closed shop' reaction that Jones had experienced in Krishnagar, he made little headway with the Sanskrit language, but by 1792 had apparently won over the pandits of Benares to the extent of being offered translations of some previously unheard-of Sanskrit texts. These showed beyond doubt that India's Manu *was* one and the same with the Biblical Noah, as Jones had speculated, and that Hindu mythology was indeed Egyptian in origin; in fact, these newly-revealed texts supported and developed Sir William Jones's theories so closely that he was happy to give over almost the entire third volume of *Asiatick Researches* to Wilford's prolix paper on the subject.

It was to Francis Wilford in Benares that Jones turned when in 1793 he received some new rubbings of inscriptions from a correspondent in Bombay. The rubbings were of a number of short inscriptions found in a complex of rock-cut temples and caves at Ellora, to the north of Aurangabad in the Deccan, which had first been brought to the Western world's attention by the Frenchman Thevenot. Soon Lieutenant Wilford was able to write back with wonderful news:

I have the honour to return to you the facsimile of several inscriptions with an explanation of them. I despaired at first of ever being able to decypher them . . . However, after many fruitless attempts on our part, we were so fortunate as to find at last an ancient sage, who gave us the key, and produced a book in Sanscrit, containing a great many ancient alphabets formerly in use in different parts of India. This was really a most fortunate discovery, which hereafter may be of great use to us.

Here was a breakthrough of awesome proportions, for it seemed Wilford's 'ancient sage' had provided him with a key that could unlock the door to India's hidden past. Thanks to the Sanskrit code book Wilford was able to report that the Ellora inscriptions were the work of the Pandava brothers, whose twelve-year exile in the jungle was recounted in that other great Indian epic the *Mahabharata*, and who in the course of their long wanderings over the subcontinent had paused from time to time to inscribe 'short and obscure sentences on rocks and stones in the wilderness'.

But there was, alas, no Sanskrit master code book holding the key to India's earliest alphabets, any more than there were messages left on rocks by the Pandava brothers, or ancient texts linking India with Egypt. Whether for financial gain, to discourage him from meddling with their sacred texts, or simply to give him what he so desperately sought, one or more of the pandits of Benares had taken Francis Wilford for a ride: both the Sanskrit code book and the hitherto unheard-of texts were fakes. Poor Wilford soon seems to have realised that the code book could not be all it was claimed to be, because nothing more was heard from him on that score. But he quite evidently failed to heed its lesson, for he continued to take at face value whatever translations were put in front of him, his enthusiasm and his credulity equally undiminished. The result was a series of bizarre papers that dominated the volumes of *Asiatick Researches* for the next fifteen years; most notorious was an extensive treatise entitled 'The Sacred Isles of the West' that purported to show how the British Isles came well within the sphere of Indian geography, and that the ancestral Indian holy land of the west known as *Sweta-dwipa*, the White Island, was nothing less than the British Isles.

But Wilford was not the only one who embarked on wild-goose chases. It had long been known that among the many piles of ruins extending across the countryside south of the walls of Delhi was one that had as its centrepiece a great *lat* or pillar of polished grey sandstone set high on a stone platform. The eccentric English traveller Thomas Coryat had seen it in 1616, and had wondered at its enormous size – ten feet round at its base and well over forty feet high – and its extraordinary sheen, which he had taken at first for that of polished brass. Much of the column was covered by lines of inscriptions written in three different scripts, one of which looked very like some kind of archaic Greek. Coryat jumped to the obvious conclusion that it was a victory column erected by Alexander the Great to mark his crushing of the Indian king Porus in 326 BCE.

From the writings of an Arab chronicler it was learned that the stone column had been brought to Delhi on the orders of the fourteenth-century Sultan Firoz Shah to add lustre to his capital. Having erected this trophy on the roof of his new palace, Firoz Shah had then called for the inscriptions to be translated: 'Many Brahmins and Hindu devotees were invited to translate them, but no one was able.'

What was known as Firoz Shah's *Lat* or 'staff' caught the attention of British antiquarians, and in 1786 a rubbing was made and sent down to Calcutta – just too late for it to be seen and examined by Charles Wilkins before he sailed for England. He would have had little difficulty in translating one of the three inscriptions, for it was written in a solid script (today known as Gupta Brahmi) he had already identified as a precursor of the more rounded pre-Devanagari form of Sanskrit he had first seen on the broken column at Badal. What would certainly have fascinated – and confounded – him was the pillar's central inscription, written in what appeared to be pseudo-Greek characters that were as much squiggles as letters. But with Wilkins gone, the efforts of Jones and others to get to grips with this mysterious writing soon petered out. 'The Nagari inscriptions are easy and modern,' wrote Sir William to one of his up-country correspondents, 'but all the old ones on the staff of Firuz-Shah drive me to despair.' This did not, however, prevent him from indulging in some wild speculation: 'I believe them to be Ethiopian and to have been imported a thousand years before Christ by the Bauddhas or priests and soldiers of the conqueror Sisac, whom the Hindus call the Lion of Sacya.'

Jones had arrived at this extraordinary conclusion by a series of quite unwarranted deductions. To begin with he had decided, like Thomas Coryat before him, that the column and its almost Greek lettering must be the work of a foreign conqueror. And from all that he had read and seen in his travels, 'the remains of architecture and sculpture in India . . . seem to prove a connection between this country and Africa'. The several cave complexes hewn from the rock in the vicinity of Bombay seemed remarkably similar to the temples of Egypt. A number of stone idols which had recently been dug up in the vicinity of Gaya in Bihar also appeared to have links with Egyptian statuary. It was clear, too, that the mysterious lettering on Firoz Shah's Lat was the same as that of the inscriptions from the caves at Ellora which had fooled Lieutenant Wilford. To Jones the conclusion was inescapable: 'All these indubitable facts may induce no ill-grounded opinion that Ethiopia and Hindustan were peopled or colonised by the same extraordinary race.' And if these two regions shared the same people, it followed that they also had a common religion: 'The Hindu religion spread probably over the whole earth, there are signs of it in every northern country, and in almost every system of worship; in England it is obvious: Stonehenge is evidently one of the temples of Boodh.'

The linking of the Boodh of the ancient Hindu chronological tables with Stonehenge was a wild card that Jones, very wisely, never played again. Even so, he had now convinced himself that this ancient law-giver was identifiable with the Egyptian god Sesostris and the Ethiopian 'Sesac . . . a conqueror or legislator who raised pillars in Yemen'. Thus it followed that Boodh or Boodha was an Ethiopian: 'Since Boodha was not a native of India, and since the age of Sesac perfectly agrees with that of Sacya, we may perform a plausible conjecture that they were in fact the same person who travelled eastwards from Ethiopia, either as a warrior or as a law-giver, about a thousand years before Christ, and whose rites we now see extended as far as the country of Nison [Nippon], or, as the Chinese called it, Japuen; both words signifying the Rising Sun. Sacya may be derived from a word meaning power . . .

but the title Boodha, or wise, may induce us to believe that he was rather a benefactor than a destroyer of his species.'

The Wilford fiasco and William Jones's wilder historical extrapolations (which make him sound like the Erich von Daniken of his day) have to be put in context. A huge corpus of information hitherto unknown and unquantified had suddenly become accessible – as if a door had been opened to a great library piled high with unread books, but one without a catalogue or a shelving system. It would be an exaggeration to say that Wilkins, Jones and Wilford were working in the dark, because always they had at their elbows the torches of their Brahmin guides; but there were areas, such as the subcontinent's early history, where no outside light had yet penetrated – and here it was that scholars like Jones tripped up, even when, as in his case, such areas formed only a small part of a uniquely wide-ranging portfolio of scholarship that illuminated everything from law and language studies to astronomy and music.

By the autumn of 1787 Jones's evident respect for their culture had won over the pandits of Navadwip and they ended their ban. Soon afterwards he was able to declare exultantly: 'I speak the language of the Gods, as the Brahmins call it, with great fluency' – a fluency that gave him access to what he termed a 'new world', a body of literature and learning almost totally unknown to the Western world. 'Suppose', he wrote in 1792 in a letter explaining to a friend in England the delightfully privileged position in which he now found himself,

suppose Greek literature to be known in modern Greece only, and there to be in the hands of priests and philosophers; and suppose them to be still worshippers of Jupiter and Apollo; suppose Greece to have been conquered successively by Goths, Huns, Vandals and Tartars, and lastly by the British; then suppose a court of judicature to be established by the British parliament, at Athens, and an inquisitive Englishman to be one of the judges; suppose him to learn Greek there, which none of his countrymen knew, and to read Homer, Pindar, Plato, which no other European has ever heard of. Such am I in this country; substituting Sanscrit for Greek, the Brahmins for the priests of Jupiter, and Valmiki, Vyasa and Kalidasa for Homer, Plato and

Pindar . . . In Sanscrit are written half a million stanzas on
sacred history and literature, epic and lyric poems innumerable,
and (what is wonderful) tragedies and comedies not to be
counted, about 2,000 years old, besides works on law (my great
object), on medicine, on theology, on arithmetic, on ethics and
so on to infinity.

As the 'father of oriental studies', Sir William Jones is generally
credited with three outstanding achievements: the establishment
of the Asiatick Society as the cornerstone of Indian studies; the
laying of the foundations of comparative philology; and the translation of major Sanskrit texts that include the ordinances of Manu,
the *Shakuntala* of Kalidasa, the *Hitopadesa* of Pilpai and the
Gitagovinda of Jagadeva. But there is also a fourth achievement to
be added, one that had far-reaching consequences for the reconstruction of Indian and Buddhist history: his identification of the
'Sandrokottos' of Classical sources.

In a paper submitted to the Asiatick Society from Madras,
Jones's old friend William Chambers had suggested that India's
pre-Muslim history could only be recovered by comparing the
names and great events recorded in documents with those 'inter-
spersed in the memories of other nations' – a methodology today
known as synchronology. This, in essence, is what William Jones
attempted with the one name from the past that stood out above
all others: that of the tyrant who according to the Greek ambassador Megasthenes had established himself as ruler of the Prasians at
his capital city beside the Ganges called Palimbothra. It was known
that Megasthenes had been sent to Palimbothra in or within a year
or two of 302 BCE, so if the identity of Emperor Sandrokottos
could be found, a starting-point for early Indian chronology could
also be established.

Jones had searched long and hard for such a name among Pandit
Radhakanta's lists of Indian kings, but without success. He and
other antiquarians had also sought to locate Palimbothra, which
Ambassador Megasthenes had placed 'where the streams of the
Erannoboas and the Ganges unite, the Ganges being the greatest of
all rivers, and the Erannoboas being perhaps the third largest'. In
his *History of Hindustan*, James Dow had confidently identified

Palimbothra with Kanauj, ancient seat of the Rajput kings of northern India before its overthrow in 1194. But Kanauj was not sited at a confluence of the Ganges and a second river, and had been dismissed as a contender by the French geographer d'Anville, who had recently published a reconstruction of ancient India based on Classical sources. In place of Kanauj, d'Anville proposed the ancient city at Allahabad which, until renamed by Emperor Akbar in the sixteenth century, had long been known as Prayag. His choice won considerable support, since Prayag was revered among Hindus precisely because it stood at the confluence of two of the most sacred rivers in India, the Ganges and the Jumna.

However, there was also a third contender. The EICo's chief geographer and Surveyor-General, Major James Rennell, had originally favoured Dow's theory – until he noted what d'Anville had overlooked: that the Greek geographer Pliny had provided two sites for Palimbothra on his maps, one of which was close to the modern town of Patna. The problem with this second site was that Patna was not known to have any ancient ruins, nor was it sited on or even near a river confluence. But the ever-thorough Rennell made enquiries at Patna, and learned of a local tradition of an earlier city named 'Patelpoot-her' that had been washed away in the long-distant past. In the course of a geographical survey of the area Rennell then discovered evidence of a dry river-bed that had once joined the Ganges just above modern Patna. 'The river Soane [today Sone],' he later wrote in his *Memoir and Map of Hindoostan*, published in 1788, 'whose confluence with the Ganges is now at Moneal 22 miles above Patna once joined it under the walls of Patelpoot-her.' Rennell had earlier written to William Jones asking him to clarify the spelling of 'Patelpoot-her', which gave Jones the firmest evidence yet that the Palimbothra of Megasthenes might have been sited at what was now Patna. But Patna could only be Palimbothra if the modern River Sone was Megasthenes' Erranoboas. Conclusive proof that this was indeed the case was delivered to Jones as he sat translating one of his Sanskrit texts: it was a reference to the River Sone under the epithet of *hiranyabahu* or 'golden-armed'. It was at once obvious that 'Erranoboas' was a Greek rendering of the Sanskrit *hiranyabahu*.

The last piece of the jigsaw revealed itself to Jones as he worked on another Sanskrit text, a verse drama entitled *Mudra-rakshasa*, which told the story of a bold young man named Chandragupta who had seized the throne of a rival and made it his own. Chandragupta had then embarked on a campaign of expansion, planning his strategy on the example of a mother whom he had witnessed scolding her child for scooping up food from the centre of a dish, where it was too hot, rather than taking it from the cooler edge of the dish. He had made his capital at Palimbothra/ Pataliputra, and there he had received ambassadors from foreign lands. 'Chandragupta' rendered into Greek became 'Sandrokottos'.

In January 1793 William Jones delivered the tenth of his annual discourses to what was now the Asiatic Society, at its new premises at the corner of Chowringhee and Park Street. 'The jurisprudence of the Hindus and Arabs being the field I have chosen for my regular toil,' he began, 'you cannot expect that I should greatly enlarge your collection of historical knowledge; but I may be able to offer you some occasional tribute, and I cannot help mentioning a discovery which accident threw my way.' He then informed his audience that he could now confidently assign both a time and a place to a known monarch of ancient India: King Chandragupta, who ruled from his capital Pataliputra, the modern Patna, from about 312 BCE (eight years before Seleucus Nikator began his attempted conquest of the Punjab) to about 293 BCE (ten years after Ambassador Megasthenes arrived at Pataliputra). 'We have solved another problem,' declared Jones, 'and may in round numbers consider the twelve and three hundredth years before Christ as two certain epochs between Rama, who conquered Silan [Ceylon] a few centuries after the Flood, and Vicramaditya, who died at Ujjaini fifty-seven years before the beginning of our era.' The all-important fixed point in history, from which a chronology of Indian kings could be built up by working both backwards and forwards, had been found.

Jones's breakthrough was more important than any of those present could possibly imagine. By an extraordinary stroke of luck Chandragupta, foundation-stone for the reconstruction of India's ancient history, also happened to be the founder of arguably the most important royal dynasty in Indian history, the Mauryas. As Francis Wilford explained, this was a family name acquired by

Chandragupta, 'who was said to be the spurious offspring of a barber: because his mother, who was certainly of a low tribe, was called Mura; and her son of course Maurya in a derivative form: and it seems that Chandragupta went by that name.' Chandragupta seized power in Magadha with the aid of a wicked priest and soon after 'made himself master of the greatest part of India and drove the Greeks out of the Punjab'. He reigned over Magadha for twenty-four years and died, according to Wilford's calculations, '292 years before our Era'. His son Varisar or Bindusara then ruled over the empire established by his father for twenty-five years and his grandson Asoca or Ashoka further extended that empire and himself ruled for thirty-six years, from 267 BCE to 231 BCE (modern historians generally stick with those dates within four or five years either way).

In the autumn of this year of discovery 1793 the Joneses had to cancel their annual visit to Krishnagar when Anna Maria suffered a serious bout of dysentery. She had been in almost constantly poor health throughout their ten years in India, and the couple now agreed that she should leave Bengal in November, with William following as soon as he could complete the 'Digest of Hindu and Muslim Law' he had been working on intermittently for some years. On 25 September he wrote to inform Lord Cornwallis that he had applied to the King to be relieved of his post – but that he would leave India with great regret, since but for the ill-health of his beloved wife the past decade would have been the happiest of his life:

> I shall leave a country where we have no royal court, no House of Lords, no clergy with wealth or power, no taxes, no fear of robbers or fire, no snow and hard frost followed by comfortless thaws and no ice except what is made by art to supply our desserts; add to this, that I have twice as much money as I want, and am conscious of doing very great and extensive good to many millions of native Indians who look up to me not as their judge only, but as their legislator.

He would stay on only as long as it took to finish his Digest, which he saw as his most important legacy to 'the twenty-four millions of black British subjects in these provinces', for 'the idea of making their slavery lighter, by giving them their own laws, is more flattering to me than the thanks of the King.'

But Jones himself was a sick man (see Plate 2), a shadow of the plump and still youthful-looking man who had first set foot on the Custom House steps a decade earlier, unknowing victim of a tumour that was diagnosed as an inflammation of the liver. Taken ill on 20 April 1794, six days later he was pronounced well enough to proceed to England. The following morning, 27 April, his nearest neighbour was roused by Jones's servants, and found him lying on his bed 'in a posture of meditation'. The only sign of life was 'a small degree of motion of the heart, which after a few seconds ceased'. He was forty-seven.

As Jones's Sanskrit translations – most notably *Sakuntala*, by the fourth-century poet and dramatist Kalidasa, and the collection of Buddhist morality fables known as *Hitopadesa*, the 'Book of Sound Counsel' – became available in Europe, they were eagerly seized upon. 'Only one name need I give you,' wrote Goethe in tribute, 'Shakuntala says it all!' No less impressed were Goethe's fellow Romantics in Germany – Arthur Schopenhauer, Johann Gottfried von Herder, Friedrich von Schiller, Franz Schubert, and Friedrich Schlegel, who spoke of an 'Oriental Renaissance' and in 1800 famously declared: 'In the Orient we must seek the highest Romanticism.' In England, however, their impact was less dramatic and the reaction to them more critical. Warren Hastings's *bête noire* Charles Grant had recently published his *Observations on the State of Society among the Asiatic Subjects of Great Britain, particularly with respect to Morals and on the means of improving them*, a broadside directed against the attitudes of men like Hastings and Jones who, he believed, had sought to 'exalt the natives of the East, and other pagan religions, into models of goodness and innocence'. Grant's call for missionary activity in India was now supported by the Evangelicals under the leadership of William Wilberforce, founder in 1798 of the Church Missionary Society.

The EICo's Board of Control continued to stand firm against calls for missionary activity until 1813, when the combination of Grant (three times Chairman of the EICo's Court of Directors between 1805 and 1815) and his allies in Parliament and the Church finally became too powerful to resist. By then Jones's promotion of Indian culture was being routinely condemned by some of London's leading opinion-formers, usually coupled with the insinuation that Jones had entertained a higher regard for Indian civilisation and for Hinduism than for his own culture and religion. In reality, Jones had found Hindu superstition just as distasteful as what he called the 'Romish impositions' of Christianity – but he had considered 'the doctrine of the Hindus concerning a future state to be incomparably more rational, more pious and more likely to deter men from vice than the horrid opinions inculcated by the Christians on punishment without end'.

In 1818 the political philosopher James Mill (father of John Stuart Mill), who had never set foot in India, brought out his hugely influential *History of British India*, which had been a decade in the writing. Mill was as much a disciple of Grant as of Jeremy Bentham, and he went to great lengths to deride Indian culture, declaring that 'everything we know of the ancient state of civilisation among the Hindus conspires to prove it was rude'. He castigated the Orientalists for encouraging the despotic barbarism of Asia by promoting the myth of a golden age, and Sir William Jones was the chief target of his scorn: 'It was unfortunate that a mind so pure, so warm, in the pursuit of truth should have adopted the hypothesis of a high state of civilisation in the principal countries of Asia.' With Orientalism still little more than a 'puny rickity child' and its founding father not long dead, its eclipse had already begun.

5

Dr Buchanan and the Messengers from Ava

A YEAR AFTER the death of Sir William Jones the protracted trial before the House of Lords of Warren Hastings, charged on twenty-three counts of having 'acted in a manner repugnant to the honour and policy of the British nation', ended with his acquittal. In that same month France invaded The Netherlands and provided the British with an excuse to annexe all the Dutch colonies, including the Cape of Good Hope and Ceylon. The occupation of Trincomalee by an expeditionary force from the Madras Presidency helped the King of Kandy put his name to a treaty that secured for the Company the island's coastal belt, previously held by the Dutch. For the King of Kandy the only alteration of consequence was the replacement of a weak neighbour by a powerful one. But in England the belief that the EICo's rule in India was tainted by exploitation was now deeply entrenched, and these doubts helped to shape the future of Ceylon: in 1798 the island's Maritime Provinces were declared a Crown Colony, to be governed directly by Britain rather than by the EICo.

The Honourable Frederick North was the man selected to be the colony's first governor. The third son of the Earl of Guilford, he was an aristocrat and a classicist, educated (like his near-contemporary Marquess Wellesley, then Governor-General of India) at Eton and Christ Church, Oxford. He could converse fluently in six living European languages and two dead ones, and was a committed aesthete: one of his first acts on arriving in Ceylon was to design and build for himself, on a commanding headland, a villa on the lines of a Greek temple which he named The Doric.

North, given a free hand in the selection of his administrative staff, gathered together a group of 'young persons' of high calibre, all bachelors like himself, who were immediately set to learning the island's main languages, Sinhala and Tamil, while they worked as assistants to the Chief Secretary, himself a former professor of history. Among their number was a Frenchman named Joseph Eudelin de Joinville, a young aristocrat 'possessed of considerable talents' who was appointed Clerk for Natural History and Agriculture. De Joinville is something of a mystery man, but evidently his abilities were sufficient to justify his being placed in charge of the extensive cinnamon plantations around Colombo, a post that allowed him to pursue his chief interest, the study of Sinhala and Sinhalese culture: his translation of the classical poem *Kokila Sandesaya* was the first from Sinhala into English. However, in March 1800 de Joinville had to put his studies to one side when he joined Major-General MacDowall's embassy to the Court of Kandy as interpreter and intelligence-gatherer.

The embassy was intended to put the Crown's relations with the King of Kandy and his ministers on a better footing. Major-General MacDowall took with him a letter from the Governor – borne, in accordance with local protocol, on the head of a messenger shielded by an umbrella – along with thirty-two cases of gifts, and a military escort of two battalions of infantry, two howitzers and four six-pounders. Despite these inducements MacDowall's mission was a failure, mirroring in almost every respect the tribulations experienced by Captain Symes on his embassy to the Court of Ava six years earlier. Having already experienced the Portuguese and the Dutch in Ceylon, the king and his ministers had every reason to fear the advance of the British into the interior of the island, and did all they could to obstruct them. Although the road from Colombo to Kandy covered barely eighty miles, it passed through wild and mountainous country and had been neglected as a matter of deliberate policy, so that there were sections made impassable by landslides and rockfalls, to say nothing of trees that appeared to have been felled on purpose to block the track. Heavy rainfall added to MacDowall's difficulties, and it took the expedition more than a month to reach Kandy, tucked away at the head of a narrow valley and surrounded on all sides by the mountains that were its main defence.

The royal palace at Kandy was discovered to be a modest two-storeyed building with a roof of gilded tiles, set within a narrow moat beside an artificial lake and surrounded by a number of temples that included a small pagoda-like structure, the Dalada Maligawa, the Temple of the Tooth. Here was housed the island's most precious relic, the supposed right molar of the Buddha. This had not, it seemed, been destroyed by the Portuguese after all: only a copy of the tooth had been sent to Jaffna, and this it was that had been seized and taken to Goa – or so the tooth's guardians were now claiming. For centuries the relic had been linked inextricably with the rulers of the island, and it was generally understood by all that whoever possessed the tooth possessed also the right to govern Ceylon. (This may explain why MacDowall and his officers were not invited to inspect the tooth, and why it was not until after the King of Kandy had been dethroned by the British in 1815 that it became available for examination.)

Curiously, the protector of this most sacred relic of Buddhism was not himself a Buddhist. For generations the Kingdom of Kandy had looked for its rulers to the Aravidu royal dynasty of South India: Tamils and Hindus, these monarchs ruled over a largely Buddhist population, and had in many instances adapted their religious practices to accommodate their subjects' beliefs. Raja Sri Vikrama Sinha, however, was an exception to this general rule; not only did he bring a great many of his Tamil relations to live in Kandy, where they exercised increasing influence, but he also introduced various Hindu customs, such as animal sacrifices, that his subjects found highly offensive.

After kicking their heels in their camp outside the town for several days, Major-General MacDowall and his officials were at last permitted to enter the royal precincts. The envoy's audience of the king was a ritual that lasted from midnight to five in the morning and involved kneeling before Raja Sri Vikrama Sinha's throne, making nine obeisances as he approached it and another three when he stood up to leave. All references to these kow-tows were excised from the official accounts, but it is plain from de

Joinville's published journal that MacDowall and his party were constrained by the royal officials to follow Court etiquette. Gifts were exchanged, and enquiries into the health of the principal parties were conveyed in hushed whispers through the medium of two interpreters and a minister and answered in the same convoluted manner. But after all, Major-General MacDowall left Kandy with nothing more substantial than vague expressions of goodwill. The main beneficiary of the expedition was de Joinville, who was promoted by North to Surveyor-General of the Maritime Provinces, a post that, in requiring him to travel through every stretch of his domain, enabled him to gather the information that went into his manuscript 'Quelques Notions Sur l'Isle de Ceylan'. This included an essay on the religions and customs of Ceylon in which de Joinville declared himself to be in no doubt that the religion of the Burmans, the Siamese and the Sinhalese was the same, and that they all worshipped Boudhou, though he was known by a different name in each country: '*Le Gaudma du Birmans, le Sommonocodom du Siamsis et le Saman Gautemé du Singulois sont sans doute la même chose.*' He also noted a striking similarity between the bell-shaped monuments called 'dageb' (more correctly, *dagoba*), said to contain the bones of their saints, and the shrines carved out of rock that he had seen inside the caves at Salsette, near Bombay.

Others besides de Joinville were also eager to learn more about what was, from a British perspective, a hitherto neglected corner of Asia. Robert Knox's *History* of 1680 was re-examined, and found to be full of valuable information. One of the first to take note of this was William Chambers, the Asiatic Society's leading light in Madras. He had also read Monsieur de La Loubère's scholarly *Description du Royaume de Siam*, in which the Frenchman had remarked on the similarities between the 'Bali' (i.e., Pali) language in which that country's laws were written and the Tamil spoken in south India – and on the apparent links between this Bali and Sanskrit. Now Chambers, like de Joinville, could see further similarities, 'From all which it should appear that *Pout*, which among the Siamese is another named for *Sommonacodom*, is itself a corruption of *Buddou* . . . The temples of *Sommonacodom* are called *Pihan*; and round them are habitations for the priests, resembling a college; so those of *Buddou* are called *Vihar*, and the principal priests live in them as in a college.' That the same religion of 'Buddou' was to be found in two regions separated by the Bay of Bengal suggested another possibility: that it might also have flourished in India. 'It will appear', concluded Chambers, 'that this worship has formerly been by no means confined to Ceylone, but has prevailed in several parts of India prior to that of the Brahmins; nay, that this has been the case even so late as the ninth and twelfth centuries of the Christian Era.'

No one read William Chambers's speculations in *Asiatick Researches* with greater interest than Dr Francis Buchanan, the ship's surgeon turned Company botanist-cum-intelligence gatherer. His response was to produce his own paper, based on Father Vincentius Sangermano's manuscripts, which he completed towards the end of 1797 and saw published in the sixth volume of *Asiatick Researches* in 1799.

Buchanan's *On the Religion and Literature of the Burmas* was the first serious account of what he chose to term 'Buddhism' to be written in English since Knox's observations published almost a hundred and seventy years earlier. It was also the first to rely on indigenous sources rather than personal observation, which makes it the first scholarly account of Burmese Buddhism to be published. 'Him they believe once to have come upon the Earth,' Captain Knox had written in his *Historical Relation*. 'And when he was here, that he did usually sit under a large shady Tree.' Now Dr Buchanan was able to confirm that this was indeed a religion founded on a historical personage, an ascetic named Godama, regarded by his followers in Ava as the most recent of four god-like Intelligences, all named Buddh, to have appeared on this earth.

The life history of this Godama Buddh was well documented: 'The books which contain the history of Godama represent him as a king, who having laid aside the ensigns of royalty, withdrew himself into a solitary place, put on the habit of a Talapoin [Burmese monk], and gave himself up to the study and practice of virtue.' At the age of thirty-five Godama had achieved a state of *Niban* (in Pali *nibbana*, in Sanskrit *nirvana* – 'extinguishing', the ultimate aim of Buddhism) which Buchanan understood to be a state of divinity: 'When we say that *Godama* obtained the *Niban*, this is to be understood as a state exempt from the four following evils: conception, old age, sickness and death. Nothing in this world, nor any place can give us an idea of the *Niban*: but the exemption of the above mentioned evils, and the possession of perfect safety, are the only things of which it consists.' Having achieved this state, Godama had then begun to work miracles and promulgate his religious laws, 'in which employment he spent forty-five years'.

As for Godama's doctrines, these consisted chiefly in observing five commandments, abstaining from ten sins, and practising good works, including the giving of alms and something that Buchanan called *Bavana* (in Sanskrit *Bhavana* – 'cultivation', thus meditation), which he defined as remembering that one is liable to vicissitudes, remembering that one is liable to misfortune, and remembering that it is not in one's power to exempt oneself from change and misfortune.

In his eightieth year Godama had died of dysentery, brought on by 'an excess in eating pork' presented to him by an admirer. Having lived 'in the practice of every good work, and having conferred salvation on every living creature, he was assumed into the state of *Niban*'. Before his death Godama had confirmed all his precepts, adding that 'the real adoration of God' did not consist in making offerings 'of rice, flowers or sandal-woods, but in the observance of his laws'. He had also recommended that after his death his statue and relics should be preserved and adored: 'These have since become objects of veneration to all the *Burmas*, wherever they are met with, but they are more particularly worshipped, with greater pomp and by greater numbers, in the *Pagodas*. These are pyramidal or conical buildings made of brick, painted and gilded on the outside. In these temples there is generally a niche in which is placed the statue of *Godama*.'

Having set out the basics, Dr Buchanan went on to draw some conclusions. Since the Burmese used a calendar that took the death of Godama as its starting-point, Buchanan was able to fix this event on the Christian calender. According to the Burmese, 2,305 years had passed between Godama's *Niban* and 1763, the year in which Father Sangermano had received his texts from the priests of Ava. From this dating, Dr Buchanan calculated that

Godama had been born 622 years before Christ and had died in 542 BCE. The Burmese belief was that the laws of Godama would be observed for five thousand years from the time of his death; as soon as this period had ended, Buchanan noted, 'the laws of *Godama* will cease to be binding, and another God must appear to promulgate a new code for the government of mankind . . . The God who will succeed *Godama* will be called *Arimatea* [Maitreya, the *bodhisattva* or enlightened being still to come].'

According to the Burmese, Buddhism had been brought to their country originally from Ceylon: 'The Cingaleze of Ceylon are Bhoodhists of the purest source, and the Birmans acknowledge to have originally received their religion from that island.' Buddhism was also to be found on Ava's eastern borders, in Siam and Cambodia; and if the Jesuit accounts were to be believed, very similar practices were also being followed to the north of Burma, in China, as well as in other corners of the Indies: Cochinchina (now Cambodia and Laos), Tonkin (Vietnam), even in Japan. Its tenets might be 'absurd', yet in 'influencing the conduct of so large a proportion of mankind' it had to be considered 'an object of great importance in the history of the human race'. Moreover, since Buddhism had evidently existed in Ceylon for many centuries, it was reasonable to deduce that at some time in the distant past it must also have flourished on the land mass lying between Ceylon and the other Buddhist counties. So Dr Buchanan was happy to support Mr Chambers, 'the most judicious of our Indian antiquaries', in his belief that Gautama Buddha must once have been worshipped in India. His own view was that 'the governing power on the banks of the Ganges, as late as about the time of the birth of Christ, was the sect of *Bouddha*. The *Brahmens* had then introduced themselves into Hindustan, and had obtained lands, and even the rank of prime minister to the great Rajah; but they had not persuaded him to change his religion; a change which when accomplished, proved equally destructive to the prince and to the people.'

This was a bold claim to make, but there was one piece of literary evidence to support it: in a Hindu history of Kashmir, *Raja Tarangani*, translated by the Persian historian Ferishta, it was stated that the forty-fifth prince of Kashmir, Raja Jennah, had 'established in his reign the Brahmeny rites', after which his successors had 'tolerated the doctrine of Bowdh' – until the reign of the fifty-ninth ruler, Raja Nerkh, when 'the Brahmens got the better of the followers of Bowdh, and burned down their temples'. According to the datings of Sir William Jones and Captain Wilford taken from the Hindu *Puranas*, this final overthrow of Buddhism by the Brahmins in Kashmir had taken place in about the middle of the fourth century CE.

What Buchanan was not so happy to support were the theories of the late Sir William on the origins of Buddhism. Politely but succinctly he demolished the great man's notion that Gautama was the same historical personage as the Ethiopian law-giver Sesac or the Egyptian god Sesostris: 'The affinity of the religion of Egypt with the present supposition of Hindustan, and the fatal resemblance of the words Sesac and Sakya, one of the names of Godama, seem to have given rise to this supposition. In my opinion, however, no two religions can be well more different than that of the Egyptian polytheist and that of the Burma unitarian.'

Egypt was at this time the object of Napoleon Bonaparte's famous experiment in scientific enquiry applied as an instrument of imperialism. In 1798 he had landed on the coast of Egypt with an invading army, and a support force of 197 savants charged with examining Egypt in terms that echoed Sir William Jones's now-famous 'Discourse' of 1784 that had launched the Asiatick Society. Baron Vivant de Denon's *Journey Through Upper and Lower Egypt*, when it was published in 1802 in French, English and German, revealed the huge gulf that existed between the cultures of ancient Egypt and India (and, taken in conjunction with his multi-volume *Description of Egypt*, first published between 1809 and 1815, established the science of Egyptology).

Buchanan's *On the Religion and Literature of the Burmas* bears no comparison with de Denon's monumental study, but it is no less of a milestone, for its publication marked the start of what has now become known as Buddhist Studies. It provoked an immediate response from Ceylon in the form of two long papers submitted to the Asiatic Society and published in the seventh volume of *Asiatick Researches* in 1801. The first was from Frederick North's Surveyor-General, Joseph Eudelin de Joinville, the second from a Captain

1. 'East View of the Hindoo Temple at Bode-Gya, in the neighbourhood of Gaya in Behar, taken by Capt. Crokatt': the earliest drawing of the Mahabodhi temple at Bodh-Gaya, probably painted by James Crockett, *c.* 1799

2. (*left*) 'Oriental Jones': Sir William Jones, founder of the Asiatic Society and father of Indian Studies, engraved from a drawing by A.W. Devis, 1798

3. (*below*) 'The Samaudh of Rajah Booth-Sain at Sara-Nat near Benares': a first drawing of the surviving Buddhist stupa at Sarnath, known today as the Dhamekh stupa, by one of Colin Mackenzie's draughtsmen *c.* 1814, copied April 1819

4. (*opposite*) Colonel Colin Mackenzie with his Brahmin and Jain pandits and his peon, with a Jain statue in the background: a watercolour copy of a painting by Thomas Hickey, *c.* 1815

ཊ୯ম্মা ক্তৃব্ধু ঘৈকেঁনে ঘান্ঘা।

শ্ৰ্ব্ব্দ নে ঘান্ঝ্বা ৱিগাবদ ৱস্মার্ষ

কন্ত্ৰেম্ংe থ্ৰিশিন্ব থ্ব্র্ম্মা

5. (*opposite*) 'The Great Muni at Baragang called Batuk Bhairav': one of the many Buddhist statues seen and admired by Dr Buchanan at the village of Baragaum, site of the then undiscovered Buddhist university of Nalanda. On the base is the Buddhist invocation beginning 'Ye Dharma hetu prabhava . . .'

6. (*right*) 'Distinct curls such as negroes have': one of Lieutenant John Bagnold's drawings from Sanchi, showing the Buddha statue found near the Great Tope, 1818

7. (*below*) The Great Tope of Sanchi, a watercolour by William Simpson painted in 1862

The landing of a Griffin at Calcutta
W. P. Sep 1833

8. (*opposite, above*) A 'griffin' or newcomer disembarks with his baggage at Calcutta: pen-and-ink and watercolour sketch by William Prinsep, *c.* 1820

9. (*opposite, below left*) The youthful James Prinsep gives his science lecture in Calcutta in 1819: painted by his older brother William's friend, George Chinnery (detail)

10. (*opposite, below right*) Aurangzeb's mosque beside the Ganges at Benares: a watercolour by James Prinsep, painted during his restoration of the building, *c.* 1824 (detail)

11. (*above*) James Prinsep's office and home, the new Mint on the Strand, Calcutta: a watercolour painted by his younger brother Thomas just after its completion, *c.* 1829

12. (*below*) James Prinsep's memorial, Prinsep's Ghat, on the bank of the Hoogly to the right of the Indiaman moored off Fort William, Calcutta: from a watercolour by William Prinsep painted just before he left India in 1840

13. British officers accompanied by Indian *munshis* explore the Shwe Dagon, the great golden pagoda at Rangoon: drawn by Lieutenant Joseph Moore, 1825

14. Mid-nineteenth-century engraving of the 'Galle-vihara at Pollonarrua', better known today as the Gal Vihara or Temple of the Rock at Polonnaruwa, central Ceylon

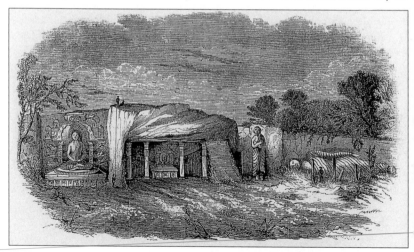

Mahony. Both had evidently drawn on Sinhalese texts written not in Sanskrit but in the equally sacrosanct language known as Pali. Both confirmed the general accuracy of Dr Buchanan's work, and provided further detail about the faith common to Ceylon and Ava. According to de Joinville, the religion had been founded by 'a man of genius' he named as *Saman* (that is, *Shramana*, the ascetic) Gauteme Boudhou:

> *Gauteme Boudhou* was the son of a king of *Giambu Dwipe* [Jambudwipa, one of the seven continents of Hindu cosmology, with Bharata or India occupying its southern quarter] called *Soudodene Maha Ragia* [Great King Suddhodana] . . . His mother was called *Maya*, or rather *Maha Maya* – he was there known under the name of Prince *Sidharte* [*Siddhartha*, 'One who has achieved his purpose', one of the earliest appellations of Gautama Buddha]. He had a son by his wife *Jassodera Devi*, who was called *Rahoule*, and who succeeded to the throne on the death of his father. Having in vain attempted . . . to become *Boudhou*, he at last made himself a Pilgrim. At the end of six years' Pilgrimage, an account of which is given in a large Volume, he became *Boudhou*, in forty-five years after, *Nivani*.

Like Dr Buchanan, de Joinville considered Buddhism to be quite separate from Hinduism – and shared his view that it was the older of the two: 'From the similarity of the two religions, there can be no doubt that the one is the child of the other; but it is hard to know which is the mother. We find the religion of Boudhou in ancient times extending from the north of Tartary to Ceylon, and from the Indus to Siam . . . I am rather of opinion, upon a comparison of the two religions, that that of Boudhou is the more ancient.'

Captain Mahony's paper was no less exhaustive, touching on every aspect of Sinhalese Buddhism from its cosmography to its current state. Mahony seems to have been a military man rather than a seafarer, almost certainly from one of the regiments of the British Army that briefly served on the island at the time of the British take-over. He had talked to priests from both religious traditions, and had learned from the Brahmins that they considered

Buddha to be one of the nine *avataras* or manifestations of Vishnu and looked upon the Buddhists as heretics, their religion being but 'one of the 339 sects or branches of the well known heresy, or rather schism, among the Hindoos'. The Buddhists, for their part, acknowledged the Hindu deity Brahma as 'first among the superior Gods, which they number in seven classes' – all of which suggested that Buddhism had emerged out of Hinduism, rather than the other way round. The Buddhist and Hindu cosmographies also appeared to have a lot in common: a belief in a multi-tiered heaven above, with the highest level being 'the seat of the most perfect and supreme bliss', and a hell below, situated 'beneath the lowest extremity of the earth'. Another shared feature, it seemed to Mahony, was the concept known as *atman*, which he translated accurately in its literal sense as a 'breath of life in man, which they compare to a leech, that first attaches itself to a body'. This leech-like soul survived death, for 'that which is termed the breath of life is immortal', but as part of a cycle of death and rebirth that ended only after many turns of the wheel of life and death: 'When men die they ascend the six Inferior Heavens, or *Deveh Loke*; are judged according to their merits by one of the most inferior Gods . . . and regenerate themselves, on the earth, either as men or brutes: which regeneration continues until they arrive at the *Brachmah Loke*, or the Heavens of the Superior Gods; and so on, by degrees, at the Triumphant Heavens, until they at length reach the Supreme Heaven.' In fact, Mahony had failed to grasp an essential difference between the two philosophies, which was that the Buddhists rejected the Hindu doctrine of *atman* entirely, teaching instead *anatta*, the absence of a permanent 'soul' or self.

Many universes had come and gone before this present one, with the Buddha – 'The word *Bhooddha*, in the Palee and Singhalai languages, implies Universal Knowledge [the modern meaning is usually given as "Enlightened" or "Awakened"]' – manifesting himself in each. 'For the government of the present universe . . . five *Bhooddhas* are specified, four of whom have already appeared: *Kakoosandeh Bhooddha, Konagammeh Bhooddha, Kasserjeppeh Bhooddha* and *Gautemeh Bhooddha* . . . At the solicitations of many of the Gods he descended on earth, and was frequently born as a man, in which character he exercised every possible virtue, by extraordinary instances of self-denial and piety . . . The last of the above mentioned four *Bhooddhas*, Gautemeh Bhooddha, is the one whose whole religion now prevails in Ceylon . . . and the fifth, *Maitree Bhooddha* [Maitreya Buddha], is still to come.'

Neither Buchanan nor de Joinville had grasped the nature of the 'law' that Gautama Buddha (as we shall call him hereafter) was said to have propagated. Captain Mahony fared no better:

The religion of *Bhooddha*, as far as I have had any insight into it, seems to be founded in a mild and simple morality. *Bhooddha* has taken for his principles Wisdom, Justice and Benevolence (in Singalese: *Booddha, Dermah, Sangeh*) from which principles emanate Ten Commandments, held by his followers as the true and only rule of their conduct. He places them under three heads, thought, word, and deed; and it may be said that the spirit of them is becoming, and well suited to him, whose mild nature was first shocked by the sacrifice of cattle. These Commandments comprise what is understood by the moral law.

Tucked away in this paragraph but mistranslated, and so misunderstood, were the three elements, known as the *triratna* or Three Jewels, that together form the basis of Buddhism: the Buddha (the Enlightened or Awakened One), the Dharma (the eternal law of the universe as discovered and preached by Gautama Buddha; thus, the Buddhist doctrine) and the Sangha (the Buddhist community of monks and laity combined). Unable to see how these three elements could form the basis for a religion, Mahony and his contemporaries focused on what they could understand while ignoring the core teachings of the Buddha. What Mahony called the 'Ten Commandments' were simply the ten rules that a novice had to accept before becoming a Buddhist monk.

As to the dating of Gautama Buddha's life, Mahony was able triumphantly to match from Sinhalese sources, and so confirm, Buchanan's date from Ava: 'He died at Cooseemarapooree, at the Court of Malleleh Raja, Tuesday the 15th of May, from which period the *Bhooddha Warooseh*, or era of Bhooddha, is dated.' He had lived for thirty-one years as a prince, had spent six years as an ascetic, and had 'exercised his functions as Bhooddha' for forty-five years, making a life-span of eighty-two – two years more than Buchanan had given him. He had achieved ultimate nirvana, and had died in or about the year 542 BCE. But where?

The Sinhalese texts spoke of Gautama Buddha as having been born as a prince in the city of Kimboolwatpuri in the country of Dumba Deeva [Jambudwipa], his father Sooddodeneh Raja and his mother Mahamaya Devee. He had expounded his laws 'in the empire of Raja Gaha Noowereh' and had died at 'Kosimarapuri at the court of King Malleleh'. None of these names or places was immediately identifiable, but both Sinhalese and Burmese versions named the country of Gautama's birth as Jambudwipa, thus the Indian subcontinent.

Mahony's sources had also provided further details of Ceylon's holy tree – the same tree that, according to Captain Robert Knox's earlier account, had come flying over from the Indian mainland and under which 'the Buddou-God at his being on earth used, as they say, often to sit'. Mahony noted that the 'Bogaha or tree of Bhooddha' was revered by the Siamese, the Burmese and the Sinhalese – and with good reason:

> It was against this tree that *Bhooddh* leaned, when he first took upon himself his divine character. A branch of the original tree is said to have been brought to Ceylon in a miraculous manner, and planted at *Annooradhepooreh Noowereh* [Anuradhapura], where to this day, a tree of that description is worshipped, and thought to possess extraordinary virtues. The *Bogaha*, or tree of *Bhooddha*, is that, I think, called in the Hindoostan the *Peepul* (*Ficus religiosa*), a species of banian with heart-like and pointed leaf. The *Singhalais*, when describing the different countries they pretend to a knowledge of, make this tree the central point, and determine the position of the place by its relative situation.

Captain Mahony and Joseph Eudelin de Joinville played no further part in Buddhist studies. The former slipped at once out of public notice, to disappear without trace; the latter remained at his post as Surveyor-General until the completion of Frederick North's term of office as Governor in 1805, when he left the island with his patron, then like Captain Mahony disappeared from the public record. Not so Dr Francis Buchanan, who in February 1802 was asked to join his second foreign embassy, Captain Knox's mission to Kathmandu.

The rulers of Kathmandu were as fearful of British ambitions as the kings of Ava and Kandy, their chief minister referring to the EICo as 'a power that crushed thrones like potsherds'. In 1793 they had given the first EICo embassy short shrift, and Captain Knox and his surgeon, arriving in Kathmandu in April 1802, were made equally unwelcome. Nevertheless, it was under these difficult conditions, amounting to house arrest inside the walls of the British Residency, that Dr Buchanan set about gathering material for his study of the religion of Nepal.

The head of the first British mission to Kathmandu had pronounced the religion of the valley to be Brahminism, 'established from the most remote antiquity in this secluded valley'. But as Buchanan made his way with Knox through the outlying villages and then through the streets of Kathmandu itself he was surprised to notice, among the many Hindu temples and shrines, structures and images that reminded him of the pagodas and Buddha figures of Ava (see Plates 16 and 17). The pagodas were more dome-like than the bell-shaped structures of Ava and Rangoon, and the most striking was to be seen on the summit of a hill just to the west of Kathmandu. On top of a large domed structure was a cube, the four faces of which bore painted eyes that gazed out across the valley in every direction: the stupa of Swayambhunath, which Dr Buchanan describes as 'the temple of the supreme deity of the Buddhists'. The Buddha images accompanying the pagodas were unmistakably similar to those he had seen in Ava, although here in the Kathmandu valley they were intermixed with statues of Brahma, Vishnu, Shiva and other Hindu deities, as well as numerous demonic figures, male and female, that he could not identify. Even the great stupa of Swayambhunath was entirely surrounded by Hindu temples with 'a great many images of Shiva'.

Hindered as much by the religious prejudices of his Brahmin munshi Ramajai Batacharji as by his own confinement, Dr Buchanan found that his enquiries into Buddhist practices in the valley made little progress: 'The doctrines of these people appeared so shockingly impious to my Brahman, that I could not induce him to converse on the subject with their learned men.' But he did discover that the original inhabitants of the valley, the Newars, followed religious practices which differed from those of the men from the surrounding mountains who had recently conquered the valley. 'The *Newars*, in point of religion, are divided into two sects,' he determined. 'The greater part still adhere to the tenets of the *Buddhs*, but they have adopted the doctrines of cast [caste].' These remaining Buddhists believed in 'a supreme being called *Sambu*, or *Swayambhu*, from whom have proceeded many *Buddhs*, or Intelligences'. Ranked among these many Buddhas but not preeminent was Sakya Singha, the Lion of Sakya, who had 'come on earth to instruct man in the true worship, and in Nepal is commonly believed to be still alive in Lhasa'.

It was soon clear to Buchanan that the Sakya Singha of the Newars was identifiable with the Gautama Buddha of Ava and Ceylon. It appeared that at some time in the past the original Buddhism practised in the valley by the Newars had been weakened by the arrival of Hindu observances, as a result of which 'a good many of the Newars had rejected the doctrine of Sakya, and adopted the worship of Shiva.' But whereas Gautama Buddha played the central role in the Buddhism found in Ava, here in Kathmandu Buddhism had been enlarged to accommodate the worship of Hindu and other still unknown deities, with a corresponding lessening of the significance of Gautama Buddha. So Buddhism appeared to come in at least two forms. Armed with this new information, which he himself barely understood, Dr Buchanan returned to Calcutta in April 1803 uniquely qualified to place Buddhism on the Indian map.

In June 1803 relations between the British and the Sinhalese took a sudden turn for the worse. In what reads today very like a dry run for the disastrous British intervention in Afghanistan in 1838, a small British force led by two companies of the 19th Regiment of Foot was sent to occupy Kandy with the aim of bullying the king and his court into submission. It arrived to find the town and palace deserted, and Kandyan forces gathered in large numbers in the surrounding hills. It soon became clear to the British commander, Major Davie, that he was in a hopeless position: his British soldiers were dying of malaria at the rate of six a day, most of the remainder were too ill to stand, and his supplies were running out. He negotiated a truce that allowed his troops to march out of the town with their arms, but leaving behind 120 British soldiers too ill to walk. When they reached the Mahawalli river, then in full flood and unfordable, the force was surrounded and ordered to surrender arms. Major Davie and two of his officers were taken back to Kandy, while the remaining British troops were massacred on the spot. Contemporary reports suggested that Major Davie's 'native' troops – 250 Malays and 140 Indian gun-lascars – were also killed, but Sinhalese accounts state that the Malays were inducted into Kandyan service and the Indians allowed to go free. However, the 120 British invalids left behind in Kandy were not spared: they were thrown into a large pit and buried alive. The three officers were imprisoned in Kandy in appalling conditions, a source of profound embarrassment to Frederick North and his successor. The last prisoner to die was Major Davie. 'My health weak and my body weaker' reads a final, pathetic note, smuggled out of his prison cell in January 1812 – almost eleven years after his capture. 'My supplies of food are small and in arrears. For heaven's sake send quickly Laudanum and opium my torture is [un]indurable.'

It was the unhappy Major Davie's fate to be held captive at a time when the expansionist policies promoted by Marquess Wellesley were in the process of being reversed. In 1805 Lord Wellesley was replaced by men with less ego and ambition, first Sir George Barlow and then Lord Minto, who were under strict orders to avoid waging war by land, and to put their finances in order. The new Governor of the Maritime Provinces of Ceylon, Sir Thomas Maitland, followed the same cautious path, suspending hostilities with the King of Kandy while strengthening the British position along the coastal belt of the island.

The sudden withdrawal of British influence plunged much of central India into chaos, allowing the weaker states to be ravaged by their stronger neighbours, the Marathas and Sikhs, and by roving bands of marauders, the Pindaris. Initially, however, Lord Minto stuck to his brief and concentrated his efforts on the con-solidation of British rule in Bengal, whose Upper Provinces now stretched as far westward as Delhi. It was at this time that Dr

Francis Buchanan, now chastened and disappointed, undertook the great statistical survey of Bengal that in early December 1811 found him and his little band of scouts, scribes and draughtsmen in the town of Gaya in south Bihar.

The Hindu pilgrimage town and its inhabitants did not impress him:

> The town looks tolerably well at a distance, but a nearer approach fills with disgust. The streets are narrow (6 to 10 feet) dirty and crooked. The galleries which serve for shops are mostly very slovenly, and even of those which are neat and gaily painted some corner or other is usually defiled by smoke or dust or cobwebs. The very best houses are rendered slovenly by cakes of cowdung for fuel patched on their walls, and the jealousy of the men prevents any reasonable number or size for the apertures intended to intromit air or light, while the small ones that are tolerated are secured by rude wooden shutters without paint or polish. In walking through the town, precautions are necessary as formerly in Edinburgh. The passenger must call out to prevent inundation from above.

Little has changed in the hundred and ninety years since those words were written, except that Gaya's population has doubled many times over.

What also struck Dr Buchanan was that many of the buildings in Gaya showed signs of having been built of salvaged rather than new materials. He had already observed on his approach that while all the temples in the area were Hindu and comparatively modern in appearance, many of the stone carvings they contained were of *padmasana* images – Buddhas seated cross-legged on lotus-flowers. Now he noted houses whose walls were patched with granite pillars 'of various lengths, thicknesses and form' bearing 'all the marks of a rude antiquity.' His suspicions were confirmed by a local Brahmin who admitted that many of the temples were indeed built with stones taken from older buildings, and that they contained religious images which were considered *nastik* (unorthodox) rather than *astik* (orthodox). 'I suspect therefore that the whole are the work of the Buddhs,' Buchanan concluded.

On 9 December 1811, his survey of Gaya completed, Buchanan took his party south through a countryside 'overloaded with plantations'. He had gone little more than two miles when above the trees he saw a stone spire. Tucked away behind a screen of banyans was a cluster of buildings rising out of piles of rubble. He had reached Bodh-Gaya (see Plate 1).

Here Dr Buchanan was met and received 'very civilly' by an elderly *sannyasi*, or Hindu ascetic, who introduced himself as the *mahant* or leader of a group of Hindu ascetics who were living in the partially restored ruins of what Buchanan termed a convent, a building which he described as 'a large square, with towers at the corners like a castle, and very few windows outwards'. Enclosed within this convent was a courtyard containing 'a plantation of turmeric, and a burial ground where several *Sannyasis* are deposited in a temple of *Siva*'. Lining the walls of the courtyard were scores of stone statues and inscribed plaques salvaged from the surrounding ruins. 'The *Mahants*', noted Buchanan, 'seem to have been at particular pains to have rescued the images although all *Nastik*, and to have placed them where they might be saved from injury.'

The *mahant* explained to Buchanan that he and his followers regarded themselves as the 'possessors' of this site. About a hundred years earlier the *mahant*'s predecessor, a *sannyasi* named Chetar Giri, had come upon the place 'in the course of his penitent wanderings'. It was 'overrun with wood and bushes', but he had 'taken up his abode' in the ruins and over the years had attracted devotees and pilgrims, becoming 'a principal object of veneration among the powerful chiefs and wealthy merchants who occasionally frequent Gaya. From these he received the various endowments which his successors enjoy.' The present *mahant* and his followers were well aware that it was a site of great antiquity, but until quite recently had had no idea of its religious significance. 'It would appear', noted Buchanan, 'that the *sannyasis* have in some degree been infected with the superstition of the place, and confounded by its numerous images, which have struck them with awe. The first *mahant* resided in the ruin of the temple, and his different successors have purposely erected several small buildings, both near the old temple, and in their convent, in which they have placed many of the most remarkable and entire images, and they have placed in the walls of the buildings raised for other purposes, a still greater number both of images and inscriptions.'

The *mahant* and his followers were notably more tolerant in their views than most Hindus: 'The *Mahant* always spoke of *Gautama* by the names of *Muni* [sage] or *Bhagawan* [Lord] . . . Among the orthodox Hindus Buddha is not considered as synonymous with *Bhagawan*, a deity, or *Muni*, a saint, but is always talked of as one personage, an incarnation of Vishnu.' But as Dr Buchanan questioned the *mahant*, the reasons for his relaxed attitude became clear: he and his disciples had remained in total ignorance of Buddhism until the arrival some years earlier of a group of foreigners. As Dr Buchanan put it, 'Some years before the king of Ava [had] sent two messengers, who in speaking Hindustani called themselves *Vazirs*, by which I know they meant officers of government. They were in search of the holy places rendered remarkable by the actions of Gautama, and took [back] with them the water of many sacred streams and pools to form a bath for their master. Both these people had books, by the assistance of which they pretended to trace the holy places, and to detail their history.' A second visitor from Ava, 'a man of some rank with several other attendants', had visited the site even more recently, claiming to be a representative of Maha Dharmu Raja, or the King of the Great Law, whom Buchanan had no difficulty in identifying as the King of Ava. From these strangers had the *mahant* learned that the site he and his followers occupied was regarded by the Burmese as holy, that it was here their god Gautama had lived, and here that the pipal tree he knew as Brahma's tree had given this same Gautama shade as he sat and meditated.

With the affable *mahant* as his guide Buchanan proceeded to explore the site, situated, as he wrote in his Report, 'a few hundred yards west from the Nilajan river, on a plain of great extent'. It was made up of three distinct areas, one of which was the so-called convent. On its north side were the foundations of a large building, '1482 feet by 1006 in its greatest dimensions', known to the *mahant* as the Rajasthan or Dwelling of Kings: 'By far the greater part of the building seems to have been a large castle or palace, which probably contained many small courts, although these have been entirely obliterated by the operation of time'.

Beside the convent and separated from this 'palace' by a cart-track was a mass of fallen walls and sunken pits. This area had been extensively plundered for building material: 'It seems to have been composed of various courts now mostly reduced to irregular heaps of bricks and stones, as immense quantities of materials have been taken away. The largest heap now remaining is at the north-east corner, where there is a very large terrace on which are two modern small temples . . . In the east end of this terrace is now making a great excavation to procure materials for building.' It was now clear where at least some of Gaya's stonework had come from: 'Indeed, it is alleged that a great part if not the whole of the images built into the walls there, as also the doors, windows, pillars and inscriptions that accompany them, have been taken from these ruins . . . All the images now worshipped at Gaya were originally in this temple as ornaments, and have had new names given to them by the Brahmans.'

The most recent excavations for building material had exposed a small chamber lined with brick, 'a cube of about 20 feet without door, window or stair'. As he examined it, Dr Buchanan remembered that some seventeen years earlier Jonathan Duncan, the British Resident at Benares, had reported the uncovering of a very similar structure. Duncan had one day received a *chit* from Jagat Singh, the *dewan* or chief minister to Raja Chait Singh of Benares, to say that he had something of interest to show him. A gang of workmen he was employing to gather building material from some ruins just outside the city had dug up a stone casket inside which was a green marble urn. They had, in Jonathan Duncan's words, been 'digging for stones from the subterraneous materials of some extensive and ancient buildings in the vicinity of a temple called Saranuth'. The ruins at Sarnath were well known, for they were dominated by two huge mounds of brick and stone surrounded by what were clearly the remains of several large buildings (see Plate 3). The site was not claimed by either the Hindus or the Jains in the city, so no objections had been raised when Jagat Singh began to tear apart the largest of the two structures for his building materials.

Having dug away the top thirty feet of the central mass, Jagat Singh's workmen had uncovered a brick chamber containing the stone casket and its marble urn. The urn, opened in Jonathan

Duncan's presence, revealed 'a few human bones . . . and some decayed pearls, gold leaves and other jewels of no value'. After deliberation it was decided to commit the bones to the Ganges and return the other objects to 'the receptacle in which they must have so long remained', which was then re-interred where it had been found. The general belief in Benares was that these were the relics of 'the consort of some former rajah or prince', but Duncan had thought otherwise. He could see no reason why, in Hindu Benares of all places, anyone would have their ashes buried rather than cast upon the sacred river. The relics could only have belonged to 'one of the worshippers of Buddha, a set of Indian heretics, who having no reverence for the Ganges, used to deposit their remains in the earth, instead of committing them to that river; a surmise that seems strongly corroborated by the circumstance of a statue or idol of Buddha having been found in the same place under ground.'

As well as this statue had been found a stone plaque bearing an inscription in archaic (Kutila) Sanskrit that the pandits at the Sanscrit College recently built by Duncan were able to translate. It had been erected by Basanta Pal, King of Gaur, and his brother, Sritha Pala, in the year 1083 of Samvat, which corresponded to 1062 CE. According to the inscription, the two brothers had come to Benares to perform worship and had 'ordered all those who did not follow the Buddhas, to embrace that sect'. Accompanying this information was what appeared to be an invocation. Its meaning had still to be resolved, but transliterated into the Latin alphabet it read:

> *Ye Dharma hetu prabhava, hetun teshan Tathagato hyavadat,*
> *teshau cha yo nirodha evem vadi Maha Shramanas.*

By the time Duncan's notice of this find had reached the Asiatick Society's offices in Calcutta Sir William Jones was dead, and there was no one among the Europeans with the knowledge, or indeed the inclination, to pursue the matter.

As Dr Buchanan now examined the brick chamber at Bodh-Gaya he came across a tablet inscribed with that same two-line invocation beginning '*Ye Dharma hetu prabhava . . .*' – and before his explorations were over he had found many more, leading him to conclude that this was probably a standard Buddhist dedication.

Immediately south of and below the ruined terrace of Bodh-Gaya was a sunken court, at its centre 'a very slender quadrangular pyramid or spire placed upon a square terrace from 20 to 30 feet high . . . It perhaps may be 150 feet high, but is not to be compared with the great temples of Pegu.' The structure was identified by the Hindu *mahant* as the 'Mahabodhi'. What was most striking about this ruined tower, in appearance very similar to a Hindu *mandir*, was its seeming antiquity:

There is nothing about this work to induce one to believe that it has been originally constructed of ruins . . . Except ornaments, the whole has been built of brick, but it has been covered with plaster and as usual in Hindu buildings has been minutely subdivided into numberless projecting corners, niches and petty mouldings. The niches seem each to have contained an image of a Buddh in plaster, and on each projecting corner has been placed a stone somewhat in the shape of a beehive and representing a temple. The number of these small temples scattered all over the neighbourhood for miles is exceedingly great. The Mandir has had in front a porch containing two stairs leading up to two upper stories that the temple contained, but the roof has fallen in, and almost every part of the Mandir is rapidly hastening to decay, except the northern and western sides of the terrace, which have [been] very recently repaired by a Maratah chief.

Clambering down into the lower court that surrounded the tower, Buchanan walked along the short avenue that led to a doorway on the tower's eastern face. After passing a number of side chambers he crossed under a 'gothic' arch to enter the main chamber:

The whole far end of the chamber has been occupied by a throne (Simhasana [lion throne]) of stone in a very bad taste, which has however been much disfigured by a row of images taken from the ruins and built upon the front of the throne on which the image of Mahamuni is seated. The image consists of clay, and is so vastly rude in comparison with all the other images as to favour very much the truth of a current tradition of the image having been gold and having been taken away by the Muhammadans. In fact the present image would appear to have been made after the sect had felt persecution and were no longer able to procure tolerable workmen.

As Buchanan emerged from the inner chamber and began to make his way round the base of the tower he noticed that its west and north sides were receiving the attentions of a group of Hindu pilgrims. The first object of their devotion was a stone, set into the terrace, bearing the impression of a pair of feet. The Hindus referred to it as Vishnupad or Feet of Vishnu, but it also had a second name, Buddhapad, the Feet of Buddha. Proceeding a few more steps to round the corner of the tower, Dr Buchanan was next confronted by the spreading branches of a mature pipal tree, *Ficus religiosa*. This, he learned, was the celebrated Brahma Pipul, revered by Hindus as a tree planted by the great god Brahma. 'The worshippers of Gautama on the contrary assert that it is placed exactly in the centre of this earth, and call it *Bodhidruma*,' noted Buchanan:

Some of them allege that it was planted by a King *Singala* before the temple was built, while the Burma messengers alleged that it was planted by *Asoka Dharma* . . . It is a fine tree in full vigour and in all probability cannot exceed 100 years in age, and has probably sprung from the ruins long after they had been deserted. A similar tree however may have existed there when the temple was entire . . . As this is still an object of worship, and frequented by the pilgrims from Gaya, some zealous person has built a stair on the outside, so that the orthodox may pass up without entering the porch and thus seeing the hateful image of Buddha.

Buchanan now set his team to work. His Hindu munshis made copies of the older inscriptions, while his draughtsmen drew the best-preserved of the hundreds of statues that littered the site. He himself toured the outlying area, taking as his guide a member of the local community of *sannyasis*, who had been pointed out to him by the *mahant* as a convert to the doctrine of Buddh. This was a great stroke of luck. The man turned out to be a Rajput, a member of the *kshatriya* or warrior caste, who had been 'converted by the messengers from Ava, and now altogether rejects the doctrines of the orthodox. This person accompanied me to each of the places in the district as had been pointed out to him as holy by the messengers from Ava, and told me what he recollected from their discourse.'

From this convert Buchanan learned that Bodh-Gaya had at one time been 'the centre of religion in India', that a great Buddhist king named Asoka had once resided there, and that it was he who had built the Mahabodhi temple:

He says that the sect so far as he knows has become perfectly extinct, and that no books relating to it are now procurable in the country. The messengers from *Ava* taught him much in the *Pali* or *Sanscrit* language, and from their books were able to discover the old places of worship, which are numerous in this vicinity, as being the native country of *Gautama*. They said on the authority of their books that the place first became celebrated by the King of *Singhala* [Ceylon] having planted a pipal tree which he calls *Buddh Brup* or the tree of Buddha and which is now called *Brahma Pipul*, and continues to be an object of worship with the orthodox. This was about two thousand two hundred and fifty years ago [i.e., about 450 BCE]. About two hundred and twenty-five years afterwards [*c*. 250 BCE] the present temple was built by King *Asoka Dharma*, King of *Magades*, who resided in the palace immediately adjacent . . . According to the messengers from Ava, Gautama died at a place called Pawa-puri, north some miles from Giriyak, where his funeral was performed by the Raja Mal sovereign of the country.

Even if Dr Buchanan failed to grasp why Bodh-Gaya was regarded by the messengers from Ava as 'the centre of religion in India', his conversation with the Rajput convert had provided him with some extremely valuable clues about the early history of Buddhism: that it was here in Bihar that Gautama Buddha had lived and taught some five or six centuries before Christ; that a great king named Asoka Dharma, ruler of Maghada, had honoured him by building the *mandir* at Bodh-Gaya; and that another, later monarch, the King of Singhala or Ceylon, had also honoured him by planting a pipal tree there.

The Buddhist convert now led Dr Buchanan eastwards across the water-course of the River Phalgu to show him the other sites associated with Gautama Buddha. One of these was the place where, to the disgust of his five companions, Gautama had ended six years of fasting by taking a bowl of thick sweetened milk from the daughter of a village headman. To Dr Buchanan's dismay, this site had been recently damaged by a British official from Gaya – the first known example of the vandalism by local government officers that marred the record of the British administration in India right up to Lord Curzon's time: 'The people say they remember it as entire as the temple of Mahamuni now is, but that it was round and solid,' wrote Buchanan in his Report. 'Mr Boddam removed many bricks for his building at Gaya, which reduced it to a mere heap. In digging for the bricks he is said to have found a stone chest containing bones and many small images . . . He also removed a stone pillar which has been erected at Sahibgunj . . . Mr Sisson [Acting Magistrate of Behar] says that Mr Boddam procured from this a small stone image of very great beauty.'

Over the next three months Dr Buchanan's caravan criss-crossed southern Bihar, uncovering other important Buddhist sites but without him ever grasping either their significance or their place in Buddhism. As before, he found numerous examples of Buddhist sculptures in Hindu temples. 'The people are totally careless in this respect,' he noted, 'worshipping males by the name of females, and female images of male deities. Nay some of the images which they worship are actually Buddhas in the most unequivocal forms.'

Three days' march north-east of Bodh-Gaya was the town of Rajgir, whose name alone, 'house of kings', hinted that it might mark 'the original seat of empire'. In the Hindu epics it was spoken of as the capital of the great king named Jaraswanda, ally of Krishna, but according to the Buddhist convert it had been the capital of a Buddhist monarch and a place where Gautama Buddha had performed many miracles. Dr Buchanan took forty-eight minutes to complete a circuit of the walls that were said to have surrounded the palace of this ancient monarch, but somehow he overlooked the almost Cyclopean walls that encircle the older of the two old cities of Rajgir. Climbing to the top of a ridge above Rajgir town Dr Buchanan saw below him 'a considerable plain surrounded by five hills held sacred by the Jain, but neglected by the Brahmans. This plain with the adjacent hills is called Hangaspurnagar [Goosetown], and is supposed to have been the situation of a city, but of this I can see no traces.' He sent out his scouts, but they reported that the vegetation was too thick to penetrate. Unseen below him were the ruins of the capital city of King Bimbisara, ruler of Maghada at the time of Buddha's teaching. What Dr Buchanan did observe, however, was that the ridge on which he stood showed signs of earlier settlement. In particular, he observed a 'hollow space with a thick ledge around it' surrounded by 'a square mass of building'. He concluded, without any real evidence, that it was Buddhist; subsequent excavations identified it as the probable site of the First Buddhist Council, attended by five hundred followers of Gautama Buddha three months after his death.

From Rajgir the survey party travelled just a few miles away to the north-west, to the village of Baragaon, where Dr Buchanan observed extensive ruins covering the plain. He was informed that these were the ruins of Kundalapura, capital of King Bhimaka of Vidarbha, father of Krishna's wife Rukmini, as described in the ancient Hindu scriptures known as *Puranas*. But he had his doubts, because the ruins were dominated by a series of large circular mounds similar to those he had seen outside Bodh-Gaya, and because of his discovery of a number of magnificent stone sculptures dotted about the site. He set his draughtsmen to draw some half-dozen of the best of these (see Plate 5), while he himself made a detailed map. He moved on, unaware that he had camped within the ruins of Nalanda, once the largest and most renowned university in Asia and the last beacon of Buddhism in India.

So the journey of discovery went on, month after month, a methodical gathering-together of miscellaneous information, among which the details of Buddhist remains were but a small part.

Three and a half years later Dr Buchanan left India for good, his body weakened by intermittent fevers, his ambitions destroyed, a man without friends. He no longer coveted the post of Superintendent of the Calcutta Botanic Garden, but advised the new incumbent to 'collect money as fast as possible and whenever you have a competence return to your native land', adding bitterly, 'Do not therefore throw any of your pearls before swine but collect largely and keep your collection for the learned of your own country.' He left Calcutta under a cloud, having lost an argument with the current Governor-General, Lord Moira – 'that animal', he called him – over the ownership of what he regarded as his private collection of natural history drawings: 144 fishes, 20 quadrupeds, 241 birds and 130 plants. 'These,' he wrote, 'the Government of Bengal at the instigation of the Earl of Moira took from me by one of those mean exertions of power, into which a weak man thrust into high authority is liable to fall.' He was also forced to leave behind all the journals and notes compiled during his seven-year statistical survey of Bengal. These were filed away among the records in the Writers' Building in Calcutta and forgotten for almost two decades. In 1838 the Government of Bengal gave permission to a Mr Robert Montgomery Martin to produce a condensed version of Buchanan's Bengal Survey, which duly appeared in print – much chopped about, and under Mr Martin's name.

A brighter note amid this wreckage of a man's fortunes is perhaps to be found in a line of the ship's log of the East Indiaman *Marchioness of Ely* which brought Dr Buchanan back to England. The list of passengers on board includes 'Dr Francis Buchanan and Miss Cornelia': was this 'Miss Cornelia' actually 'Miss Cornelia Buchanan', possibly a natural daughter by an Indian *bibi*? A footnote attached to this entry adds: 'Landed the above passengers 28th August, 1815, off the Isle of Wight.'

No hint of 'Miss Cornelia' is to be found in later records; but then, Dr Francis Buchanan left a trail of confusion behind him by taking his mother's name, Hamilton, in order to inherit her property in Scotland. There he settled into the life of a country laird, married late in life and fathered two children. His son wrote of him in 1880 that he had 'spent the evening of his life in beautifying his home, in arranging his family charters and papers and carrying on extensive correspondence with his old, his literary and his scientific friends'. But by that change of name this man of many parts caused posterity to subdivide him into four persons. Dr Francis Buchanan, Dr Francis Hamilton, Dr Francis Hamilton-

Buchanan, and Dr Francis Buchanan-Hamilton all crop up in accounts of the period, and all have some claim to fame. Perhaps now that these four avatars are once more united in one person, posterity will give the doctor his due.

6

Three Englishmen and a Hungarian

BETWEEN SEPTEMBER 1818 and September 1819 three young men arrived in the Indies to take up their first posts as government servants. Born within months of each other at the turn of the century, George Turnour, Brian Hodgson and James Prinsep were to follow very different courses in their chosen fields, each in his own territory – Ceylon, the Himalayas and Bengal. After serving long apprenticeships, in the 1830s they joined forces for six eventful years that transformed Indian historical studies, a renaissance of Orientalism that outshone the golden age of Sir William Jones. Yet all too soon mental breakdown and death deprived it of its driving force, and but one was left to soldier on in self-imposed solitude.

The Honourable George Turnour was effectively the first to set foot in the East, for his father had been one of the select band of administrators brought to Ceylon by Frederick North in 1798, and he was among the first Britons to be born on the island. Sent back to England to be educated like so many later sons and daughters of empire born overseas, like them he continued to hanker after the land of his birth and early childhood, and in 1818 returned to the island as a cadet in the Ceylon Civil Service.

Ceylon was by then totally in British hands. In 1814 the increasingly tyrannical King of Kandy, Raja Sri Vikrama Sinha, had perpetrated a series of ghastly killings of his Sinhalese subjects prompted largely by his desire to transform Buddhist Kandy into a faithful copy of the Hindu city of Madura. 'One scene of horror and bloodshed rapidly follows another, till the tragedy is wound up' was how a contemporary, Dr John Davy, summed it up. At the request of the Kandyan chiefs, the British Governor of the Maritime Provinces intervened and the Kandyan monarch was dethroned – only to be replaced by another foreigner, George III.

Clause 5 of the Act of Settlement of 1815 stated unequivocally, if remarkably, that 'The religion of Budhoo, professed by the chiefs and inhabitants of these provinces, is declared inviolable, and its rights, ministers, and places of worship are to be maintained and protected.' But this guarantee was not enough. 'It may be observed,' wrote Dr Henry Marshall, an unusually dispassionate witness of these proceedings, 'that civilised nations assume a sort of inherent right to regulate the policy of the more barbarous nations, humanity being frequently assigned as the pretext for subjugating a country, while conquest is the real and ultimate object of commencing hostilities.' Having restored order to the country, the British took it upon themselves to govern it. 'The Kandyans', continues Dr Marshall, 'used to enquire when the English intended to return to the maritime provinces. "You have now", said one, "deposed the king, and nothing more is required – you may leave us." . . . Conversing on this subject, a subordinate chief observed to an officer, that the British rule in the Kandyan country was as incompatible as yoking a buffalo and a cow on the same plough.'

This incompatibility led to the Kandyan Rebellion of 1817–19, a desperate bid by the chiefs of Kandy, encouraged by Buddhist monks, to regain their powers and privileges. It began with its leader, the gallant chieftain Maha Dusave Keppetipola, dismissing the British troops sent against him with the words: 'It is not proper for us as Sinhalese to shoot you down with your own guns – go, therefore, return your guns to your Governor and tell him that the whole of Uva, Wellasssa and Bintenne has risen in rebellion.' It ended with Keppetipola's public beheading as he sat in the Buddhist posture of meditation beside the lake at Kandy (his head was purloined by Dr Henry Marshall and later presented by him to the Phrenological Society of Edinburgh). 'The natives never met us boldly and fairly in the field,' complained Dr Davy, the Governor's physician and author of *An Account of the Interior of Ceylon and of its Inhabitants* (and younger brother of the celebrated scientist Sir Humphry Davy). 'They would way-lay our parties, and fire on them from inaccessible heights, or from the ambush of an impenetrable jungle; they would line the paths through which we had to march with snares of different kinds – such as spring-guns and spring-bows, deep pits, lightly covered over, and armed with thorns etc.' The British response to this guerrilla warfare was a ruthless scorched-earth policy. However, what finally broke the back of the Sinhalese revolt was the British administration's seizure of the island's most precious treasure, the Relic of the Tooth, which had previously been smuggled out of Kandy secreted in the robes of a *bhikkhu*, a Buddhist monk.

As a matter of policy the relic was returned and reinstalled in its little temple beside the royal palace, where it was examined by a party of British officials that included Dr John Davy. He found it to be secured within no fewer than six jewelled onion-shaped caskets of gold: 'Never was a relic more preciously enshrined,' Davy wrote. 'Wrapped in pure shoot-gold, it was placed in a case just large enough to receive it, of gold, covered externally with emeralds, diamonds and rubies, tastefully arranged. This tasteful and very valuable bijou was put into a very small *karandua* [casket], richly ornamented with rubies, diamonds and emeralds.' This second case was lodged within another slightly larger gold casket 'very prettily decorated with rubies' which was, in its turn, encased within three others. When unwrapped from its gold sheets the relic itself proved to be 'discoloured by age' and 'of a dirty yellow colour, excepting towards its truncated base, where it was brownish'. Dr Davy was not impressed: 'Judging from its appearance at the distance of two or three feet (for none but the chief priests were privileged to touch it), it was artificial, and of ivory, discoloured by age.' His drawing of the tooth shows a large molar approximately 3.7 centimetres in length with a long curving root and a crown with a radius of 0.9 centimetres. For all Dr Davy's doubts, it does indeed appear to be the molar tooth of an adult male *Homo sapiens*.

Young George Turnour played no direct part in these unhappy proceedings. Much of his early time as a civil servant was spent in minor posts learning the languages of the island, Sinhalese and Tamil. There, no doubt, he was happy to accept the general view of his countrymen, as set down by Dr Davy, that Sinhalese culture had little to offer. Dr Davy took the view that the Buddhist religion of the island was a highly moral one, but he much regretted that 'such a system of morality should be associated with such a monstrous system of religion – a compound of the coldest materialism, and the grossest, offering nothing consolatory, or intellectual, or dignifying, or rational'. He was also of the opinion that the Sinhalese had no written history: 'They possess no accurate records of events, are ignorant of genuine history, and are not sufficiently advanced to relish it. Instead of the one, they have legendary tales; and, instead of the other, historical romances, which are the more complete the more remote the period is to which they belong.' What they did have – or were rumoured to have – were religious works 'so extensive that no individual has studied the whole of them; and so obscure, as to be frequently unintelligible, affording reason to the hostile Brahmens to remark, that "the Boodhists are like the dumb, who dream and cannot explain the dreams".' These texts were written in 'a learned and dead language – the Pali, derived from and said to be very similar to Sanskrit, and common to the priests of Ava and Siam, as well as that of Ceylon.'

In the mid 1820s George Turnour was posted away from the British capital to become the Collector and Magistrate at Ratnapura, the island's 'city of gems', situated in lush forest country on the western slopes of Adam's Peak. In these idyllic surroundings he began to study Sinhalese culture to a degree that won the confidence of the local Buddhist priests – very much as Charles Wilkins had with the Brahmins in Bengal forty years earlier. The Buddhist monk who was Turnour's language teacher agreed to teach him Pali and, after he had made some progress, brought him a manuscript of the most valued text on the island, known as the *Mahavamsa* or Great Chronicle. As the two began to work their way through it, Turnour realised that this was not only a history of the island from the time of the arrival of Buddhism, but also an invaluable history of Buddhism itself. A second volume, the *Mahavamsa Tika*, provided a prose commentary on the main book, helping him to arrive at a more accurate reading. In 1826 Turnour moved to Kandy, the former capital, and there set to work translating the *Mahavamsa* into English.

While George Turnour pursued his Pali studies at one end of the subcontinent, Brian Houghton Hodgson was following his own wider course of scholarship at the other. Unlike Turnour, with his aristocratic background, Hodgson was a grammar-school boy from Macclesfield whose father was a local banker fallen on hard times. One of his father's friends was, however, influential enough to be able to nominate him for a post in the Company, and Hodgson was duly groomed for the Indian Civil Service, first at the EICo's college at Haileybury and then at Fort William College in Calcutta. Within months of his arrival in Bengal Hodgson's health broke down. Had he stayed in the plains he would almost certainly have joined the scores of young chancers buried in South Park Cemetery, but by a stroke of luck one of only two civil appointments in the Himalayan foothills fell vacant and he was made assistant to the Commissioner of Kumaon.

Kumaon had come under British rule at the conclusion of the Nepal War in 1815 – the inevitable outcome of the expansionist policies of both the EICo and the Gorkha rulers of Kathmandu. The losers were forced to relinquish some of their recent gains to the victors and to accept a permanent British Resident in Kathmandu, a post filled initially by The Honourable Edward Gardner. In 1820 Gardner was joined by Brian Hodgson, who became his political assistant and secretary. Apart from a spell in the Political Department in Calcutta in 1823, when his frail constitution once again let him down, Hodgson remained in Nepal until 1846, from 1833 onwards as Resident. In social and career terms this was the ultimate backwater, but Hodgson was more than happy to stay put. Sure-footed diplomacy was called for in calming the Nepalese court's fears over the EICo's imperial ambitions while at the same steering clear of the many court factions vying for power, but even so he had plenty of time to pursue his own wide-ranging interests, all stemming from an insatiable curiosity about the country in which fate had placed him. What was by Hodgson's own admission 'foreign to my pursuits' was the study of Buddhism; nevertheless, 'my respect for science in general led me cheerfully to avail myself of the opportunity afforded, by my residence in a Bauddha country, for collecting and transmitting to Calcutta the materials for such investigation'. His initial aim, then

– simply to gather documentary material on the subject for others to study – led him indirectly to 'an old Bauddha residing in the city of Patan', one of the three principal cities in the Kathmandu Valley. Because of the continuing restrictions placed on British diplomats by the Nepalese Government, together with what Hodgson describes as the 'jealousy of the people in regard to any profanation of their sacred things by an European', he had to rely on a Nepalese member of his staff to act as a go-between. That first contact eventually supplied a list of Buddhist scriptures and then, as relations further improved, an offer from the 'old Bauddha' to supply the texts themselves: 'His list gradually enlarged as his confidence increased; and at length, chiefly through his kindness, and his influence with his brethren in the Bauddha faith, I was able to procure and transmit to Calcutta a large collection of important Bauddha scriptures.'

Between about 1820 and 1823 Hodgson sent no fewer than 218 Sanskrit texts to the Asiatic Society, where they were acknow-ledged by the Society's Secretary, Dr Horace Hayman Wilson, and then ignored. More donations of manuscripts followed, including two complete sets of the Tibetan canon of Buddhist literature known as the *Kanjur* or 'translation of the commandments of the Buddha'. A third set, together with a large number of Sanskrit manuscripts, Hodgson sent at his own expense to the Collège de France in Paris. His compatriots responded with indifference; the French made him a member of the Légion d'honneur and struck a gold medal in his honour.

Hodgson's relations with the Buddhist from Patan, Amrita Nanda Bandya – 'the most learned Buddhist then, or now, living in this country' – developed into an abiding friendship. In 1827 he was able to persuade the Nepalese authorities to allow the old man to visit him at the British Residency, where the two spent many hours closeted together. The first fruit of this duologue was a set of written answers in reply to a list of questions. Question 8, for example, asked: 'What is the reason for Buddha being represented with curled locks?' Answer: 'In the limbs and organs we discrim-inate thirty-two points of beauty, such as expansion of forehead, blackness of the eyes, roundness of the head, elevation of the nose, and archedness of the eyebrows; so also the having curled locks is one of the points of beauty and there is no other reason.' Question 12 asked for an explanation of the differences between the Buddhism practised by the Newars of Kathmandu Valley and that followed by the lamas of Tibet, and produced a curious answer that can be seen as an allegorical explanation of the manner in which the Buddhism practised in the Kathmandu Valley had been modified by the Hindu revival in India initiated by the ninth-century Brahmin reformer Sankaracharya:

The *Lamas* [of Tibet] . . . carry their orthodoxy to a greater extent than we do [in Nepal] . . . the *Buddhamamargi* practice of *Bhote* [Tibet] is purer, and its scriptures more numerous, than ours . . . Insomuch, that it is said, that *Sankara Acharya, Siva-Margi*, having destroyed the worship of *Buddha* and the scriptures containing his doctrine in *Hindustan*, came to *Nipal*, where he also effected much mischief; and then proceeded to *Bhote*. There he had a conference with the *Grand Lama*. The *Lama*, who never bathes, and after natural evacuations does not use topical ablution, disgusted him to that degree, that he commenced reviling the *Lama*. The *Lama* replied, 'I keep my inside pure, although my outside be impure; while you carefully purify yourself without, but are filthy within', and at the same time he drew out his whole entrails and showed them to *Sankara*; and then replaced them again. He then demanded an answer of *Sankara*, who, by virtue of his yoga, ascended into the heavens.

This confrontation between the two faiths apparently concluded with the Grand Lama of Tibet pinning the shadow of the Brahmin reformer to the floor with his magic knife and so killing him (a case of wishful thinking: the historical Sankaracharya almost certainly died peacefully in Benares in about 820 CE).

Realising the limitations of this question–and–answer method, Hodgson concluded that he must read the texts himself. Reluctantly he set about learning Sanskrit, but made slow progress, not least because he was now devoting most of his attention – along with much of his official salary – to other far more appealing areas of study. 'He has seldom had a staff of less than two and twenty persons of various tongues and races employed as translators, collectors, artists, shooters and stuffers,' wrote the botanist Dr Joseph Hooker of the Hodgson of later years, adding that it was through this combination of 'unceasing exertions and princely liberality' that he 'unveiled the mysteries of Buddhism, chronicled the affinities, languages, customs and factions of the Himalayan Tribes and completed a natural history of the quadrupeds and birds of these regions'. The first of these accomplishments Hodgson continued to regard as burdensome. 'I pore over the pictorial, sculptural and architectural monuments of Buddhism,' he wrote to his sister in 1833. 'But the past chiefly interests me as far as it can be made to illustrate the present – the origin, genius, character and attainments of the people.' What he did not tell his sister was that his isolation had for some years been lessened by the companionship of a *bibi*, a Moslem mistress with whom he had formed a 'domestic connection' resulting in two much-loved children. He had also by then established his own menagerie within the grounds of the British Residency, consisting of 'a wild tiger, a wild sheep, a wild goat, four bears, three civets and three score of our beautiful pheasants'.

B. H. Hodgson's sojourn in the Himalayas is remarkable for its duration, but it was not unique: even in this early period of British expansion others were busy making inroads into and over the mountains, particularly in the Western Himalayas. Among these pioneers were Dr William Moorcroft and Dr James Gerard, two more of those remarkable EICo surgeons for whom doctoring was chiefly a means to other ends. While wandering through the mountain regions that today form the Indian states of Himachal Pradesh and Ladakh, both men reported back to the Assistant to the Agent to the Governor-General in Delhi, Captain James Kennedy, who had made a base for himself on a vantage-point high above the Sutlej river at a tiny village called Simla. In July 1822 Dr Moorcroft wrote from Leh to say that he had come across a most extraordinary traveller, a Hungarian vagabond named Alexander Csoma de Koros. He had been in central Asia for the last three years, and had a remarkable story to tell. Born in Transylvania in 1784, Csoma de Koros had been obsessed from an early age with the idea of discovering the identity and origins of the Hungarian people, then an oppressed minority. Of the various theories about their origins, the one he favoured was that they were descendants of the tribes of Attila the Hun whose original homeland lay somewhere to the east of the high Pamirs. After years of study and preparation, Csoma de Koros had set out for central Asia in the belief that he could trace his people's homeland through language roots. He had reached Leh by way of Alexandria, Aleppo, Bokhara, Kabul and Srinagar, and was now intent on entering Tibet.

With characteristic enthusiasm, Dr Moorcroft proposed that the Government of Bengal should fund the young Hungarian's researches into the Tibetan language, and on its behalf gave him some money and books before continuing on his own journey, one that saw him tracing Csoma de Koros' steps in reverse as far west as Bokhara and dying soon afterwards.

Two and a half years after Dr Moorcroft's report, Captain Kennedy received a letter from Csoma de Koros himself. Following his encounter with Dr Moorcroft he had, by his own account, set himself to learn Tibetan, in order to 'penetrate into those numerous and highly interesting volumes which are to be found in every monastery', and to this end had journeyed to Yangla in Zanskar and there applied to the head lama: 'By the able assistance of that intelligent man, I learned the language grammatically; and became acquainted with many literary treasures shut up in three hundred and twenty large printed volumes, which are the basis of all Tibetan learning and religion. These volumes, divided into two classes, and each class containing other sub-divisions, are all taken from the Indian Sanskrit, and were translated into Tibetan.' He regarded himself as indebted to the EICo for the money Dr Moorcroft had lent him in the Company's name, and intended to repay that debt by making the fruit of his researches freely available to the Asiatic Society. His letter ended with a plea for continued support so that he could complete his studies: 'There is yet in Asia a vast terra incognita of Oriental literature. If the Asiatic Society of Calcutta would engage for the illuminating of the map of this terra incognita I shall be happy if I can serve that Honourable Society with the first sketches of my research.' Grudging government approval was given, together with a small stipend of fifty rupees a month.

In 1827 Csoma de Koros was visited in Zanskar by Dr James

Gerard, who was travelling through the region with the ostensible purpose of eradicating smallpox through inoculation. Reporting to Captain Kennedy, he described the primitive conditions under which the Hungarian was studying at his isolated monastery. He was living 'like one of the sages of antiquity, and taking no interest in any object around him, except his literary avocations . . . He sat at his desk wrapped up in woollens from head to foot, and from morning to night, without an interval of recreation or warmth, except that of his frugal meals, which are one universal routine of greasy tea . . . In this situation he read from morning till evening without fire, or light after dusk, the ground to sleep upon and the bare walls of the building for protection against the rigours of the climate.' Dr Gerard found the Hungarian to be by turns gloomy and vivacious, self-pitying and anxious, but 'highly pleased with the prospects of unfolding to the world those vast mines of literary riches'. He also noted that both teacher and student were extremely dirty. The former exhibited 'a singular union of learning, modesty, and greasy habits; and Mr Csoma in this last respect vies with his learned companion.'

Dr Gerard's report was followed by a second letter from Alexander Csoma de Koros. He had compiled a Tibetan grammar and a Tibetan–English dictionary which he would like to see published, and he enclosed a fifty-five-point review of Tibetan religious literature. This was passed on to the Secretary of the Asiatic Society, Dr Wilson, who appears to have ignored it, as he had ignored Brian Hodgson's Sanskrit texts.

However, Csoma de Koros had also made contact with Brian Hodgson in Kathmandu, and from their respective eyries in the mountains the two now began a learned correspondence – the one armed with a mass of Sanskrit manuscripts on the Buddhism of Nepal, the other with access to an even larger pile of Tibetan documents printed from woodblocks in a script based on Indian Devanagari but written in the Tibetan language. Each was now able to fill gaps in the other's learning, but the greatest gain came from the validation of information. Csoma de Koros was able to confirm to Hodgson the accuracy of what the latter had learned from his Patan Buddhist – that the Tibetan texts were translations of Sanskrit texts from India: 'The Tibetans have derived their religion and literature in general from India, commencing about the middle of the seventh century after Christ, and have formed their alphabet in imitation of the Devanagari letters. Several Tibetan scholars resided for many years in India, and became well acquainted with the Sanskrit literature of the Buddhists in that country. Learned pandits were invited many times to Tibet to assist the Tibetans in the translation of the Sanskrit works.' According to Tibetan sources, the doctrine taught by Gautama Buddha had been compiled in three stages: 'It was first collected immediately after his decease by three of his principal disciples, whose names are mentioned. The second collection was made one hundred and ten years after the death of Shakya [Gautama Buddha] in the time of King Ashoka or Asoka. The third in the time of Kanishka, the king, four hundred years after the death of Shakya, when the followers of Buddha had separated themselves into eighteen different classes of sects.' These texts provided the material for the Tibetan *Kanjur*, brought over the Himalayas by Indian gurus in the tenth and eleventh centuries when the last outposts of Buddhist learning in India were facing extinction.

After three more years of unremitting study Csoma de Koros applied for permission to come down to the Indian plains. The response from the Asiatic Society was equivocal, to say the least, and it is impossible to avoid the conclusion that it, in the person of its Secretary Dr Wilson, did not take to this most dedicated but also most idiosyncratic of scholars. However, the Government of India considered that a Tibetan grammar and dictionary would be valuable aids to trade, and authorised the despatch of funds to enable the Hungarian to proceed to Calcutta. He arrived there in May 1831 and at once placed himself and his literary treasures at the Government's disposal. The Tibetan texts sent down to Calcutta by Brian Hodgson were still lying unread in the archives of the Asiatic Society, so he was put to work cataloguing Hodgson's books, on a Government salary of a hundred rupees a month – with the Secretary insisting that this payment be limited to a two-year period. The vexed question of where the unwashed foreigner should sleep was solved when the Society's Treasurer, a Bengali named Babu Ram Sen, offered him a room in his own house.

Csoma de Koros's *Tibetan Grammar* and *Tibetan–English*

Dictionary were ready for publication, but the Asiatic Society was unwilling to pay for their printing. However, one of his translations did find its way into print at this time, a Tibetan *sutra* or scripture that was seen and read by the French traveller Victor Jacquemont. This first glimpse of the mysteries of Vajrayana Buddhism was greeted with incomprehension: writing to a friend in May 1832, Jacquemont declared it to be 'unspeakably boring. There are some twenty chapters on what sort of shoes it is fitting for lamas to wear. Among other pieces of preposterous nonsense of which these books are full, priests are forbidden to take hold of a cow's tail to ford a swift river. There is no lack of profound dissertations on properties of griffins', dragons', and unicorns' flesh or the admirable virtues of hoofs of winged horses. To judge by what I have seen of these people and what M. Csoma's translations tell us about them, one would take them for a race of madmen or idiots.'

The issue of the *Grammar* and *Dictionary* dragged on for months. At the end of 1832 Dr Wilson retired as Secretary of the Asiatic Society, and as he prepared to leave Calcutta he let it be known that he thought the two books would be best published in England, and that he was prepared to take the manuscripts with him to facilitate this. His proposal was stoutly resisted by the incoming Secretary of the Asiatic Society, who argued to the Government of Bengal that it should regard 'Mr Csoma's labours as of national interest' and accordingly pay for the two books to be printed and published in Calcutta, the costs being 'trifling compared with the importance of the work to literature'. It was he who corrected the English portion of the text, oversaw the casting of the new Tibetan fount, arranged for copies of the *Tibetan Grammar* and *Tibetan–English Dictionary* to be sent to all the learned societies of Britain and Europe, and ensured that their author was proposed and elected an Honorary Member of the Asiatic Society.

New quarters were also found for de Koros, at the back of the Asiatic Society's premises, although from a thumbnail portrait recorded by an artist named Schoefft, a visiting Hungarian compatriot, we know that he continued to live and work in Calcutta in very much the same style as he had in Ladakh and Zanskar. 'I never saw a more strange man than him,' wrote Mr Schoefft. 'He lives like a hermit among his Tibetan and other works, in the house of the Asiatic Society, which he seldom leaves. Of an evening he takes slight exercise in the grounds, and then causes himself to be locked up in his apartment . . . He was cheerful; often merry, his spirits rose very considerably when we took the opportunity of talking about Hungary . . . He proposed remaining for ten years longer in the country, to enable him to glean whatever he could find in the old writings . . . I began to suspect, however, that he would never see his native land again.'

The new Secretary of the Asiatic Society was James Prinsep, the third member of the trio of young sophomores of the Class of 1818–19. James's father John Prinsep has already appeared briefly in these pages with his description of his arrival in Calcutta at the time of Warren Hastings. After sixteen years in India Prinsep *père* retired with a modest fortune of £40,000, part of which he used to buy himself a seat in Parliament and part to set himself up in London as a businessman. He made enemies of the Government, the Evangelicals and the Board of Directors of the EICo by attacking their Indian policies and advocating free trade. He failed in a bid for re-election, failed in his ambition to become a Director of the EICo, and failed in business. 'Granpapa Prinsep had had a wonderful career,' wrote his grandson Sir Henry Thoby Prinsep in an unpublished memoir entitled 'Three Generations in India'. 'He went to India young, and is said to have been the first introducer of indigo plantation. He made two fortunes and lost both. In his zenith of prosperity he lived in one of the princely frescoed houses in Leadenhall Street – afterwards a part of the India Office; but after a second failure he was too old to go out to India again. They gave up all they had to their creditors, even to grandmama's settlement, £30,000 thrown into Chancery, and her jewels and watch, and were very ill-off. She used to tell the story with much glee of how they lived in an attic, across which she put a curtain to make two rooms, and cooked herself; and how the three boys, James, Tom and Augustus, had but one pair of trousers between them and went out by turns!'

It was in these very straitened circumstances that young James Prinsep grew up as an adolescent in Bristol, the seventh son of his father, a blond, blue-eyed and unusually shy child who was thought to be 'slow of apprehension'. Lacking a formal education but showing an aptitude for mechanics and model-making, James was apprenticed at fifteen to a rising young architect named Augustus Pugin. In Pugin's workshop he applied himself so diligently as a draughtsman that his eyesight began to deteriorate and his apprenticeship had to be abandoned – an early sign of both his capacity for concentrated effort and his physical vulnerability. His father procured him a cadetship with the EICo which James declined, asking that the prize be given to his younger brother Thomas. An opening in the EICo's Mint in Calcutta was then offered to him, on the understanding that he secure the necessary qualifications. This was more to James's liking, and after periods of study at Guy's Hospital (for the chemistry) and at the Royal Mint he was appointed assistant to the Assay Master in Calcutta. Thomas had by then completed his one-year cadetship at the Company's Military College at Addiscombe, so the brothers were able to sail to India together, arriving at Calcutta in September 1819. A portrait copied by his sister Emily in 1822 from an earlier drawing that must have been done just before his departure for India shows James looking as pretty and ineffectual as the young Keats.

On hand to welcome them and help them settle in were two of their older brothers, Henry Thoby, a member of the Bengal Civil Service, and William, a merchant. The Calcutta Mint was then situated in Church Lane, opposite St John's Church, and it was here that James Prinsep presented himself.

The Assay Master and Director of the Calcutta Mint was Dr Horace Hayman Wilson, whom we have already encountered as Secretary of the Asiatic Society. Here was another of those medical men whose professional skills were regarded by the EICo as less valuable than their knowledge of science. Dr Wilson had joined the Company as an assistant surgeon on the Bengal establishment, but was at once diverted to take over the running of its Bengal Mint; his personal desire was to become the leading Sanskritist of his age. 'Excited by the example of Sir W[illia]m Jones,' he later wrote, 'I entered on the study of Sanskrit with warm interest as soon after my arrival in India in 1808 as official occupation allowed.' By the time of James Prinsep's arrival in Calcutta, Wilson had achieved his ambition: the EICo had just published his Sanskrit–English dictionary to universal praise, and having been appointed its Secretary in 1811 he now dominated the proceedings of the Asiatic Society of Bengal in much the same way as his hero Sir William Jones had thirty years earlier – but with one crucial difference. Whereas Jones had extended his own and the Society's enquiries into every field, Wilson concentrated on the translation of Sanskrit texts – he made the first English translation of the Sanskrit history of Kashmir, *Raja Tarangani* – and on overseeing the studies of Calcutta's Hindu College, which under his direction became the first public institution in India to teach English literature and European science to its students. Such spare time as he had he devoted to his one abiding hobby – amateur theatricals. This was all very laudable – except that Wilson was the Secretary of the Asiatic Society for twenty-two years, and fruitful as this period was for him and his own work, it was not similarly productive for Indian studies in general. With its 'Orientalist' philosophy coming increasingly under attack both at home and in India, the Asiatic Society needed a champion, supported by powerful protectors, who was also an enthusiast able to guide and co-ordinate the activities of its members. It wanted a second William Jones, and Dr H.H. Wilson, for all his scholarship, was no Jones.

A second Jones had in fact already come and gone, in the person of a brilliant young scholar of Oriental languages who in 1806 had become Professor of Hindustani at Fort William College. It was later said of Dr John Leyden that in the following four years he did 'about as much for Asia [that is, Asian philology] as the combined scholarship of centuries had done for Europe'. Appointed Assay Master of the Calcutta Mint in 1810, he was being groomed to take over the pivotal role of Secretary to the Asiatic Society from the soon-to-retire Dr William Hunter when he was invited by the Governor-General to join him as his Malay interpreter on a military expedition to Java. Within weeks of his arrival in Java Dr Leyden was dead. It was said that he had entered an 'unventilated native library' and there contracted a fever, which killed him in three days. So it came about that for want of a better man the Asiatic Society had been saddled with Wilson, a diligent but narrow-minded standard-bearer whose talents were more suited to the Oxford to which he retired (to take up the newly-endowed Boden Professorship of Sanskrit) than they were to British Bengal.

7

Tigers, Topes and Rock-Cut Temples

IN THE absence of a presiding genius at the centre during the Wilson years, the Asiatic Society's members increasingly went their own way – as exemplified by the career of the EICo's leading surveyor and map-maker, Colonel Colin Mackenzie.

Like his fellow Scot Buchanan, Mackenzie was a late starter, an Outer Hebridean whose first ten working years were spent as a customs officer on the Isle of Lewis. Drawn to India by an interest in Indian mathematics, it would seem, he initially enlisted in the Madras Infantry in 1783, before transferring to the Engineers to become a military surveyor and siege engineer. Almost as soon as he set foot in Madras, Colin Mackenzie had begun to formulate plans to write a history of India – but the wars against Tipu Sultan and the French, the taking of Ceylon's maritime provinces in 1795–96 and the subsequent topographical surveys of newly-won territories all combined to frustrate his wider ambitions. All this campaigning and surveying did however have the advantage of taking him far off the beaten track, leading to his discovery of a number of hitherto unrecorded Hindu and Jain sites. He also acquired a band of loyal followers, British and Indian (see Plate 4). 'He employed,' noted an observer, 'at an immense expense, various individuals to collect objects of antiquarian research throughout all parts of India, but more especially in the peninsula . . . As their employer had the singular art of inspiring them with a portion of that zeal which animated his own mind, their reports are in general highly interesting and replete with much valuable statistical as well as antiquarian observation.'

As the years passed Colin Mackenzie became increasingly single-minded, using his purse and his position to secure for his private collection every curio that came his way, be it ancient coin, engraved copper plate, manuscript, statue, or carved stone frieze. And where such articles could not be purchased or carted away, he ensured that one of his team of draughtsmen made a sketch or a copy. In 1797, while surveying on the borders of Madras and Hyderabad, Mackenzie received reports that slabs of finely-carved stone were being used as construction material by a local prince-ling, the Raja of Chintapalli, in the process of building a new town beside a temple of Shiva. He arrived at the village of Amrawati (now Amaravati) to find the Raja's workmen digging into a vast circular hill well over five hundred feet in circumference with a solid core composed entirely of bricks. A section of the lower rim of the hill had been exposed, and revealed a wall of finely-carved stones unlike anything he had seen before. 'The Rajah', noted Mackenzie, 'eagerly came over to inspect the place, and perceiving that it was the most curious of the several mounds he had caused to be opened, conceived that it might conceal something of value; as most places so marked are generally the receptacles of hidden treasures, he commanded the mussulmen [Muslims, who were living there] to move elsewhere, as he designed to form a garden there, and a reservoir at the centre.' There was nothing Mackenzie could do, so he contented himself with noting the name of the place, and moved on.

In 1811 the Governor-General Lord Minto was visited in Calcutta by a civil servant named Stamford Raffles, his Agent at the Company's Settlement on the island of Penang. This remark-able young man had joined the EICo at the age of fourteen as a humble clerk in East India House, but his expertise in all matters pertaining to the Indies trade had elevated him within ten years to the post of Assistant Secretary in the EICo's service at Pulo Penang, off the coast of Malaya, newly annexed from the Dutch East India Company. He had very soon proved himself indispensable, becom-ing the Company's key man on the spot. Raffles was acutely aware that as long as the Dutch retained control of the island of Java, the last of their remaining possessions in the Indies, the EICo's trade route to China would be under threat, a perception that took him to Calcutta to persuade Lord Minto to lead an invading force against Java. This ran counter to the EICo's policy of non-interference, but could be justified as a blow against Napoleon Bonaparte, now holding sway over most of Europe. The invasion duly took place, and in 1811 Stamford Raffles became Java's lieutenant-governor, with ambitious plans to transform the archipelago into a British trading area.

With Raffles went Colin Mackenzie, by now Surveyor-General of the Madras Presidency, charged with mapping this newest British possession and gathering all available intelligence about it. One of the first fruits of this survey was the discovery, in the caldera of an extinct volcano at the very centre of the island, of a mound many times larger than that at Amaravati. Mackenzie himself never saw the site, for in August 1813 he took some long-overdue leave, so it was left to a Dutch engineer named H.C. Cornelius to uncover the mound, known locally as Chandi Borobudur. The trees and undergrowth covering the site were felled and cleared with the help of two hundred villagers, and layers of volcanic ash and earth removed to reveal a vast stone monument, in scale and form quite unlike anything seen before by any European. When in May 1815 Stamford Raffles came to inspect the work, he found himself standing before what was later known to be the largest and most spectacular single structure in south-east Asia: it was a miniature cosmos, dedicated to the Buddha, in the shape of a stepped pyramid of stone some sixteen thousand square yards in area and rising to more than ninety feet, made up of five rectangular terraces topped by three concentric terraces (the sixth and outer terrace was not discovered until the excavations of T.W. Izerman, begun in 1885). The galleries of the lower terraces were adorned with more than fifteen hundred intricately carved panels – since recognised as the most extensive and complete collection of Buddhist reliefs in the world.

In the absence of Colin Mackenzie it fell to Stamford Raffles to draw together and write up the research his surveyor had started. From local Muslim records he established that Islam had effectively obliterated Buddhism on the island in the thirteenth century and that the Borobudur area had been deserted for some time before that, possibly as a result of volcanic activity. His conclusion was that this 'prodigious monument' had been built between the eighth and tenth centuries CE (later historians were able to determine that it was raised by three generations of kings who ruled briefly over mainland and insular south-east Asia, begun in 778 and completed in 824 CE). With the assistance of one of Mackenzie's Engineer officers, Captain Godfrey Baker, and a team of draughtsmen, Borobudur was drawn and surveyed. But before the work could be completed the battle of Waterloo was fought and won, and the concluding treaty restored Java to the Dutch. Stamford Raffles was forced to quit the island and retire to the derelict pepper factory of Bencoolen in Sumatra, where he wrote his *History of Java* and laid the groundwork for the famous coup of 1819 that founded Singapore and secured Malaya for the British.

Although Colin Mackenzie had good cause to regret his premature departure from Java, he spent his leave well, travelling up the River Ganges as far as Hardwar and adding to his extensive collection. In Delhi he inspected the stone column known as Feroz Shah's Lat. He visited Bodh-Gaya, which (on the evidence of the several drawings made there by his draughtsmen) had been considerably tidied up since Dr Buchanan's visit three years earlier. At Benares he met the increasingly eccentric Colonel Wilford, and took the opportunity to continue the diggings at the ruins of Sarnath started by Dewan Jagat Singh twenty years earlier (see Plate 3), uncovering a number of statues and reliefs which were added to his collection. The largest of the two domed structures on the site had been demolished, but the second mausoleum still remained largely untouched. Local legend held it to be the cenotaph of a legendary king named 'Rajah Booth-Sain'.

Mackenzie left this structure untouched, but its conical shape put him in mind of the great hill he had seen some seventeen years earlier on the northern border of Madras Presidency. In 1816 he returned to Amaravati with his team of assistants and draughtsmen – only to find that the hill he had watched being excavated for its bricks by the Raja of Chintapalli was now little more than a shell, with a large tank or square reservoir dug into its centre. It was obvious that this was indeed the remains of what Mackenzie termed a 'tope', from the Pali word *thupo* (in Sanskrit, *stupa*) used to describe a reliquary containing the ashes of a Buddhist saint. It was also clear that the tope had once been entirely surrounded by a paved walkway some twelve feet broad, enclosed inside and out by a monumental stone colonnade. Most of the stone from this colonnade had gone: large numbers of pillars and beams had been used to form a flight of steps leading down into a nearby bathing tank, while hundreds of slabs had ended in the walls of a nearby Saivite temple and other buildings.

A cursory dig uncovered one last section of the railing still in place, made up of about a hundred and thirty pillars and slabs in all, every one a work of art 'very neatly executed'. Many of these carved bas-reliefs portrayed detailed narrative scenes of past events or legends – bejewelled kings parading through cities on elephants, receiving the homage of admirers or dallying with semi-naked women, ordinary men and women performing everyday tasks in their villages (see illustration overleaf). There were also carved images that Mackenzie believed to be of Jain rather than Buddhist iconography, although he could not understand their significance: a pair of footprints, a pipal tree, a regal parasol, an empty throne and, most notably, a spoked cartwheel – all being adored or worshipped by men and women.

Mackenzie's eight European and three Indian draughtsmen made careful drawings of more than a hundred of the best bas-reliefs. Three sets of drawings were made, of which Mackenzie sent one to the Asiatic Society in Calcutta and another to the EICo's Court of Directors in London, keeping the third for himself. He also arranged for some eighty-eight of the stones to be moved to the nearby regional centre of Masulipatam, where they were cemented into a curious temple-like structure known as 'Mr Robertson's Mount'. Another seven were sent to the Asiatic Society's Museum in Calcutta. It was just as well. The next Orientalist who visited Amaravati – Walter Eliot of the Madras Civil Service, in 1845 – found that 'every fragment of former excavations' had been 'carried away and burnt into lime'.

In that same year, 1816, Colin Mackenzie was made Surveyor-General of India. He was now sixty-one, ancient by Anglo-Indian standards, and he was beginning to feel his age. Opportunities to get out into the field with his dedicated band of pandits and

draughtsmen dwindled, but in 1820 he (or possibly one of his draughtsmen acting on his instructions) made a brief foray south to Orissa to explore a number of antiquities reported in the vicinity of the Hindu holy city of Bhubaneswar. One was at Dauli, just a few miles to the west of the city: an isolated rock standing on the edge of the plain below a low ridge. One entire face of this rock, measuring some fifteen feet by ten, was covered with an inscription – recognised by Colonel Mackenzie as being 'in the very identical character which occurs on the pillars at Delhi', written in that curious pseudo-Greek script that had baffled Sir William Jones and others, and which he himself had seen inscribed on Feroz Shah's Lat outside Delhi. His men made copies, and the party returned to Calcutta. But before he could take the matter any further, Colin Mackenzie died of fever near Calcutta on 8 May 1821.

It was left to a Mr Stirling to publish the research into the Dauli rock inscription begun by Colin Mackenzie. 'There are, I think, two eminently remarkable circumstances connected with the character used in the above inscription,' he wrote. 'The first is the close resemblance of some of the letters to those of the Greek alphabet.' Six of the characters found on these inscriptions – A, E, Λ, Σ, K, O – were, indeed similar to letters of the Greek alphabet, but there still remained more than thirty characters that were nothing like Greek. It was, however, the second circumstance that made this lettering truly remarkable, 'the occurrence of it in sundry monuments situated at widely distant quarters of India . . . Any reader who will take the trouble of comparing the Khandgiri [i.e., Dauli] inscription with that of Firoz Shah's Lat at Delhi, on the column at Allahabad, on the Lat of Bhim Sen in Sarun [see illustration overleaf], a part of the Elephanta, and a part of the Ellora inscriptions, will find that the characters are identically the same.' It also seemed that the Dauli inscription was Buddhist rather than Hindu or Jain, for according to Mr Stirling, 'The Brahmins refer to the inscription with shuddering and disgust, to the *Budh Ka Amel*, or the time when the Buddhist doctrines prevailed, and are reluctant even to speak on the subject.'

As Mr Stirling's report implies, more polished stone columns similar to but less well-preserved than Feroz Shah's Lat had been found – including one at Allahabad, the largest section of which had been used by an over-zealous public works engineer as a road-roller. Copies of their inscriptions in that baffling archaic pseudo-Greek lettering had been sent to the Asiatic Society, where no one spotted that the three most important – from Delhi, Allahabad and Dauli – had much more than a shared script in common. What aroused much greater interest was the news that the EICo had paid out the enormous sum of £15,000 to the widow of the late Colonel Colin Mackenzie to secure the bulk of his antiquarian collection (the largest ever amassed by a private individual in India in the nineteenth century). Much of the statuary and many of the coins and other antiquities gathered by Mackenzie helped lay the foundations of the Indian collections of the Bodleian Library, the British Library and the British Museum in Britain – and, by way of the Asiatic Society's Museum, of the Indian Museum in Calcutta. The bulk of Mackenzie's 1,600 manuscripts and papers was handed over to the care of Dr H. H. Wilson, who was far too busy with his translations and his theatricals to do more than catalogue and then sit on them.

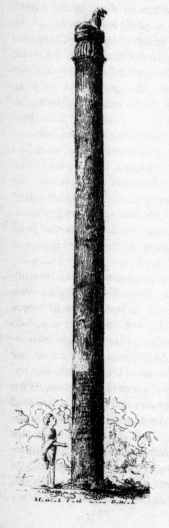

Although Mr Stirling's note on the Dauli rock inscriptions was eventually brought to the attention of members of the Asiatic Society, two of the most exciting discoveries to be made in India in the course of the nineteenth century were initially ignored by that august body. Both resulted directly from the opening-up of the Indian interior brought about by the protracted wars between the EICo and the warlords of the Marathas, the Hindu hill peoples of the Western Ghats, whose armies had wreaked devastation in central India in the wake of the collapse of Mughal power.

In the Cold Weather of 1818–19, as the battle for supremacy in central India known as the Third Maratha War reached its conclusion, a commissariat train under the command of one Major Henry Taylor made camp beside the road leading north towards Gwalior, two days' march out of Bhopal at a place called Bhilsa (today Vidisha). A party of Bengal Native Infantry officers – probably out with their fowling pieces or hog-spears for the customary spot of late-afternoon *shikar* in the surrounding countryside – crested the levelled summit of a nearby hill and found themselves among a large cluster of mounds. Dominating the site was one domed structure so remarkable (see Plate 7) that at least three of the officers – Captain Edward Fell, Lieutenant John Bagnold and Ensign George Roebuck – returned later to make a fuller exploration. While the two more junior officers sketched, Edward Fell set down a brief report, later forwarded to the *Calcutta Journal*, in which it was published in July 1819. 'On a table land of a detached hill', he wrote, 'is an ancient fabric of a hemispherical form, built of thin layers of free-stone, in the nature of steps, without any cement and, to all appearances, solid . . . The monument (for such I will call it) is strengthened by a buttress of stone masonry, 12 feet high and 7 broad, all around the base, the measured circumference of which is 554 feet.'

Like Mackenzie's tope at Amaravati, the monument was surrounded by 'a colonnade of granite [in fact, sandstone] pillars, 10 feet high, distant from each other a foot and a half, connected by parallels also granite, of an elliptical form, united by tenons.' The difference was that here, the colonnade and its gateways were almost complete: 'At the East, West and North points are gateways, plain parallelograms, the extreme height of which is 40 feet and the breadth within the perpendiculars 9 feet.' At Amaravati the great pillars that had held up the gateways had fallen, and the intricately carved panels that once decorated them were either lost or lying undiscovered under the earth. But here at Sanchi three of the four gateways were still standing and – almost miraculously – they were largely undamaged.

Captain Fell despaired of doing justice to the 'magnificence of such stupendous structures and exquisitely finished sculptures', but described as best he could the three standing gateways, each made up of two vertical pillars supported by stone dwarfs or elephants, that were crossed by three beam-like architraves. Every inch of these pillars and cross-beams was decorated, and every space between, above and below was filled with carved figures of elephants and riders (see illustration overleaf), horses and riders, sinuous maidens, lions, gryphons, more elephants and more people – 'figures in groups, some standing, others sitting cross-legged, others bowing, all with joined hands, and in the act of worship'.

Every panel told a story, but what the story was Fell had no idea. One (see illustration opposite) depicted 'a small convex body in a boat, the prow of which is a lion's head and the stern the expanded tail of a fish, over which is suspended a long cable. In the boat are three male figures, two of whom are rowing and the third holding an umbrella over the convex. The vessel is in an open sea, in the midst of a tempest; near it are figures swimming and endeavouring by seizing piles to save themselves from drowning. One, on the point of drowning, is making an expiring effort to ascend the side.' But Captain Fell soon found himself running out of words, and was reduced to the conclusion that here was something quite beyond his experience, for it would be 'hardly possible to conceive sculpture more expressive of feeling than this'.

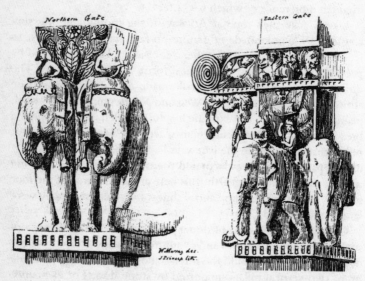

As news of the extraordinary carvings at Sanchi began to spread through the regimental masses of the Bombay Army the site received other visitors, including a Captain Johnson, political assistant to the British Resident at nearby Bhopal, who had been given permission by the Nawab of Bhopal to dig into the central tope in search of treasure. He opened it from top to bottom and, according to an observer, 'found the whole solid brick-work,

without any appearance of recess or open space of any kind'. Fortunately, Captain Johnson then lost interest.

Opinion among these first European visitors was divided as to whether this was a Buddhist or a Jain site. In a small shrine just to the east of what soon became known as the Great Tope of Bhilsa (better-known today as the Great Stupa of Sanchi) a larger-than-life-size stone statue was found which Lieutenant Bagnold for one believed to be a representation of Buddha. As he sketched the image (see Plate 6) he took particular care to examine the way the hair on its head had been chiselled and declared himself satisfied that the statue was that of an African: 'I am positive after very careful examination of the hair of this and several other images that the sculpture represents distinct curls such as negroes have.' The difficulty faced by Bagnold and others was that the carvings on the Great Tope itself did not appear to show any Buddha images: what they did not then know was that its carvings represented the earliest phase of Buddhist iconography, when it was still considered disrespectful, and contrary indeed to Gautama Buddha's wishes, to show any likeness of him. Both here at Sanchi and at Amaravati the stupas were richly adorned with depictions of the major events in the life of Gautama Buddha and the legendary tales of his earlier incarnations as told in the *Jataka* – but without ever portraying the Buddha in anthropomorphic form. He was represented in aniconic form alone: by the prints his feet left, by the unoccupied throne or saddle upon which he sat, by a parasol above an empty space. In this first phase it was the symbols of Gautama Buddha's teaching that were objects of veneration: the *chakra* or Wheel of Law that represented Gautama Buddha's teaching; the pipal or *bodhi* tree as well as the stone slab at its base known as the *vajrasana* or Diamond Throne, where Gautama Buddha had achieved enlightenment; and the image of the stupa or tope itself, worshipped because it contained relics of Gautama Buddha or his chief disciples in the form of ashes and bone fragments.

Sculpture in one of the Compartments of the Bauddha monument at Sanchee.

Drawings of the Great Tope of Bhilsa were circulated in Calcutta but seem to have cut no ice with Horace Hayman Wilson or the other luminaries of the Asiatic Society. Their response to a second and perhaps even more astonishing discovery was equally negative, possibly because this too was made outside Bengal and might therefore have been perceived as being outside their province.

From 1819 onwards stories had been circulating in military circles of a cave complex somewhere in the wild frontier regions of Berar, on the borders of the Bombay Presidency and the territories of the Nizam of Hyderabad. In February 1824 a young lieutenant in the 16th Lancers, James Alexander, took some local leave from his regiment and went into the hills north and west of Aurangabad for a spot of *shikar*. This was unexplored country, and Alexander was warned to beware of the 'stony-hearted' Bhils, the aboriginal hunters who lived in the forests of Central India and were widely regarded as hostile savages. He took note and camped in the Khandesh plains beneath a low plateau cut into by a number of deep, wooded ravines that provided ideal cover for the sport Alexander and his companions were after – tiger, leopard, bear, wild boar, and the large deer known as *sambhar*.

Out of the deepest of these ravines flowed a river known as the Waghewa or Tiger Valley, reputedly the haunt of tigers, and it was to this that Alexander directed his attentions with the help of a local guide. 'I mounted early in the morning,' he wrote in his account of his discovery, set down five years later at the Royal Military College at Sandhurst,

> arrayed in my Muselmani [i.e., Moslem] costume, and accompanied by a couple of servants and a guide, all of us well armed with sabres, pistols, and hunting spears . . . Directing our steps towards an opening in the deeply serrated hills, we arrived at the debouche of the glen. A low whistling was heard above us to the left, and was quickly repeated from the opposite cliffs. This proved to be the Bhils intimating to one another that strangers were approaching. The guide evinced strong symptoms of fear; but on being remonstrated with, and encouraged with the hope of a handsome present, he proceeded onwards. Some of the Bhils showed themselves, peeping out from behind the rocks. They were a most savage-looking race, perfectly black, low in stature and nearly naked. They seemed to be armed with bows and arrows.

Despite their hostile appearance, the Bhils made no effort to halt the *shikaris* but allowed them to continue unmolested. They followed the river upstream as it entered a steep-sided gorge, and then turned a corner to find themselves at a point where the water had dug deep into the black basalt rocks to form a horseshoe-shaped canyon. Strung out before them in a five-hundred-yard semi-circle on the outside of the bend were a series of caves set high on the sheer rock face. Each had its own portal of carved stone arches, pillars and architraves, some supported by stone elephants, others richly decorated with scores of human figures – but all hacked and chiselled directly out of the rock.

As Alexander and his companions clambered up the steep hillside and began to explore the more accessible of the caves, it became clear that the site had been abandoned for centuries, unknown to all except the Bhils:

The fetid smell arising from numerous bats, which flew about our faces as we entered, rendered a continuance inside, for any length of time, very disagreeable. I only saw one cave with two storeys or tiers of excavated rock. In it the steps from the lower apartment to the upper had been destroyed by the Bhils. With our pistols cocked we ascended by the branch of a tree to the upper range of chambers; and found, in the middle of one of the floors, the remains of a recent fire, with large footmarks around it. In the corner was the entire skeleton of a man. On the floor of many of the lower caves I observed the prints of the feet of tigers, jackals, bears, monkies [*sic*], peacocks etc.

The caves were of two distinct types. Five had been carved out to resemble church-like interiors, divided by two rows of columns into a central nave with a vaulted ceiling complete with stone roof beams and side aisles that continued behind the apse. At the centre of this apse, lit by a large horseshoe-shaped window above the entrance, was a domed memorial resembling a scaled-down stupa (more properly, a *chaitya*, a stupa without a relic inside) hewn, like everything else, out of the solid rock. The remaining caves were simpler in construction, mostly taking the form of rectangular halls whose inner walls were lined with doors leading to small stone cells, each complete with a stone sleeping platform. The former were quite evidently places of worship, the latter the living quarters of monks (see Plate 18).

'That these excavations served for the retirement of some monastic society I have no doubt,' observed Lieutenant Alexander. He had seen something very similar at the now well-known caves at Kanheri and Ellora, which were perhaps more impressive in the quality of their exterior carvings. What was different here at Ajanta – and set these caves apart from anything yet seen in India – were the interiors, for every surface of every one of the twenty-six finished caves had at one time been painted. Here were 'paintings in fresco, much more interesting, as exhibiting the dresses, habits of life, pursuits, general appearance and even features of the natives of India perhaps 2,000 or 2,500 years ago, well preserved and highly coloured, and exhibiting in glowing tints, of which light red is the most common, the crisp-haired aborigines of the sect of the Buddhists, who were driven from India to Ceylon after the introduction of Brahminism' (see Plate 19).

In fact, the cave-paintings of Ajanta were far more astonishing than James Alexander could have imagined from the limited glimpses he had of them by the light of a burning torch that afternoon in February 1824. Large areas had mouldered away over the centuries, but more than enough remained to show the consummate artistry with which they had been executed, particularly in the modelling of the human form. A window into the past had been thrown open to reveal a brightly-lit world peopled not only by gods and demi-gods but by lesser beings of flesh and blood, every aspect of whose living and dying was depicted, from the king in his palace to the hermit in his jungle cave: scenes of love and war, triumph and adversity, pageantry and poverty – each crowded scene rendered more complete by details of dress, ornament, utensils, weaponry, musical instruments, and much more besides. Many of the paintings showed haloed Buddha-figures surrounded by floating beings that might be construed as angels, but the most striking images were those of bare-breasted men and women of quite extraordinary grace and beauty: sad-eyed monarchs clasping lily-flowers in one hand and consorts in the other, of queens and princesses riding in state on elephants or being pampered by handmaidens who gossiped and giggled together (see below).

The caves contained a number of stone images that Alexander, like his fellow-officers at Sanchi, immediately construed as having features 'of African cast, with curled hair and prominent lips', although he was greatly puzzled by the lobes of the ears, which were 'elongated and hang upon the shoulders'. After exploring the lower caves, the party tried to reach a second tier set higher up the cliff: 'We clambered upon our hands and knees until stopped by a precipice; and not having ropes, we were unable to reach the caves up above. We therefore gave up the attempt in despair, and after we had partaken of a slight repast, and a *chilum* had been smoked in one of the best lighted and finest excavations, we returned to the horses.'

Lieutenant Alexander felt himself incapable of conveying the magnitude of what had for so long remained hidden in those extraordinary caves – and those who followed him to Ajanta found the task no easier. Four years after Alexander's lone expedition a Mr Ralph and his military friend Captain Gresley rode out to the site from Aurangabad in a series of 'breakneck marches, galloping over stony roads and rocky torrents at the rate of ten miles an hour', and then spent three ecstatic days exploring the caves from end to end, each by turns uttering exclamations of wonder and expressions of regret. Mr Ralph, like Lieutenant Alexander, considered his powers of expression inadequate, and so contented himself with recording snatches of the conversation that passed between them as he and Gresley moved from one mural to the next:

'What a wonderful people these must have been! Remark the head dresses. Now is this a wig or curly hair? All the statues, the curved figures of Buddha have them. How can I say? First wigs were made to present hair, and then hair dressed to look like wigs. 'Tis the shape of your Welsh wig, and rows of curls all over. Then the head dresses and ornaments are different from every thing we now see. These are chiefly domestic scenes – seraglio scenes – here are females and males every where, then processions and portraits of princes which are always larger than the rest. The subjects are closely intermixed – a medallion is twelve or fifteen inches in height, below and above, closely touching, are other subjects. I have seen nothing monstrous. No, certainly there is nothing monstrous except where we see some figures evidently designed for ornament, as in the compartments of the ceiling. The ceiling – aye, every thing but the floor and larger statues and small figures – every thing has been painted. It is done while the plaster is wet – it is fresco painting. I have seen the operation while going about in Rome. It has been dug off, scraped and knocked off with iron instruments. See how the stone itself has been broken!

'Now Ralph, look here: can you see this figure? No. Bring the torch nearer. Give me the torch. You can see it better now. Hardly! Let us light dry grass. Bring grass now: place it here. Now watch while the light is strongest: you may now see the whole figure. This is a prince or some chief. It is a portrait. Observe how well fore-shortened that limb is – yes I can see it now: but throw water on it – now the colours are more vivid. Here is a lovely face – a Madonna face. What eyes! She looks toward the man. Observe, these are all Hindu faces – nothing foreign. All the sweet countenances are of one complexion. R., now remark. Here are three beauties in this apartment – one an African, one copper-coloured, one of a European complexion. Yes, and how frequently we see these intermixed. See this, R., is a fair man – yes, I think he is a eunuch. Another – he has his hand round her waist, and she one hand on his shoulder. Observe – many love scenes, but little gross or grossly indecent: no nudities – nothing like the shocking sculptures on the outside of the temples in Talingana . . .

'I wish I could make out this story; there certainly is a story. Here is a fair man of full age, dressed in a robe and a cap like some monk. Here is next to him a half-naked Brahmin, copper-coloured with shaven crown and single lock on his head. Here is a man presenting him with a scroll on which something is written. He has come to a crowded court – he has come to an audience. What can all this be?'

Mr Ralph and Captain Gresley pondered long and hard over whose work these paintings and sculptures might be, and to what religion they belonged. 'We must form theories,' declared the former to his companion. 'We cannot remain awake and not do so.' Gresley was of the opinion that whoever had dug out the caves at Elephanta and Kanheri was also responsible for the work here at Ajanta – 'Some nation of conquerors who landed at Elephanta, coming from Egypt. First began there, and then got 2 or 300 miles to the eastward.' Wherever these conquerors had come from, both men were sure they were Buddhists. However, on their last day on the site they were joined by Dr James Bird, surgeon at the British Residency in Sattara, together with his Brahmin pandit, who both declared that this was the work of Jains. Ignoring the protests of Ralph and Gresley, Bird took a crowbar to a well-preserved mural portraying the signs of the zodiac and prised off four painted figures.

At the instigation of Dr Wilson's successor as Secretary of the Asiatic Society, Mr Ralph's expressive stream-of-consciousness report eventually appeared in the pages of the *Journal of the Asiatic Society of Bengal*. This was in 1837, seven years after Lieutenant James Alexander's account had been published in London, in the first volume of the *Transactions of the Royal Asiatic Society*.

It is tempting to interpret the founding of this latter body – the Royal Asiatic Society (RAS) – in England in 1823 as a rebuke to the intellectual inertia of the Orientalist movement in India as represented by the Asiatic Society during Dr Wilson's tenure of office as Secretary, but in fact it was a the natural outcome of the process initiated by Sir William Jones in India, since the RAS was formed by a group of retired Company men – Henry Colebrooke, Sir John Malcolm, Sir Alexander Johnston and others – who had all in their younger days in the East been admirers of Jones. The civil servant and Sanskrit scholar Henry Colebrooke had played a leading role in the affairs of the Asiatic Society for a decade until his retirement to England in 1814, and over the next few years others of a similar frame of mind had joined him in retirement, so that when he first mooted the idea of a learned body modelled on the Asiatic Society and with virtually the same aims, it was widely welcomed. More than a dozen highly respected Orientalists attended the first discussions, among them the newly knighted Sir Charles Wilkins, the pioneer Sanskritist.

At the inaugural meeting of the RAS, held in March 1823 at the Thatched House Tavern in St James's Street, Colebrooke delivered a speech about the aims of the Society which was very much in the style of Sir William Jones's original Calcutta discourse, declaring that 'nothing which has much engaged the thoughts of man is foreign to our enquiry . . . We do not exclude from our research the political transactions of Asiatic states, nor the lucubrations of

Asiatic philosophers . . . Nor is the ascertainment of any fact to be considered destitute to us.'

By the end of the year the RAS had enlisted no fewer than 343 members, and by the end of its second year it had found premises in Grafton Street in which to hold its monthly meetings as well as house all the books, manuscripts, maps, drawings, works of art and other items donated by members and well-wishers. It had been envisaged from the start that the transactions of the RAS should be published in much the same form as the Asiatic Society's *Asiatick Researches*, but on a more regular basis. In the event it was not until 1829 that the first volume of *Transactions of the Royal Asiatic Society* appeared, to be soon afterwards renamed the *Journal of the Royal Asiatic Society* (*JRAS*).

Among the many donations made to the RAS in this early period was a collection of manuscripts acquired by its Vice-President, Sir Alexander Johnston, during his seven-year term of office as Ceylon's Chief Justice and President of Council. A keen moderniser, Johnston had played the leading role in pushing through a number of reforms that included the introduction of the jury system, the emancipation of slaves, and the setting-up of universal popular education on the island – policies that undermined the authority of the Sinhalese nobility and undoubtedly contributed to the revolt of 1817. In a letter accompanying the donation of a collection of manuscripts, drawings and watercolours to the RAS, Johnston explained that these had been presented to him by a group of 'Buddhist Jurymen' whom he had been questioning on 'the state of Buddhism, Astrology, and the worship of Demons'. That same interest had led to his acquisition of a number of manuscripts written in Sinhalese which set out 'the most important points of Buddhist literature, sacred and historical'. The most prized of these was a text that was said to be a version of the *Mahavamsa*, Ceylon's Great Chronicle, the most revered and, reputedly, the oldest of the historical records of the island. This had been translated for Sir Alexander into Sinhalese from the original Pali by a 'well-known intelligent native' named Raja-pakse.

In 1824 the EICo went to war against the Kingdom of Ava. It had no option but to do so since the King of Ava, known to his subjects as 'the golden presence, fortunate king of the white elephants, lord of the seas and earth', had taken it into his head that he could secure Bengal for himself and had invaded Sylhet, only 225 miles from Calcutta. The war was a disaster for both parties. It cost the Company in excess of thirteen million pounds sterling and the lives of fifteen thousand soldiers of the Bengal Army, amounting to three-eighths of the invading force, most of them from malaria and typhoid. The Kingdom of Ava was forced to pay a one-million-pound indemnity, to give up its claims on Assam, Manipur, Cachar and Jaintia, and to cede to the EICo in perpetuity the coastal territories of Arakan and Tenasserim.

In Britain the Burma War was seen as a great novelty and aroused much public interest. Coloured prints of British troops marching through lush green landscapes dotted with golden pagodas, or strolling beside the vast edifice known as the Shwe Dagon or Golden Pagoda – which served as a military outwork during part of the campaign – caught the public imagination (see Plate 13). Captain Frederick Marryat, who had been in charge of naval operations at the taking of Rangoon (and later wrote a series of much-loved adventure stories for boys), returned with a magnificent souvenir in the form of a statue of Buddha, which was placed in the vestibule of the British Museum 'as a trophy of British valour'. People wanted to know more about the country and about its picturesque religion – and that demand was met by a retired West Country bookseller named Edward Upham, a Fellow of the Society of Antiquaries and a member of the RAS. Upham knew absolutely nothing about Buddhism – but he knew a man who did, for he had met Sir Alexander Johnston at the RAS and was aware of the collection of Sinhalese manuscripts he had lodged there.

These gentlemen now combined forces to produce two books. The first, a three-volume work entitled *The Sacred and Historical Books of Ceylon*, purported to be 'the most genuine account which is extant of the origin of the Budhu religion, of its doctrines, of its introduction into Ceylon, and of the effects, moral and political, which these doctrines had from time to time produced upon the conduct of the native government and upon the manners and usages of the native inhabitants of the country.' The second was a popular account of Buddhism – *The History and Doctrine of*

Budhism, popularly illustrated: with notice of Kappooism, or demon worship, and of the Bali, or planetary incantations of Ceylon – published by Mr Upham in London, Bath, Exeter and Paris.

Both books drew on the same source material, an English translation of three of Ceylon's most valuable religious texts: the *Mahavamsa*, the *Rajavali* and the *Rajaratancari*. These were Pali texts said to have been 'carefully revised and corrected by two of the ablest priests of Buddha on that island' and then translated into Sinhalese by Sir Alexander Johnston's official translators 'under the superintendence of the late native chief of the cinnamon department, who was himself the best native Pali and Singhalese scholar in the country'. These Sinhalese translations had then been translated into English by Mr Upham with the help of his friend, the Reverend Mr Fox, 'who resided in Ceylon for many years as a Wesleyan minister'.

It all seemed perfectly proper. Mr Upham claimed to have drawn on the writings of M. de Joinville, Dr Buchanan, Dr Leyden and others, but his main source, he declared, was Sir Alexander Johnston's copy of the *Mahavamsa*. In the light of what was contained therein, Mr Upham could announce that 'we have now a map before us of that vast portion of that human race, who derive their opinions and faith from Budhist doctrine'. Buddhism, he declared, had now been 'traced back to a very early period in Hindustan, where, for a very long time, it exercised supreme control. After ages of sanguinary wars, it was finally expelled and rooted out of India; and its vanquished followers fled in all directions from their relentless persecutors, the Hindu Brahminists.' As for the founder of Buddhism, Upham could now state unequivocally that 'the Gaudma Buddha was an Indian, and moreover, an historical personage . . . The legends are precise on this point: they all rest upon Indian machinery, and all converge on one centre, the Buddhist sovereignty of Magadha . . . It is manifest that a powerful Buddhist monarchy was established on the banks of the Ganges.'

So far, so good – but then Mr Upham went on to proclaim with equal authority that the 'theatre of Gaudma's actions and existence' and the 'chosen scene of the Buddha's preachings and miracles' was not India at all, but Ceylon. In fact, Ceylon was nothing less than the fountain-head of Buddhism and the scene of a great Buddhist civilisation (see Plate 14).

Both books were well received in England – and why not, since they carried the imprimatur of a very senior member of the judiciary who was also a leading light of the RAS. Upon the recommendation of the Secretary of State for the Colonies, copies were sent to the Government of Ceylon. As soon as news of them reached George Turnour in Kandy he abandoned his own translation of the *Mahavamsa*, on which he had been working for the past two years.

Sir Alexander Johnston received the plaudits of his peers – quite literally so, on one occasion, when Lord Gray stood up in the House of Lords to declare that his friend had 'immortalised his name' with his work in Ceylon – while Mr Edward Upham went on to write, in quick succession, histories of Egypt, the Ottoman Empire, and China.

8

James Prinsep the
Scientific Enquirer

SOON AFTER his arrival in Calcutta in 1819 young James Prinsep had attended a couple of meetings of the Asiatic Society, from which he decided it had little to offer a modern-minded young man like himself. 'The meetings are always rendered sleepy', he had written to his father, 'by the presence of the marquess [the Governor-General, Lord Moira, created Marquess Hastings in 1817] and the Bishop [the Bishopric of Calcutta had been created in 1813] – the former a bar to conversation and the latter to argument. Manuscripts and surveys are the only objects presented . . . so there is no advantage in commencing a high subscription.' He saw himself as a scientist, a practical man with advanced ideas, and was dismayed to find how few of these had reached Bengal.

Despite a warm welcome from his brothers William and Henry Thoby, James's first letters home to his father were filled with misgivings. Through William he had met two outstanding native Bengalis, the wealthy merchant Dwarkanath Tagore (grandfather of the Nobel Prize-winner Rabindranath Tagore) and the celebrated reformer Ram Mohun Roy, a 'most eloquent Englishman and a most philosophical Hindoo'. But they were the exceptions to the general rule that Calcutta society divided along racial lines. He had expected to find the Indian population sharing in 'the perfect equality and freedom existing among the English', but found instead that equality was not 'so general as the constitution framed for them would have led me to suppose – I never expected to find the highest natives excluded from European society nor to see Indian servants beaten about like slaves'. To add to his disappointment, his own position as assistant to the Assay Master at the Calcutta Mint was anything but secure. When James arrived in Calcutta the Assay Master himself, Dr H. H. Wilson, was away up-country, having gone to Benares to reorganise the local EICo mint there, leaving the Calcutta Mint in the charge of the man James was supposed to be replacing, a Persian scholar named Dr Atkinson whose only qualification appeared to be his close friendship with Wilson. James Prinsep soon discovered that Dr Atkinson had been busy 'making strong exertions, thro some powerful men gone to England, to get confirmed in his appointment in this Mint, or else to be made Mint Master'. Dr Atkinson was after his job, in fact.

Determined to prove his worth, James spent every daylight hour at the mint, at the same time dreaming of setting up an EICo-sponsored science laboratory which might 'furnish many a useful discovery and many an advantage to the Company, in the examination of Salt, Opium, Nitre, and other natural productions of this Country'. He wrote home asking for scientific journals and pieces of scientific apparatus to be mailed out, and towards the end of his first year in Bengal derived intense satisfaction from giving his first public lecture on modern scientific advances, demonstrating 'for the first time, the combination of Steel, Gold and Platinum' in a 'set of the most showy experiments'. The lecture became the subject of a portrait by his brother William's friend George Chinnery, which shows James at twenty-one very much as William Prinsep describes him: cheerful, and now full of self-confidence (see Plate 9).

In September 1820 James was ordered to proceed to Benares to take over as Master of the mint there. He began the journey up-river a month later, hiring an additional *budgerow* or country-boat to carry all the scientific apparatus, books and papers he had by now acquired. Writing to his father from a mooring-point on the Ganges identified only as 'Sickly Gully', he described the new delights to the eye after the 'the miserable monotony' of Bengal:

Here are the Rajmahal Hills covered with woods descending completely into this magnificent river, with sometimes a

Mosque or Hindoo Temple overhanging the water-worn bank – masses of brick-work jutting above the water and offering unspeakable difficulties to my Dandies [boatmen] in tracking my Budgero thro' a current of about 8 knots. The climate is quite altered, too; sharp cold mornings and dryness of the air proclaimed by the curling of the backs of all my Calcutta-bound books, and the quick evaporation of the ink from my pen. We travel here just as comfortably as we live, with all servants and conveniences about us, and if it were not for the tediousness of the progress . . . nobody would refuse assent to its being more pleasant than Stage Coach conveyance.

Sailing up-river between Calcutta and Benares was a slow and laborious process – though the current was sluggish, it was a distance of almost seven hundred miles – and it was late November by the time James arrived at his destination. 'A real town, extensive and of stone' is how he described Benares to his father. 'The Ghats on the banks of the sacred Ganges are really superb. A few sketches will however do much more in the way of description than all I could say.' All the Prinsep brothers were accomplished artists. William was the acknowledged master (see Plates 8 and 12), but to judge from the lithographs published in *Views and Illustrations of Benares* and the few sketches that have survived, James was scarcely less talented. From an unpublished memoir written by William we learn that his younger brother 'soon made himself the most popular man in the North West, the centre of all science & fun'. The shy child 'slow of apprehension' had grown into an ebullient adult brimming with self-assurance. Ignoring the Orientalists in the Civil Station at Benares – dominated by Colonel Wilford and Dr Yeld, the Secretary of the Sanscrit College – James and a Monsieur Duvaucel formed their own little circle, a Literary Society that also went in for amateur theatricals. This became known as the 'Society for the Suppression of Vice', because it kept the young bachelors of the station too busy 'scene painting, carpentering and acting' in a miniature theatre James created by converting part of his bungalow to have time for more carnal pleasures. An unfinished drawing of a number of young European males lounging at ease beside a group of Indian musicians suggests that James and his circle enjoyed listening to Indian music – a taste that had by now become distinctly unsahibish and not quite pukka. Meanwhile, in his home laboratory James began to design and build a number of scientific instruments, including a pyrometer that could measure more accurately the heat of the furnaces at the mint, and a balance that was for many years considered the 'most exact and delicate then existing even in Europe, inasmuch as it showed the variation of 3/1000th part of a grain'. These and other scientific contributions secured his election as a Fellow of the Royal Society in 1828.

By following his father's old Indian custom of early rising, James was able to 'conclude all the arduous duties of my office before breakfast, so as to return from the Mint, a distance of three miles, long before the hot winds attain their maximum temperature – before any of my friends, these Civilians, think of entering their Kutcheries [government offices]. From 10 o'cl. the day is entirely my own.' Although these leisure hours were in large part spent in his laboratory, James was also able to devote himself to more ambitious projects. In December 1821 he wrote to his father that he was 'busy about rather a stupendous work of labour, just for my amusement this cold weather, making an accurate map of this Holy City, a work never yet undertaken . . . A copy <u>elegantly illustrated</u> is to go to the Government, who will thus spare me the trouble of copying it for the Magistrate and other authorities. Another will be in Nagree [Devanagari] for the benefit of Hindoos.'

In the event, his map of Benares took James Prinsep almost two years, for it was drawn to sufficiently large scale to show every single dwelling in the city. But it was only the start of a number of remarkable voluntary labours by which he left his mark – in the most literal sense – on Benares. His second significant project was the draining of a series of pools and swamps at the back of the city, a source of malarial agues and fevers, by means of a tunnel that ran under part of the city into the river. According to his brother William, its success made him very much the local hero: 'After draining the swamp which used to decimate with death the back part of the city by means of his famous tunnel, the native community presented him with the ground which was of great value from its proximity to the city, he levelled it, and caused a large Bazar to be erected upon it, and presented it again to the town, an act of almost chivalric generosity seeing that he was then "poor" himself.'

We learn from William that James's prospects were still under serious threat: 'I find from my correspondence that at this time . . . I was warning him against Wilson who, having him appointed Mint Master [in Benares], had chosen his friend Dr Atkinson as his Assay Master [in Calcutta] meaning when he visited England to get him confirmed and so have James out altogether.'

James's next challenge was the dismantling, stone by stone, of one of the city's landmarks – the mosque of Aurangzeb, which had begun to slip into the river. Having strengthened the foundations and added a series of abutments, he then rebuilt the mosque (see Plate 10). Once that was completed he took some local leave in order to visit his brothers in Calcutta. There were now two more Prinseps in the city: George, who joined William's mercantile firm, and Charles, who was a member of the Calcutta bar. Despite a cheerful family gathering at Christmas, James returned to Benares 'a sadder man than I had ever seen him'. Part of the reason, as William later recorded in his memoir, was that he had fallen in love:

He had been seriously smitten with regard for our sweet Lucy [the sister of Thoby Prinsep's new wife], but thinking that he observed a preference for his brother Tom, he at once withdrew, though with an aching heart. He had also been refused by the Court of Directors to be placed under a Civil Indenture, and he knew that Atkinson would succeed in putting him aside in the Calcutta Assay Office, so that, poor fellow, he had good cause for depression, but his ever busy mind soon gained its composure though his correspondence with me became very sad. Very soon after James's departure brother Tom proposed to Lucy but unsuccessfully, and he left us in miserable plight to bury himself in the unhealthy employment they had given him of cutting a canal through the Salt water lake east of Calcutta.

His hopes doubly dashed, James Prinsep threw his energies into the largest engineering project he had so far undertaken: the building, at the request of a wealthy Hindu merchant and philanthropist, of a stone bridge across the River Karamnasa, outside

Benares on the road to Calcutta. 'This bridge was a curious instance of the advantages of scientific knowledge over plain college instruction,' wrote his elder brother admiringly:

> The Govt Engineers had pronounced the work impossible from the nature of the soil and the force of the current during the rainy season. James merely asked for permission to build it with funds entirely supplied by a native Gumashta [the philanthropist] . . . A superstition existed that the waters of this river were so defiling to a good Hindoo than none could safely cross it except on the back of a Brahmin at one of the fords. Now as the great road for pilgrims lay across that river, an enormous income was reaped by the priests by that occupation; so no wonder that the work of erecting a bridge was pronounced impossible . . . However, the Governor-General decided as it was a private enterprise for a really good object, possession of the ground should be given to my brother who, without any other assistance than from native artisans, completed a good and substantial stone bridge of three arches, in one part having to drive in stone piles into quicksands one over another until he could make a solid foundation. What better monument to his memory could he have than the blessing of every Hindoo walking dry footed across this accursed stream.

In March 1828 it was officially announced that Dr Atkinson was to succeed Dr Wilson as Assay Master, finally putting paid to James's hopes of promotion – or so it seemed, until July of that same year when, as brother William put it, 'a circumstance occurred which changed our James's fate entirely'. Atkinson was found to have been falsifying his accounts, and the matter was judged serious enough to be brought before the new Governor-General, Lord William Cavendish Bentinck, who ordered Atkinson's immediate dismissal and return to England. At the same time it was decided that the Benares Mint could be dispensed with, since the new Government Mint being constructed on the Strand in Calcutta would be large enough to provide all the coinage the Bengal Presidency required. James was ordered to close down the Benares Mint and return to Calcutta.

Just as James Prinsep's ten-year tour in Benares was drawing to a close, financial disaster struck Calcutta, hitting virtually every member of the British community in Bengal and beyond. When the EICo's Charter had come up for renewal by Parliament in 1813 only one of its monopolies had been retained: the China tea trade. John Company had long ceased to be anything but a loss-making headache to its shareholders – and indeed to Parliament, which was constantly having to bail it out. It had been grudgingly allowed to plot its own course, in part because Britain could not afford to allow France a second chance to restore its fortunes in the East but equally because the EICo's bureaucracy and army had built up such momentum that there was no easy way to dismantle the system that would not invite catastrophe – a quandary neatly encapsulated in Robert Clive's famous dictum, 'To stop is danger-ous, to recede ruin'.

Freed from the old constraints by the terms of the charter renewal of 1813, private traders had flocked to Calcutta to make money wherever they could, leading to the rapid growth of what became known as agency houses – umbrella companies involved in every sort of mercantile enterprise that might generate business and profit. The agency houses also acted as unsecured savings banks for the British community in Bengal, whose members cheerfully deposited their savings in the expectation of doubling or trebling their money within a few years. Inevitably, as the agency houses overextended themselves, an initial boom in the early 1820s was followed by a bust.

The largest of the agency houses was Palmer & Co., of which William Prinsep was a senior partner. By Christmas 1828 it had become clear that, in common with the other major agency houses, Palmer & Co. could no longer meet the demands of its creditors. In February 1829 the heads of the six leading businesses in the city met 'to look into our budget and see what could be done to save us'. It was decided that William Prinsep should lead a delegation to the *shroffs* or money-lenders of Benares in an effort to buy more time. It was a wasted journey, but it gave him the opportunity to see and admire all his brother had done there over the preceding decade. 'I was truly proud of my wonderful brother,' he wrote, 'when I heard the native gentlemen of the city speak of him with almost adoration for all he had done and was doing for them, and to their great astonishment (for I dare say it was the only instance known to them of any European gentleman devoting his time and talents for their benefit) all for love! He took no reward, and made not a rupee of profit from any of the large sums they gave him to lay out upon the important works.' Before William returned to Calcutta he and James went out together to admire and sketch the city's sights, 'the only bar to my complete happiness being the too frequent reference to my gloomy fears for the future from which I could see no hope of escape'.

William Prinsep's memoir for the year 1830 begins: 'Oh what a year of sadness this is! – of loss – of death – of terrible trial.' The crash had come, amounting to a total loss of 130 million rupees affecting over eleven thousand creditors, British and Indian. Palmer & Co. suffered the greatest loss, leaving William a ruined man. The assets of all the partners were seized, including the grand house in the Strand that William and his barrister brother Charles and their respective families had shared: 'Everything in the way of books, furniture and pictures, carriages and horses were brought to sale by auction, and realised much more than all claims upon our estate. The balance went to the credit of the general estate. My wife's trinkets were valued and paid for by my dear brothers and presented to her. I was allowed to keep my watch and my sketch books with some drawing materials; but all my pet design books and some well chosen pictures passed into other hands and I never saw them again.' Not long after this day of reckoning Thomas Prinsep, the youngest of the brothers in India, fell from his horse while returning from his engineering work on the salt water lake canal outside Calcutta, and died without regaining consciousness.

Only the arrival of James Prinsep in Calcutta to take up the long-delayed post of Deputy Assay Master helped to lighten the gloom. 'His residence amongst us was to my wife and myself a solace of all others the most comforting,' wrote William. 'Kindhearted James . . . took good care that my children should not want . . . but the winding up of the affairs of Palmer & Co's was weary work. The balance sheet showed claims to the extent of 3 millions, of which nearly one half was for the estates and trusts that passed through our hands, the custom having been to make the members of these great firms the Executors and Trustees of all marriage settlements because of the handsome rate of interest given for capital so placed in our hands to trade with.'

Having finally secured his position, James Prinsep might have been expected to spend most of his working hours at the new Government Mint that now dominated the Strand Road, a magnificent temple to Mammon built in the style of the Parthenon, with rows of massive stone columns rising from a high platform to support a heavy portico (see Plate 11). He chose, however, to devote himself to completing the engineering project his recently-deceased brother Thomas had started: the digging of canals and the installation of a series of locks to form a waterway around Calcutta linking up with the network of rivers running through the Ganges delta. This was done with the full approval of Lord William Bentinck, and the arrangement clearly suited both Dr Wilson and his Deputy, between whom a certain *froideur* had developed as a result of the former's overzealous championing of his friend Dr Atkinson. Nevertheless, James was not a man to bear a grudge, and the breach had certainly been healed before the end of 1831 – when, with Wilson's encouragement, James Prinsep at last become a member of the Asiatic Society.

What seems to have brought him in was the opportunity to apply scientific method to the new discipline of numismatics. Over the previous two decades thousands of ancient coins had been sent in to the Asiatic Society from all over India, including a large collection assembled by Colonel James Tod, for many years Resident to the Rajput states in Western Rajasthan. Most of these coins were copper, but more recently a number of gold coins had come from a most unlikely source, a French mercenary soldier named General Jean-Baptiste Ventura who had once fought for Napoleon Bonaparte but was now in the service of the Sikh ruler of the Punjab, Ranjit Singh. In 1830 Ventura had found himself encamped with his troops south of the town of Rawalpindi (in what is now northern Pakistan). Nearby was a domed monument known locally as the Manikyala tope, said to have been built by the gods. It had been seen and reported on as early as 1808 by Mountstuart Elphinstone, the head of an EICo embassy to the

Kingdom of Kabul (now Afghanistan), who had found it to be 'a solid structure on a low artificial mound . . . built of large pieces of a hard stone . . . decidedly Grecian'.

Having nothing better to do at the time, General Ventura had set his sappers to work on the ruin. His first approach, from the side, produced nothing but brick and rubble, so he started again, sinking a shaft from the highest point of the tope. Three feet down, his men came across some coins. As the digging continued more were found, and then several chambers containing stone caskets and metal reliquaries filled with a few scraps of cloth, pieces of jewellery and yet more coins – both copper and gold (see below).

Relies found in the Tope of Manikyala.
Principal deposit

inscription on brass cylinder.

It was the coins that first caught James Prinsep's interest and drew him into Indian studies – not because of their metal content, but because of the lettering stamped on them. Both Dr Wilson and Colonel Tod had begun to classify their coins and had made some headway with the coins of the pre-Muslim eras stamped in

Devanagari, where it was possible to read the characters and match them to the names of rulers given in the dynastic charts drawn up by Jones and Wilford. James Prinsep had at this point no more than a shaky grasp of spoken Hindustani and understood not a word of Sanskrit, but the challenge of identifying and then classifying coins purely by the images and letters stamped on them appealed to his scientific bent. He very quickly discovered that he had a natural aptitude for absorbing, analysing, comparing and matching multiple inputs in the form of groups of symbols – the essential qualifications of the code-breaker – as well as an exceptional capacity for sustained concentration. The combination of these two gifts was what set him apart as a near-genius – but it was a lethal one.

As more coins came in from the Punjab, sent by others who had followed General Ventura's example and carried out their own excavations, the task became easier. A number of coins bore dual inscriptions, one in Greek and the other in a second lettering that was incomprehensible but had obvious links with the Greek text. Further discoveries in the far north produced magnificent silver coins that were entirely Greek both in iconography and lettering – the coinage of Alexander the Great's Macedonian successors. Among them was the stamp and profile of that Seleucus Nikator who had sent his ambassador Megasthenes across the Indus to fraternise with Emperor Chandragupta of Magadha at Pataliputra. These and other dynasties Prinsep painstakingly identified and matched, sometimes confirming and sometimes rewriting the genealogical charts of Jones and Wilford: the so-called Indo-Scythians (more properly, Kushans) who had ruled in the Punjab and Afghanistan in the first three centuries of the Christian era; the Guptas who had ruled over northern India in the fourth and fifth centuries; the Valabhis who had followed them in Gujarat; the Chauhans, Paramaras, Rathors and other ruling clans of central and northern India who came to call themselves the Rajputs; the Senas of Bengal; the Kadambas of North Kanara; the Rashtrakutas of the Deccan; and others.

By the time Dr H. H. Wilson left Calcutta in 1832 to take up the Boden Chair of Sanskrit at Oxford, James Prinsep was more than qualified to succeed him both as Assay Master at the Mint and as Secretary of the Asiatic Society, which he did in January 1833.

In the first role he immediately pushed for a number of long-overdue reforms, including the standardisation of weights and measures and the introduction of a uniform coinage based on a hundred-gramme copper rupee to be known as the Company Rupee. This last was introduced in 1835, when the copper rupee, cast from a die designed by James and bearing the British sovereign's head, displaced the old silver currency of Bengal. For his own comfort James installed outside his office an ingenious steam-driven device that not only powered a lathe and a series of *punkahs* or fans hanging from the ceiling but also operated some kind of musical organ – so that he could at the same time work, keep cool, and enjoy music.

Nor were his scientific researches neglected. From brother William's memoir we learn of the visit of a French balloonist named Monsieur Robertson, who arrived in Calcutta in 1835 – direct from the Tivoli Gardens in Paris – with a large silk balloon in his baggage but without the gas to fill it. James Prinsep came to the rescue, setting up his own gas-making apparatus on the open ground at Garden Reach and thus enabling the balloonist to ascend 'almost perpendicularly into the sky', to the delight of a vast crowd: 'The whole river was covered with one mass of boats, bringing out the entire population to see what to them was so wonderful, and the roar of thousands of "Wah Wahs" of delight was curious to hear.'

Unfortunately, M. Robertson ignored James's warning not to tug too hard at a delicate valve controlling the flow of gas and, as William recalled:

He had barely reached the height of a mile when it was observed that the balloon was collapsing. He had evidently broken the valve and the gas was escaping. By the greatest good luck the empty silk formed a kind of cup in the netting and saved the man's life, by acting as a kind of parachute and so breaking his fall as to allow him to escape with only a few severe bruises . . . Financially the whole thing was a terrible failure and my brother paid severely for his love of science, but the public saw it for nothing of course. No more gas was made and we never heard more of the balloon.

Soon after returning to Calcutta in 1830 James had taken over the editorship of a monthly periodical entitled *Gleanings of Science*, to which he had for some time been the chief contributor. Later, when he was offered the post of Secretary to the Asiatic Society, he proposed to the Committee that it should change its name to the Asiatic Society of Bengal, to avoid confusion with its London offspring the Royal Asiatic Society, and that its journal, *Asiatick Researches*, should be merged with *Gleanings* to become the *Journal of the Asiatic Society of Bengal* (*JASB*). *Researches* was a relic of the eighteenth century, a bulky and expensive quarto tome that appeared so irregularly and infrequently as to be almost useless as a medium for the propagation of the latest advances and discoveries. The smaller octavo-sized *Journal*, cheaper to produce, could be compiled and published monthly as a magazine and then bound annually – and he would himself edit it, at no cost to the Society. In the event, another three issues of *Asiatick Researches* were published, but its fate was sealed by the appearance in January 1832 of a bound volume of the first twelve monthly issues of the *JASB*. This double role – secretaryship of the Asiatic Society and editorship of the monthly journal – enabled James Prinsep to instil new life and vigour into Indian studies to a degree exceeding even that of the golden years of Sir William Jones.

Like Sir William, James Prinsep made it his first aim to expand the scope of the Society's studies by enlisting 'the industry and talents of all who cultivated scientific or literary pursuits connected with the East', which he achieved as much by force of personality as by hard work. The first volume of the *JASB* carried an appeal and a warning: the Asiatic Society of Bengal would only flourish 'if naturalists, chemists, antiquaries, philologers and men of science, in different parts of Asia, will commit their observations to writing, and send them to the Asiatic Society in Calcutta'. If such communications were 'long intermitted', the Society would languish; if they ceased, it would die.

Among the many who now responded to this call was a lieutenant of Engineers named Alexander Cunningham. Writing about his hero many years later, Major-General Sir Alexander Cunningham had no doubts as to what had first drawn him to

James Prinsep: it was his 'ardent enthusiasm, which charmed and melted all who came into contact with him. Even at this distance of time (1871), when a whole generation has passed away, I feel that his letters still possess the same power of winning my warmest sympathy in all his discoveries, and that his joyous and generous disposition still communicates the same contagious enthusiasm and the same strong desire to assist in further achievements.'

That 'ardent enthusiasm' is perfectly illustrated in the following extracts from three of Prinsep's letters to that young lieutenant, written between 11 and 12 May 1837: 'Here are two plates addressed to me,' reads part of the first. 'Quarto engravings of 28 Saurashtra coins, all Chaitya reverses, and very legible inscriptions which are done in large on the next plate. Oh! But we must decipher them! I'll warrant they have not touched them at home yet. Here, to amuse you: try your hand at this.' But by 7 a.m. the next day the inscriptions had already been deciphered and Prinsep was writing a follow-up: 'You may save yourself any further trouble. I have made them all out this very moment on first inspection . . . Every one of them gives the name of his father of blessed memory, and we have a train of some eight or ten names to rival the Guptas!! Hurra! I hope the chaps at home won't seize the prize. No fear of Wilson, at any rate! I must make out a plate of the names in ours added to Steuart's, and give it immediate insertion . . . Bravo, we shall unravel it yet.' A third missive followed hard on the heels of the first two, with yet more new readings, ending with the Hindi exhortation '*Chulao bhai, juldee puhonchoge*' – a phrase familiar to every Anglo-Indian who ever travelled in a *palki* or palanquin because it was the cry uttered by the palki-bearers to encourage each other on the road: 'Go on, brother, we shall soon get there.'

Since Sir William Jones's time, the advances in Indian studies he and his British contemporaries had made had been all but thrown away, and the French were again showing the way. In 1814 the Collège de France in Paris set up the first European chairs in Chinese and Sanskrit. The first holder of the Chinese chair was Jean Pierre Abel Rémusat, who in 1822 founded the Société Asiatique de Paris, with himself as Secretary. The chair in Sanskrit was first held by Léonard de Chézy – among whose students were Auguste Wilhelm Schlegel (brother of Friedrich), who later held the first chair in Sanskrit in Bonn, and the brilliant phililogist Eugène Burnouf. In 1818 these three savants were joined in Paris by the German traveller and sinologist Heinrich Julius von Klaproth, who made no secret of his disdain for the British Orientalists in India and treated their work with 'ineffable contempt'. In 1833 Burnouf succeeded de Chezy as Professor of Sanskrit at the Collège de France, declaring at his inaugural lecture that 'we must not close our eyes to the most brilliant light that may ever have come from the Orient . . . It is more than India, gentlemen, it is a page from the origins of the world, of the primitive history of the human spirit, that we shall try to discover together.' It was at this juncture and against this background of fierce academic rivalry that the talents of Turnour, Hodgson, Csoma de Koros and Prinsep were now brought together, with the last now perfectly placed to provide the driving force.

No one welcomed Prinsep's appointment as Secretary of the Asiatic Society with more pleasure than Brian Hodgson in Kathmandu, who soon became a most valued correspondent. In 1833 and 1836 James Prinsep brought out special issues of *Asiatick Researches* concentrating on Indian geography, geology, zoology and anthropology, with a number of contributions from Hodgson on these subjects. Hodgson was also continuing with his Buddhist studies, drawing on the Nepalese texts that his 'old Bauddha' from Patan had obtained for him and on the papers on Tibetan Buddhism that Csoma de Koros sent him. Out of those came his findings that both forms of Buddhism had been greatly influenced by the teachings of *tantra*, the employment of esoteric texts as meditation rituals, probably introduced from eastern India, where the Hindu *shakti* cult involving religious empowerment through ritual sexual intercourse had its origins. This was a far cry from the Buddhism that Buchanan, de Joinville, Knox and others had written about, leading Hodgson to make a deduction of considerable importance regarding its early evolution: that there were two very different forms of Buddhism – a basic form to be found in Ceylon, Ava and south-east Asia; and a more esoteric and evolved form practised in the Himalayas and beyond:

It is clear that the Baudda religion, as cultivated in Nepal, is far from being so simple and philosophical a matter as has sometimes been imagined. The objects of worship are far from being limited to a few persons of mortal origin, elevated by superior sanctity to divine honours, but embrace a variety of domifications and degrees more numerous and complicated, than even the ample Pantheon of the Brahmans . . . There can be no doubt, that they are recognised by the Bauddhas of Tibet and Chinese Tartary, and some of them are traceable in China. It is very doubtful, however, if they form part of the theocracy of Ceylon, Ava and Siam. In the first of these we find inferior divinities, some of them females, worshipped, but they do not, as far as any description enables us to judge, offer any analogy to the similar beings reverenced in Nepal. In Ava and Siam, nothing of the kind occurs, although in the existence of *nats* [pre-Buddhist spirits incorporated into Burmese Buddhism], it is admitted, that other animated creatures than man and animals exist.

Here is a first cautious delineation of the historic division of the Buddhist world between the followers of *Theravada* or the Doctrine of the Elders (sometimes referred to as *Hinayana*, the Lesser Vehicle), based on the Pali Canon preserved in Ceylon, and *Mahayana* or the Great Vehicle, the umbrella that covers all the other sects and schools of Buddhism.

It was now also apparent to Hodgson that Buddhism had emerged out of Brahminical early Hinduism, rather than the other way round – and that its origins were entirely Indian:

The Buddhists themselves have no doubts upon either point. They unhesitatingly concede the palm of superior antiquity to their rivals and persecutors the Brahmans; nor do they in any part of the world hesitate in pointing to India as the cradle of their faith. Formerly we might be pardoned for building fine-spun theories of exotic origin upon the African locks of Buddha's images: but surely it is now somewhat too late, in the face of the abundant direct evidence which we possess against the exotic theory, to go in quest of presumptions to the time-out-of-mind illiterate Scythians, in order to give them the glory of originating a system built upon the most subtle philosophy, and all the copious original records of which are enshrined in Sanskrit – a language which, whencesoever primevally derived, had been, when Buddhism appeared, for ages proper to the Indian continent. The Buddhists make no serious pretensions to a very high antiquity; they never hint at an extra Indian origin . . . The Chinese, the Tibetans, the Indo-Chinese, the Ceylonese, and other Indian islanders, all point to India as the father-land of the creed . . . That Buddhism was, in very truth, a reform or heresy, and not an original system, can be proved by the most abundant testimony of friends and enemies. The oldest *Saugata* works incessantly allude to the existing superstitions as the *Mara-charya*, or way of the serpent, contradistinguishing their reformation thereof as the *Bodhi-charya*, or way of the wise; and the Brahmanical impugners of those works invariably speak of Buddhism as a notorious heresy.

9

Triumph and Disaster

JAMES PRINSEP's shake-up of the Asiatic Society of Bengal soon began to pay handsome dividends. A revived interest in the sub-continent's hidden past spread throughout the scattered British community as correspondents from every corner of the land were encouraged to add their tuppence-halfpennyworth of local knowledge. A Lieutenant Alexander Burnes of the Bombay Native Infantry, soon to be lionised in England as 'Bokhara' Burnes, sent in a report from Bamian in western Afghanistan of two 'colossal idols', one male and one female, carved out of a rock face, said to have been made 'at about the Christian era by a tribe of *kaffirs* [infidels]' (see illustration overleaf); from the same country Dr James Gerard reported seeing hundreds of topes spread across the plains outside Jelalabad and Kabul; while a third traveller, calling himself Charles Masson and claiming to be an American but actually a deserter from the British Army, wrote to say that he had in three years accumulated more than six thousand copper coins, 'besides silver ones, many rings, signets and other relics', from one small area of Afghanistan alone. Meanwhile, in India itself, a string of revelations emerged in response to Prinsep's appeal for more information on Bhilsa (Sanchi), Ajanta, Bodh-Gaya and other sites that had been noted but not fully reported on.

One such response came from Captain George Burney of the 33rd Bengal Native Infantry and concerned an inscribed black marble slab he had found set against the wall of the Hindu

Mahant's convent at Bodh-Gaya. He had been escorting a party of foreign visitors to this and other sites in Bihar – Burmese envoys from the King of Ava, sent on a mission to India to find what they declared to be the holy places of Buddhism. It was they who had first spotted the marble slab, and it caused great excitement because they recognised the writing on the slab as an early Burmese version of Pali. According to the present mahant occupying the site the stone had been removed for safe-keeping from its original location on the orders of the resident mahant at the time when the site was being excavated for bricks. Captain George Burney's brother was the British Resident in Ava, and it was he who now provided a translation which showed the plaque to have been erected to commemorate repairs carried out on the main pagoda by two Burmese missions in the mid-thirteenth century. The inscription further stated that the original shrine had been erected by a great king named Theeri Dharma Thauka or Excellent Keeper of the Law, grandson of King Tsanda-goutta. This King Theeri Dharma Thauka had reigned for forty-three years between the Burmese years 214 and 255, or 330 to 289 BCE, and was a figure of great consequence, reported Colonel Henry Burney:

> According to the Burmese history, *Tsanda-goutta* reigned for 24 years between the Burmese sacred year 162 and 186, or BC 382 and 358. He is also described as having been of the race of *Mauriya* . . . The son of this king, who was called *Bheindoo-*

Thara . . . reigned for 28 years and was succeeded by his son *Theeri Dharma Thauka*, who is also named *Athauka*, in the sacred year 214 or BC 330. The Burmese always use a soft *th* for *s*, and hence *Athauka* is evidently the same as *Asoca-Verdhana* and *Asoca* in Sir W[illia]m Jones's and Colonel Wilford's lists of the kings of Magadha. This prince appears to have restored or established more extensively the religion of Gaudama, and hence the Brahmins of India have probably destroyed all accounts of his government; but the Burmese possess copious details, and the latter half of the second volume of the *Myamma Maha Yazawen-dau-gyee*, or large Burmese royal history of kings, is filled with accounts of this king's reign. He is described as a Mauriya king of Magadha, as the grandson of *Tsanda-goutta*, and as having held his capital at Pataliput, which the Burmese consider with Major Rennell to have stood on the site of the present town of Patna.

Everything fitted. Tsanda-goutta was the Mauryan emperor Chandragupta about whom ambassador Megasthenes had written and whose subsequent dynasty had been tentatively sketched in by Jones and Wilford. His grandson was Asoca, Asoka or Ashoka, also known as Dharma-Ashoka or Asoka of the Law. In his translation of the Hindu history of Kashmir, *Raja Tarangani*, Dr H. H. Wilson had identified this Ashoka (as he is now known) as an important figure in north Indian history who had expelled barbarian invaders, but had added a footnote he later had cause to regret. 'The faith of Asoka is of very little moment, as the prince himself is possibly an ideal personage,' Wilson had written. 'The passages in the original show that Asoka was a worshipper of Siva. It is not improbable however that he permitted heretical, possibly Bauddha doctrines, to be introduced into the kingdom during his reign.' But if the Buddhist texts were to be believed, Ashoka was much more than a king who had permitted the practice of Buddhism: he was a Buddhist himself, and an extremely influential one, for according to the Buddhist royal chronicle, 'Four years after his accession Asoka resolved to erect 84,000 monuments to the memory of Gaudama Buddha in different parts of his realm . . . His brother, son and daughter all assumed the priesthood and rejected the throne. The son, prince Maheinda, proceeded to Ceylon and established the Buddhist religion there.'

But even before this remarkable news from Ava could be published, James Prinsep received startling confirmation from another quarter that Ashoka Maurya was more than just another name in a list of kings. It came from George Turnour in Kandy, in the form of a note on work in progress which was soon afterwards published in the back pages of the *Ceylon Almanac* for 1833. For reasons that were not immediately apparent, Turnour had gone back to his abandoned translation of the *Mahavamsa*, Ceylon's Great Chronicle, and these were the first fruits of his efforts – what he termed 'An Epitome of Ceylonese History', a chronology of the kings of Ceylon that listed 165 kings from the first year of the Buddhist Era (begun on the day of Gautama Buddha's death), or 543 BCE, to the year of the accession of King Sree Wickrema Raajasingha in 1798. Also set down in the Great Chronicle were all the noteworthy events relating to the progress of Buddhism on the island, revealing that it had been introduced during the reign of the seventh king listed, Devenipeatissa, who came to the throne in 306 BCE and ruled for forty years. King Devenipeatissa had 'induced *Dharmaasooka*, sovereign of the many kingdoms into which *Dambadiva* [*Jambudwipa*] was divided, and whose capital was *Pattilipatta*, to depute his son *Mihindoo* and his daughter *Sanghamitta*, with several other principal priests, to *Anooraadhapoora*, for the purpose of introducing the religion of *Buddha*. They arrived in the year 237, the first of this reign, and the eighteenth of that of *Dharmaasooka*. They established Buddhism, propagating its doctrines orally.'

According to Turnour's account, Ashoka's son and daughter had devoted their lives to the organisation of Buddhist communities throughout Ceylon and had died there in the reign of King Uttiya in 267 BCE. In the eighteenth year of his reign, 289 BCE, King Devenipeatissa had asked King Ashoka for a cutting of the sacred pipal tree under which Gautama Buddha had achieved Buddhahood: 'The *bo*-tree was brought and planted at *Anooraadhapoora*, on the spot where the sacred trees of former Buddhas had stood.' In the same year Prince Mihindoo had also obtained corporeal relics of the Buddha himself: 'The right jaw-bone of *Buddha* was obtained from *Sackrayaa* himself, and a cup full of other relics from *Dharmaasooka*.' This had been followed by an impressive building programme on the island: 'The king built the *wihare* and *daagoba* called *Toohpaaraamaya*; in which the jaw relic was deposited; 68 rock temples with 32 priests' chambers on *Mihintallai*; the *Maha wihare*, the *Issaramooni wihare*, the *Saila chytyia* daagoba; and the *Tissa-raamaya daagoba* and *wihare*; and formed the *Tissa-wewa* tank. *Anoola*, the principal queen, and many inferior wives of the king, assumed priesthood.'

Turnour also provided a detailed account of the history of the island's famous Relic of the Tooth. For its first eight hundred years it was in Kalinga (modern Orissa), a trophy often fought over by rival rulers. Then the island's fifty-fourth ruler, King Maha Sen, sent a deputation to King Ghoohasew of Dantapura in Kalinga to collect the tooth, which arrived on the island in 301 CE. Ten centuries later it was captured by Malabars from the Indian mainland but swiftly recovered by King Prakrama Bahu III. During the troubled centuries that followed the Relic of the Tooth was frequently moved from one hidden location to another to keep it safe. In 1560 the Portuguese supposedly seized it from Jaffna – as recounted in an earlier chapter – but this was a copy and not the real tooth, which was kept hidden until it was considered safe to reveal the deception six years later.

This outline was followed in 1836 by Turnour's full translation of the first twenty chapters of the *Mahavamsa*, covering the first three centuries of Ceylon's history, from 587 BCE to 307 BCE. It was the result of more than ten years' work, and it came with more than a hundred pages of introduction in which he not only described the historical background of the text but also gave a full account of what he called 'one of the most extraordinary delusions, perhaps, ever practised on the literary world'.

This delusion was to be found in Mr Edward Upham's *Sacred and Historical Books of Ceylon* and *History of Budhism*, the two books that had halted Turnour in his tracks more than a decade earlier (see pages 136–9). George Turnour chose his words very carefully. He did not use the words 'fraud' or 'deception', but both were implicit in his detailed setting-out of the evidence suggesting that much of what Mr Upham had written was nonsense – and in his explanation of why he was now determined to do all in his power to 'prevent these *Sacred and Historical Books of Ceylon* and the *History of Budhism* (also published under that right honourable gentleman's auspices) being recognized to be works of authority'. George Turnour then proceeded to tear both books to pieces: 'It is scarcely possible for a person, not familiar with the subject, to conceive the extent of the absurdities involved . . . It is no burlesque to say that they would be received, by a Ceylonese buddhist, with feelings akin to those with which an Englishman would read a work, written by an Indian . . . which stated – that England was the scene of the birth of our Saviour; that his ascension took place from Derby peak; and that Salisbury cathedral stood on Westminster abbey.' What was even more damaging, from Turnour's point of view, was that Upham's two publications had received widespread support in official quarters and had been written in close consultation with Sir Alexander Johnston. Such circumstances must inevitably cast doubt on his own translation of the *Mahavamsa*: all he could do was set out the Romanised text of the Pali side by side with his translation, so that his work could be fairly judged by other oriental scholars.

It is impossible to miss the undercurrent of anger and sarcasm running through these introductory pages. Although Turnour was careful not to impugn the motives of Sir Alexander Johnston, it is clear that he regarded him as having been just as much at fault as Mr Upham. There had been a 'signal failure on the part of Sir A. Johnston' in allowing his translators to produce 'a compilation of their own' and 'a mutilated abridgement' in place of genuine translations. Perhaps these translators had 'totally misunderstood the late chief justice's object' – yet it was strange that 'Sir A.' should have thought his chief translator to have been 'the best Pali and Singhalese scholar in the country', because George Turnour had himself met the man in court when sitting as a magistrate and had found him to be quite unable 'to speak, much less write, the shortest connected sentence in English'. In fact, Turnour had been obliged 'to employ an interpreter not only to interpret his Singhalese answers in English to me, but to interpret my English questions in Singhalese to him, as he was totally incapable of following me . . . He must therefore (unless he has practised a most unpardonable deception on Sir A. Johnston) be at once released from all responsibility.'

There was of course more than a slight element of pique in all this. With his bogus translation, Upham had not only taken the shine off of Turnour's own work but had robbed him of the glory he felt should have come his way. George Turnour was well-connected – one of his grandfathers was the Earl of Middleton and the other a French duke – and he had powerful friends in Ceylon. Nevertheless, it took courage to point the finger at a man who was both a pillar of the judiciary and an important figure in the world of Asian studies. It could easily have ended his career. In the event, Sir Alexander Johnston chose to remain silent, and his translations from the Sinhalese are no longer listed in the catalogues of the RAS, which suggests that he quietly removed them and disposed of them. Even so, he remained active in the RAS, as chairman of its Corresponding Committee and then vice-president, until his death in 1849.

Turnour's *History of Ceylon* – his translation of the *Mahavamsa* – remains a milestone as much in Buddhist studies as in the study of Ceylon's early history. First compiled several centuries before the Venerable Bede's *Historia Ecclesiastica Gentis Anglorum* and the *Anglo-Saxon Chronicles*, it remains the most powerful riposte to Mill, Macaulay, Trevelyan and others who have sneered at South Asia's lack of early historical records. It showed that Pali was central to Buddhism as the language in which the earliest Buddhist texts had been set down – if not as the form of Sanskrit spoken in Maghada at the time of Gautama Buddha. It provided a mass of corroborative information on the chronology of the kingdoms of the Indian mainland. It shone a lot more light on the life of Gautama Buddha in Maghada, the subject of the *Mahavamsa's* first chapter; on the early development of the Buddhist *sangha* after the Buddha's death; and on the subsequent spread of the Buddhist faith both on the mainland and in Ceylon, in the process devoting considerable space to the actions of the 'illustrious and powerful monarch Asoka' and his immediate family.

King Ashoka had come to the throne in the traditional manner – by killing all his brothers in a war of succession – and had then embarked on the equally traditional policy of extending his kingdom by making war on his neighbours. Eight years after his coronation he had attacked and conquered Kalinga, and the slaughter he had there effected had wrought a complete change in his personality and thinking. It may be that he was nominally a Buddhist before Kalinga; afterwards, he underwent a true conversion and, as Dharma Ashoka, Protector of the Law, spent the rest of his life seeking to apply Buddhist principles to the government of his Indian empire. He went on pilgrimage to Gautama Buddha's birthplace, to the scenes of his enlightenment and his first teaching – and to the site of his *mahaparinirvana*, or 'great ultimate extinguishing', where he caused the several stupas containing Gautama Buddha's ashes and bones to be opened and the relics recovered, to be afterwards reburied within no fewer than 84,000 stupas distributed throughout his realms. His piety, together with that of his son and daughter, helped the Buddhist faith to spread not only to Ceylon but to other countries to the north and west.

Whatever Sir Alexander Johnston and his fellow grandees in London may have thought of Turnour's efforts, others had no doubts about their value. 'Had your Buddhist chronicles been accessible to Sir W. Jones and Wilford,' wrote James Prinsep enthusiastically, 'they would have been greedily seized to correct anomalies at every step.' They would now enable him and others 'to clear away the chief of difficulties in Indian genealogies, which seem to have been intentionally falsified by the Brahmans and thrown back into remote antiquity, in order to confound their Buddhist rivals'.

Enormously exciting as these and other advances were to the Orientalists in India and to those in Europe who shared their ideals, they took place against a background of political change that was to have far-reaching consequences – as much for Indo-British relations as for Indian studies. In 1819 the political philosopher James Mill, author of the *History of British India*, had acquired a position of major influence at India House – initially as the EICo's Assistant Examiner of Correspondence. Over the years his influence widened as his anti-all-things-Indian philosophy gained adherents. The College founded in 1800 at Fort William by Lord Wellesley as an 'Oxford of the East', where young civilians could study under Indian pandits and munshis, was soon eclipsed by the growth of the EICo's East India College at home in Haileybury, where the students were instructed by English scholars from Cambridge. A later Governor-General, Lord Hastings, had presided over the founding of the Hindu College (1816), the Calcutta Book Society (1817) and the Calcutta School Society (1818), all of which had the laudable aim of educating young Indians in their own and in English culture. But within a space of fifteen years the curriculum of these and such institutions as the Scottish Church College and other missionary-led bodies had grown increasingly sectarian, promoting English ideas to the detriment of Indian studies. Under the combined pressure of utilitarians, churchmen, rationalist philosophers and jurists – very few of whom ever set foot in India – the EICo and its Governors-General were finally moved to introduce a series of reforms intended to end, in Mill's words, 'the vice, the ignorance, the oppression, the despotism, the barbarous and cruel customs that have been the growth of ages under every description of Asiatic misrule'. Their zealotry found expression in the person of Lord William Bentinck and his seven-year administration as Governor-General of British India between 1828 and 1835.

Before he left for India Lord William was heard to remark to James Mill, 'It is you that will be Governor-General', the clear implication being that he would be governed by Mill's political thinking. Bentinck's plan to demolish the Taj Mahal and sell off its marble may well have been no more than a canard put about by his enemies, but many of his more ambitious schemes went ahead – all based on the belief that India could only awake from the slumber of centuries if it were remodelled on English lines. The rallying-call for these 'Anglicist' reforms was Macaulay's devastating polemic known somewhat misleadingly as his 'Minute on Education', put before Lord Bentinck in Calcutta in February 1835. Macaulay's argument was that Indian civilisation was worthless. Sanskrit was 'barren of useful knowledge' and 'fruitful of monstrous superstitions'. Nothing was to be gained by the study of Indian history, full as it was of fantastical tales and 'abounding with kings 30 feet high, and reigns thirty thousand years long'. It was in India's best interests that it should abandon its own demonstrably useless culture and adopt another that was conspicuously successful. This would be best done by introducing a system of education based on the English language that would create 'a class of persons,

Indian in blood and colour, but English in taste, in opinions, in morals, and in intellect'.

The Governor-General's response was to appoint Macaulay President of the General Committee of Public Instruction and give him a free hand. 'His Lordship in Council', Macaulay announced in March 1835, 'is of opinion that the great object of the British Government ought to be the promotion of European literature and science among the natives of India and that all the funds appropriated for the purposes of education would be best employed on English education alone.'

Macaulay's ideas were bitterly contested in Calcutta, by both Indians and Britons – the latter in large part because of the speed and scale of the proposed reforms. The notorious 'Minute' was supposed to be confidential, but within days of its submission the contents were known throughout Calcutta, provoking a public outcry: 'In the course of two days a petition respectful in language but strong in the points to which it averted was signed by upwards of 8,000 educated Mahommedans and a similar petition in regard to the Sanscrit College [that is, the Hindu College] was under preparation by the Hindus.' This quotation comes from an unpublished memoir written by the son of Henry Thoby Prinsep. Entitled 'Three Generations', the memoir more than hints that it was the author's father who leaked the confidential paper and organised the opposition. James's elder brother Henry Thoby had become Chief Secretary to the Government in 1834, the same year in which Macaulay arrived in Calcutta to take up the post of Legal Member of the Governor-General's Council. He now became Macaulay's fiercest opponent and refuted point by point the arguments set out in the 'Minute', which provoked Macaulay to respond with his own counter-criticisms. According to a contemporary, the two men 'butted at each other like bulls, blind to everything but their own joust of brains, and the contest was not advantageous to either'. Since Lord William sided with Macaulay, Prinsep's position soon became untenable, and the Governor-General declared to his Chief Secretary that it was 'impossible under such circumstances that our acting together can any longer continue'. A diplomatic sick-note was procured and Henry Thoby was sent on a long sea voyage to recover his political health.

Other Orientalists also spoke out, though to little avail. From Kathmandu Brian Hodgson wrote a series of letters to the Calcutta newspaper *The Friend of India*, published under the title 'Preeminence of the Vernaculars or The Anglicans Answered', warning that if 'Macaulayism' triumphed it would 'help to widen the existing lamentable gulf that divides us from the mass of people'. He himself argued for an inclusive middle way that would allow the regeneration of India to take place through the introduction of English learning – but not at the expense of the vernacular languages and Indian culture: 'Let then the foundation be broad and solid enough to support the vast superstructure. Let us begin in the right way, or fifty years hence we may have to retrace our steps, and commence anew! Sound knowledge generally diffused is the greatest of all blessings; but the soundness of knowledge has ever depended and ever will on its free, and equal, and large communication.'

Despite this opposition, the Macaulayites won the day. A year later Macaulay was able to write to his father in triumph, telling him that 'our English schools are flourishing wonderfully . . . It is my firm belief that, if our plans of education are followed up, there will not be a single idolater among the respectable classes in Bengal thirty years hence.'

Throughout the dispute James Prinsep had sided with his brother, but he was a comparatively lowly figure in the political hierarchy of Bengal and, as past events had shown, his position as Assay Master of the Government Mint was far from secure. But he was Editor of the *Journal of the Asiatic Society of Bengal* and it was in its pages that his disgust at the turn of events found expression. In the Preface to the journal's fourth volume, published at the end of 1835, he condemned 'a measure which has in the face of all India withdrawn the countenance of Government from the learned natives of the country, and pronounced a verdict of condemnation and abandonment on its literature'. Now an 'epoch of interdiction' had begun, and he wondered what the outside world must make of it:

The unbiassed spectator beholds, at one period, the Government accusing itself of doing nothing for Indian learning and making amends by establishing colleges and patronizing

publications and translations . . . Anon, it beholds it throwing up
all the works half translated or half printed; and withdrawing all
the scholarships and exhibitions, which had been instituted for
the encouragement and support of poor native students; annul-
ling most of the appointments which heretofore were held out
as temptations to the study of the classical languages by
Europeans – and leaving the completion of the *Mahabharat* to
the charity of private subscription; along with the statistical
information collected by Buchanan; the geographical and geo-
logical by Moorcroft, Voysey and Herbert.

The work of the Asiatic Society of Bengal was now more
important than ever, for 'while the Asiatic Society supplies,
however feebly, the patronage lost elsewhere, India need not be
wholly dependent upon France and Germany for its editions of
the Sanskrit classics, and for the development of the ancient
history and philology of the nations under British rule.'

Yet these were not bad times for all the Prinsep brothers. In June
1835 William, the artist and businessman, was formally discharged
from the bankruptcy court and allowed once more to trade under
his own name. After the crash of 1830 he had teamed up with a
Bengali and a Jew to sell indigo and raw silk by auction, and their
business had prospered to the extent that he had been able to pay
off the bulk of his debts. Two old friends, William Carr and
Dwarkanath Tagore, now made him a full partner in their firm
Carr, Tagore & Co., which quickly became the most successful
trading house in Bengal. With his fortunes restored he was able to
buy one of the grandest old mansions in Garden Reach, commanding the best views up and down the river. His brother James,
meanwhile, had found himself a wife in Harriet Aubert, who
'made his new house at the Mint a happy home'. In May of the
following year a boy was born to Harriet, but died within three
days. Two years later a second child was born, a girl. A brief letter
home to James's mother dated 31 May 1838 records that the child
was accidentally named 'Eliza' rather than the intended 'Elizabeth'
by her godmother at the christening, adding: 'I was very anxious
to have her named <u>Nanaia</u> after a female beauty on some of my
ancient coins, but was overruled!'

Numismatics and the unravelling of the past had by now become James Prinsep's passion.

Though they seem never to have met, Prinsep and Brian Hodgson had become close friends through their correspondence, although the irregularity of communications between Calcutta and Kathmandu meant that their letters frequently crossed. In 1835–6 much of this exchange of ideas was taken up with the continuing mystery of that most curious writing in pseudo-Greek characters first noted on Feroz Shah's Lat outside Delhi, but now known to be replicated in at least four other sites. One of these Brian Hodgson had himself reported almost a decade earlier in a letter ignored by Dr Wilson. Now he wrote again, giving details of two standing polished stone columns, identical to Feroz Shah's Lat, to be found in north Bihar (see illustrations overleaf). The first, which carried the inscription, he had discovered at Mathiah (today, Lauriya Nandgarh), a few miles south of the main entry point into Nepal, an area of 'pestilential jungle where now the tiger, wild boar, and wild buffalo usurp the soil, and a deadly malaria infects the atmosphere for three-fourths of the year'. The second column carried no inscription, but bore a magnificent stone lion perched on the capital at the top. Found at the village of Basarh in the district of Tirhut, forty miles due north of Patna beside the banks of the River Gandaki, it was known locally as Bhim Sen's Lat.

At Prinsep's request this second site was visited by a Mr Stephenson, who reported to the Society that the lion on the pillar faced directly on to a domed brick tope. A Hindu fakir had taken up residence at this tope and was selling what appeared to be rather well-made clay images of Hindu deities. Mr Stephensen had purchased the best of these and, after washing off the dried clay, found that it had been modelled on the base of a stone sculpture:

This fragment of sculpture represents the lower part of a figure of Buddha, sitting cross-legged, according to the custom of the east, with the arms resting across the upper part of the thigh. On the soles of the feet (which are turned up), and on the palms of the left hand, is represented the lotus flower. The back of this fragment is beautifully sculptured, with two lions standing in an

The Radhia Pillar.
in zilla Sarun.

The Bakhra Pillar.
in Tirhut.

The Mound and Dehgope at Kesariah. in Tirhut.

erect position, upon two elephants. On each side of the base is cut a lion half couchant with a small female figure in the centre. The stone is the same as that of the pillar, viz. a red fine grained sandstone, very hard. On the lowest part of the fragment is an inscription in Sanscrit, which the Pandits of this part of the country cannot as yet decypher.

As so often in this story, coincidence now pushed matters on. As James Prinsep was examining a copy of this inscription with the Reverend William Hodge Mill, Principal of Bishop's College, Calcutta and Vice-President of the Asiatic Society, a copy of a second inscription was delivered to the premises of the Asiatic Society. This had come from Benares.

Prinsep's curiosity regarding the great tope at Sarnath had first been aroused while he was still living in Benares. A delegation of Jains made up of members of the two major sects in Jainism had come to him with a request to 'open the building at their expence [sic], that it might be ascertained to which party (Digambari or Swetambari) the enclosed image might belong. My departure from Benares alone prevented my satisfying their curiosity in 1830.' The subsequent success of General Ventura's excavations in the Punjab then persuaded Prinsep that the Sarnath tope should be opened in the same way, so he had written to Captain Thoresby, Secretary of the Sanscrit College in Benares, and to another young officer based there whom he knew to be an enthusiastic antiquarian and numismatist, Lieutenant Alexander Cunningham of the Royal Engineers, offering to bear the labour costs himself if they would organise the digging. As it happened, Cunningham had already started to excavate on his own initiative. Having first ensured that no religious group in the city would take offence, he had erected a ramp to give his labourers access to the dome of the tope and had then begun to sink a shaft down from the top. At a depth of ten and a half feet he had come across a small stone slab bearing a short inscription. This he had showed to the pandits of Benares but, failing to get a satisfactory response, had then sent a copy of it down to Prinsep in Calcutta:

The facsimile reached me, as I have before stated, while the Tirhut image [the inscribed base of the statue found by Mr Stephenson at the tope in Basarh] was under examination, and it immediately struck me from one or two prominent letters, as well as from the general appearance of the whole, that the two inscriptions were substantially the same, although the characters of the two differed as much from one another as the Nagari from the Bengali alphabet. Upon shewing them to Govind

Ram Shastri, Mr Wilson's intelligent Pandit, and comparing the letters with the Tibetan and Gya forms of the Sanscrit alphabet, the identity of the two was confirmed, and several words made out, among them the titles '*Tathagata*' and '*Maha Sramana*'.

Prinsep had by now taught himself enough Sanskrit to know that *mahasramana* meant 'great ascetic', but *tathagata* was still a puzzle, although it was known to be associated with Gautama Buddha (today this epithet is generally translated as 'One who walks in the right path' or 'One who follows the way of his predecessors'). With the help of the Reverend William Mill and a Ceylonese convert to Christianity named Ratna Paula, Prinsep was able to produce a Romanised text which showed that despite their different scripts the Sarnath and Bakhra inscriptions were identical, but for two synonymous words. The Romanised text read:

> *Ye dharma hetu prabhava hetun teshan tathagato hyavadat teshau cha yo nirodha evem vadi maha sramunas.*

Just weeks later Prinsep, thumbing through the early numbers of *Asiatick Researches* produced in Sir William Jones's time, realised he was looking at the same formula: 'Turning by accident to the copy of the inscription on an image of Buddha, found along with two urns in the excavations at Sarnath, made in the year 1798, and described by J. Duncan in the 2nd volume of the Asiatick Researches, I was much pleased to discover the identical sentence, *Ye dharma hetu prabhava*, etc.' Further reading through back numbers of *Asiatick Researches* showed that Dr Francis Buchanan had also noted the inscription at Bodh-Gaya, which he had characterised as 'the usual pious sentence of the Buddhists' (see Plate 5).

The news of the identification of a 'standard' Buddhist formula elicited an immediate response from Hodgson in Kathmandu. 'I hasten to tell you', he wrote, 'that your enigma requires no Oedipus for its solution in Kathmandu, where almost every man, woman and child, of the Bauddha faith can repeat the *confessio fidei* (for such it might be called), inscribed on the Sarnath stone . . . As I was looking over your Journal my Newari painter came into the room. I gave him the catch word, "*Ye Dharma*", and he immediately filled up the sentence, finishing with "*Tathagata*".' With the help of his old friend from Patan, Amrita Nanda Bandya, Hodgson came up with the following translation:

The cause of all sentient existence in the versatile world, the Tathagata hath explained.
The Great Sramana [Ascetic] hath likewise explained the cause or causes of the cessation of all such existence.

The meaning of this formula, Hodgson added, was that 'Bauddha hath revealed the causes of mundane existence, as well as the causes of its complete cessation, implying, by the latter, translation to the eternal acquiescence of Nirvritti, which is the grand object of all Bauddha vows . . . Nothing can be more complete, or more fundamental, than this doctrine.'

Prinsep now showed the Sanskrit declaration to his reclusive librarian, Alexander Csoma de Koros. At first the Hungarian failed to recognise it, but he agreed to look at his Tibetan texts, and within days reported that he had found 'the very sentence, agreeing word for word with the Sarnath version, in three volumes of the *Kahgyur* [*Kanjur* – the Tibetan Canon] collection'. A further search produced another fifteen examples. Csoma de Koros was further able to explain that the Dharma declaration was the preamble to the standard compendium of the precepts of Buddha, so familiar to Buddhists that it was not felt necessary to set down more than the first two sentences.

Thanks to Brian Hodgson's generosity a large number of Tibetan religious texts had by now become accessible to Western scholars, the first to make use of them being Csoma de Koros in Calcutta: the twentieth and last volume of *Asiatick Researches*, published in 1836, contained two important articles on Tibetan Buddhism by him. The first explained the significance of the *Kanjur*, which was nothing less than the complete Canon of Tibetan Buddhism, consisting of 108 volumes translated into Tibetan from the north Indian form of Sanskrit known as Prakrit. The second provided a great deal more information on the life and death of Gautama Buddha that both confirmed and added to that already obtained by Buchanan, Turnour and others.

Whether these sources were Tibetan, Nepalese, Burmese, Siamese or Sinhalese, it was now clear that they all had a common origin in Pali. Although there were minor variations, what they agreed on was that Gautama Buddha or Shakya Sinha, Lion of the Sakyas, had chosen to be incarnated in the house of Suddhodana, a warrior-king of the Shakya tribe residing at Kapilavastu, through his queen Maya Devi. He had been born not far from Kapilavastu at the garden or grove of Lumbini, 'whither she [the queen] had gone with great procession for her recreation', not from her womb in the usual way but 'of her right side, she being in a standing position, and holding fast the branch of a tree'. Named Siddhartha or 'Aim Attained', the prince had spent all his youth and early manhood in Kapilavastu; he married at sixteen, and his wife Yasodhara bore him a son who was named Rahula. Despite his father's best efforts to shelter him from the realities of life, Prince Siddhartha had witnessed the realities of disease, old age and death. Filled with alarm and disgust, he resolved to become an ascetic in order to seek freedom from rebirth and suffering.

At the age of twenty-nine Siddhartha left his home and family in secret – an act known as the Great Departure – to become an ascetic under the tutelage of a Brahmin sage at a place named Vaisali. When this failed to satisfy him he journeyed south to the city of Rajagriha, capital of the powerful kingdom of Maghada, where he was welcomed by its monarch, King Bimbisara. Here again he failed to find a guru with answers, and abandoned Rajagriha for the wooded hills of Uruvila, a day's journey to the south, where he applied himself more fully to asceticism and was joined by five companions. For six years he devoted himself to the most extreme mortification, without avail. Realising that these privations were weakening his faculties, he then went to the bank of the nearby Nairanjana river, washed himself and accepted food from a village maiden, whereupon his five companions deserted him and went to Benares. He recovered his strength, crossed the river, accepted a bundle of grass from a grass-cutter and sat upon it under the shade of a pipal tree, vowing not to leave the spot until he attained complete enlightenment. He meditated, overcame the hosts and temptations of the demon Mara, and in one night of full moon achieved *bodhi* and became a Buddha, or Awakened One. As

Gautama Buddha, he continued his meditations beside the Bo-tree or Tree of Awakening for seven weeks, 'perfecting himself for his great purpose', before proceeding to Benares as Tathagata, 'He who walks in the right path'.

In the deer park of Sarnath outside the city of Benares Gautama Buddha found his five former companions and expounded to them his doctrine, known as the First Turning of the Wheel of the Dharma, and soon afterwards preached the 'four excellent truths', usually called the Four Noble Truths. The five companions became his first disciples, and another sixty joined him as he made his way back to Rajagriha. The King of Magadha offered him a home, and the court physician gave him an orchard where he established his first *vihara* or monastic settlement.

Gautama Buddha spent the next forty-five years preaching the Dharma (in Pali, *Dhamma*), the Law of the Universe as discovered by him and taught by him, thus the Buddhist doctrine. He resided chiefly at Rajagriha and at Sravasti, where Prasenajit, King of Kosala, adopted Buddhism. Two other great kings also converted. His royal father sent many messengers inviting him to return to Kapilavastu, but only after the ninth did he agree to go home. King Suddhodana was then converted and the Shakya tribe adopted the faith, so that henceforward Gautama Buddha also became known as Sakyamuni, the Sage of the Sakyas. As the numbers of his followers grew, Sakyamuni established rules for the members of his community, the *Sangha*, made up of both monks and nuns and lay members. Growing weary in old age, Sakya at last left Rajagriha and began to journey north. In the country of the Mallas near the city of Kush or Kushinagar, in the plains some distance short of Kapilavastu, he fell ill. In his eightieth year, lying between a pair of *sal* trees, he achieved *mahaparinirvana*, the Great Final Deliverance. After his cremation his ashes were gathered and placed in eight urns, which after several days of adoration were placed in a 'magnificent pyramidal building', the first stupa.

The most significant difference between the two emerging Buddhist traditions lay in the dating of the Buddha's death. According the Sinhalese, Burmese and Siamese texts, his *parinirvana* took place 218 years before the consecration of Ashoka, whereas Nepalese and Indian sources placed it exactly a hundred years before this event. Cross-checking against Greek sources suggested 268 BCE as the most probable date for Ashoka's consecration, placing the final extinguishing in 486 BCE (according to the 'long' chronology) or 368 BCE (according to the short; just to muddy the waters further, Buddhist orthodoxy in Sri Lanka and south-east Asia today places the *parinirvana* in the year 543 BCE, while the general tendency among modern historians is to bring it forward into the fourth century BCE).

Thus, by the end of 1836 the Indian origins of Buddhism had been established beyond doubt, together with the main biographical facts of the philosopher who had come to be called Gautama Buddha, Tathagata, Sakyamuni, Mahasramana, and more than a score of other names. It was now apparent why the Mahabodhi tower had been raised at Bodh-Gaya, why there was a stupa at Sarnath – and why the envoys from Ava who had come looking for the holy places associated with Gautama Buddha had also visited Rajgir, ancient Rajagriha, where Gautama Buddha had set up his first *vihara* under the patronage of King Bimbisara.

But there were another five sacred sites the Burmese had failed to locate: Lumbini, where Prince Siddhartha had been born; his father's capital, Kapilavastu, where he had spent the first twenty-nine years of his life; Sravasti, the capital of Kosala, where Gautama Buddha and his followers had gathered annually during the Rains; Vaisali, where Gautama Buddha had given his last sermon; and Kushinagar, where he had died. The manner in which Buddhism had evolved and spread through Asia in the centuries following the death of its founder had still to be established – as had the reasons for its disappearance from India. It had still to be determined who had been responsible for the building of the great topes at Sarnath, Bhilsa (Sanchi), Amaravati, Manikyala and elsewhere – and, above all, who had ordered the mysterious pseudo-Greek inscriptions to be carved on the polished columns and great boulders whose diverse locations suggested ever more strongly the existence of some unknown Buddhist civilisation in India's past.

10

Prinsep and the Beloved of the Gods

O N NEW Year's Day 1837 James Prinsep wrote to his now widowed mother in England: 'Seventeen short years have I sojourned in this splendid Indian pilgrimage . . . let me again and again return thanks for the blessings that have fallen to my lot, above all for that of <u>content</u> without which there can be no real happiness.'

His days were now spent in a frenzy of activity. In his capacity as Secretary of the Asiatic Society of Bengal he regularly exchanged news and information with a dozen learned societies and universities in Europe, scores of learned men and many times that number of less distinguished enthusiasts scattered far and wide across the subcontinent – to say nothing of the more avid correspondence he maintained with an inner circle of like-minded individuals that included Hodgson in Nepal, Turnour in Ceylon and, increasingly, his young protégé Alexander Cunningham. Among the many who sought him out and demanded his attention was the French traveller Jacques Stocquelier, who later said of him that 'from the deepest antiquarian researches, and the pursuits of chemical discoveries, down to the lighter occupations of the drama, James Prinsep had a head for all, and a time for all . . . As there was nothing too intricate, so there was nothing too playful (that was not irrational) to engage a mind thus constituted.'

What was now increasingly engaging this remarkable mind was the matter of the mysterious pseudo-Greek lettering first identified on Feroz Shah's Lat in Delhi, which James now referred to as 'Delhi No. 1'. As early as 1833 he had called for someone with linguistic skills 'to engage upon the recovery of this lost language', and to do it quickly, before the 'indefatigable students of Bonn and Berlin' beat them to it. When no one responded to his call he joined forces with William Mill to address the problem himself. As a first step he got an Asiatic Society member, Lieutenant Burt, to take an impression of the Allahabad pillar. Like the Delhi pillar, this carried long inscriptions in both Delhi No. 1 and the early Sanskrit script (Gupta Brahmi) – already 'broken' by Charles Wilkins almost half a century earlier but subsequently forgotten – which became 'Delhi No. 2'. The first defeated them, but they did better with Delhi No. 2 and were able to read the Gupta Brahmi inscription on the Allahabad pillar as a victory declaration, carved on the orders of a king named Samudragupta, son of Chandragupta, who had 'uprooted' nine kings and conquered much of central India. This information presented something of a puzzle, until it was realised that there were at least two ancient monarchs of the name Chandragupta, and that the Allahabad inscription was the work of the second, the founder of the Gupta dynasty of the third and fourth centuries CE, rather than of the earlier Chandragupta, founder of the Maurya dynasty.

The first real step forward came in 1835, when Brian Hodgson sent in his copy of the inscription he had found on the Radhia pillar (at Lauriya Nandgarh) in the Terai country, the narrow belt of jungle immediately south of the foothills of the Himalayas, between Nepal and Bihar. Prinsep responded almost immediately, in a state of great excitement. He had placed Hodgson's transcript beside his copies of the Delhi No. 1 from Feroz Shah's Lat and the Allahabad inscription – with startling results: 'Upon carefully comparing them . . . I was led to a most important discovery, namely that all three inscriptions were identically the same.'

Prinsep's subsequent appeals now brought to light two more inscriptions in the Delhi No. 1 script, both carved on rocks. One was from the Dauli rock in Orissa, first discovered by Mackenzie and subsequently reported on by Stirling. The other was from the opposite side of the country, at Girnar in Gujarat, where it had been first spotted by Colonel James Tod on a journey from Rajasthan to the coast. He described it as 'a huge hemispherical mass of dark granite, which, like a wart upon the body, has protruded through the crust of mother earth, without fissure or inequality, and which, by the aid of the "iron pen", has been converted into a book'. Unable to make any sense of the writings, which he believed to be Greek in origin, Tod had made a copy of two of the sections into which the rock face had been divided – enough to show that it and the Orissa rock carried passages of text that were also all but identical to those on the pillar inscriptions.

Exciting as these discoveries were, they only heightened the aura of mystery surrounding the inscriptions and what they might have to say. As Prinsep put it, 'Whether they mark the conquests of some victorious raja; whether they are, as it were, the boundary pillars of his dominions, or whether they are of a religious nature . . . can only be satisfactorily solved by the discovery of the language.'

Prinsep surmised that the language of Delhi No. 1 must be an early form of Sanskrit, so he began by trying to match the letters with the Gupta Brahmi script he and William Mill had earlier deciphered. The outcome was disappointing, although he believed he had identified a number of consonants. He next tried drawing up tables listing the number of times each individual letter appeared in the Delhi and Allahabad inscriptions, in the hope that this would identify common letters or words. This was even less successful, and led him to conclude that he was not dealing with pure Sanskrit, as he had supposed. After two years of fruitless puzzling he put the project to one side to concentrate on other matters.

In March 1837, as the Cold Weather months began to give way to the Hot Weather, the issue of Delhi No. 1 suddenly came alive again. It had been decided that the Allahabad pillar should be restored to its original vertical position, and a committee had been set up at the Asiatic Society of Bengal to determine how best to do this. It was judged that a lion couchant and capital similar to that on the pillar at Bakhra should be added, and the task was given to Colonel Edward Smith, Superintending Engineer for the Public Works Department of the Central Provinces. The outcome was not a success – Alexander Cunningham commented tersely that the carved lion resembled 'a stuffed poodle stuck on top of an inverted flowerpot' – and the pillar was subsequently re-erected without lion or capital. However, Smith's involvement in the project led to a request from Prinsep for some accurate drawings of the sculptures at the Great Tope at Bhilsa (Sanchi) – and Smith obliged by providing not only the desired drawings but also accurate copies of some two dozen brief inscriptions cut into the pillars and stone railings surrounding the Great Tope. All were in the now very familiar lettering of Delhi No. 1 (see illustration opposite).

Prinsep decided that these short inscriptions could only be records of donations. He knew of other sites where such inscriptions had been incised in Gupta Brahmi or more modern Sanskrit, and felt there was every reason to suppose that the Sanchi inscriptions must similarly record the names of those who had paid for or donated sections of the railing or the gateways – and must also, therefore, include the word 'gift' or 'gifted'. Arranging the separate scraps of paper on which Colonel Smith had copied the inscriptions, Prinsep was struck by the fact that almost all terminated in the same two characters: a snake-like squiggle and an inverted T followed by a single dot: 𐀥⊥. He further observed that the letter ⎖ appeared frequently before or near to this terminal word – and, as luck would have it, only a day or two earlier, working on some coins from Saurashtra, he had determined that the equivalent letter represented the genitive singular, 'of', the equivalent of the Pali *ssa* and the Sanskrit *sya*. If his hunch was correct, then the general structure of each sentence was something like 'So-and-so of, the gift'. The Sanskrit word for gift was *danam* and this seemed to fit the characters 𐀥⊥, 'teaching me the very two letters, *d* and *n*, most different from known forms, and which had foiled me most in my former attempts.' Once these three characters and sounds – d, n and s – had been identified, James began to make speedy progress in breaking down the rest: 'Since 1834 also my acquaintance with ancient alphabets had become so familiar that most of the remaining letters in the present examples could be named at once on re-inspection. In the course of a few minutes I thus became possessed of the whole alphabet.'

Inscriptions from Sanchee.

taken in facsimile on paper by Capt. E. Smith. Eng.ʳ

Prinsep lith.

the same on Nᵒˢ 19 and 25

On 23 May James wrote an excited note to Alexander Cunningham in Benares:

My dear Cunningham,

Hors de department de mes etudes! . . . No, but I can read the Delhi No. 1 which is of more importance; the Sanchi inscriptions have enlightened me. Each line is engraved on a separate pillar or railing. Then thought I, they must be the gifts of private individuals where names will be recorded. All end in 𑀤𑀦 – that must mean 'gift' or 'given'. Let's see – 𑀇𑀲𑀧𑀸𑀮𑀺𑀢𑀲𑀘𑀲𑀸𑀫𑀦𑀲𑀘𑀤𑀦

Isa-pâlitasa-cha Sâmanasa-cha dânam

'The gift of Isa-Palita (protected of God) and of Samana'

He had indeed broken the code of Delhi No. 1. The short inscriptions from Sanchi thought to be no more than 'trivial fragments of rude lettering' had provided the key to 'the alphabet and language of these ancient pillars and rock inscriptions which have been the wonder of the learned since the days of Sir Wm Jones'. For several days and nights during the hottest month of the year he had pored over the Sanchi inscriptions again and again until the means of deciphering them had suddenly become apparent. Later he described this moment of inspiration as being 'like most other inventions, when once found it appears extremely simple; and, as in most others, accident, rather than study, has had the merit of solving the enigma which has long baffled the learned.' In reality, it had been neither simple, nor arrived at by accident.

On 7 June 1837, on what must have been a stiflingly hot evening, James Prinsep addressed those few members of the Asiatic Society of Bengal who had not left Calcutta seeking refuge from the heat. Word of his momentous breakthrough had spread among his intimates, but the manner of its accomplishment and what it revealed James had kept to himself. Now he began by explaining stage by stage how he had built up a working alphabet for Delhi No. 1, beginning with his assumption that the common endings to the Sanchi inscriptions must be related to 'the offerings and presents of votaries'.

The alphabet, made up of thirty-three basic characters based on syllables, was simple but ingenious. Aspirated letters, for example, were formed in most cases by 'doubling the simple characters; thus, **ⵁ** *chh*, is the double of **ⴅ** *ch*; **ⵔ** *th*, is the double of **ⵂ** *t*; **D** *dh*, is the half of this; and **⊙** *th*, is the same character with a dot as a distinguishing mark'. Once its workings had been established it had become clear to Prinsep that he was dealing with the early vernacular form of Sanskrit, now known as Prakrit, found in all early Buddhist literature, which had much closer links with Pali than with Gupta Brahmi. 'There is a primitive simplicity in the form of every letter, which stamps it at once as the original type whereon the more complicated structure of the Sanscrit has been founded. If carefully analysed, each member of the alphabet will be found to contain the element of the corresponding member, not only of the Deva-nagari, but of the Canouj, the Pali, the Tibetan, the Hala Canara, and of all the derivatives from the Sanscrit stock.'

It was now possible to translate almost every one of the Sanchi inscriptions sent in by Colonel Smith. They were indeed records of the names of donors, often with an additional word or two about their status or occupation. Some were short and straightforward – as, for example, No. 15 on his list (see illustration page 181). This he read as *Kadasa bhichuno danam*, and translated as 'The gift of Kada, the poor man'. Others were more complex and presented problems that would require further elucidation.

Having, as he put it, 'become possessed of the master-key of this ancient language', Prinsep next turned to the coins in the Society's collection that were still undeciphered:

Foremost among these was the series of coins conjecturally, and, as it now turns out, correctly designated as the Buddhist series; and of these the beautiful coin discovered by Lieutenant A. Conolly at *Kanauj*, attracted the earliest notice from the very perfect execution and preservation of the legend. The reading of the coin was now evident at first sight, as **ⵛ ⴆ ⵕ ⴆ ⴑ** *Vippa dèvasa*; which, converted into its Sanscrit equivalent will be *Vipra devasya*, the coin of Vipra Deva. On reference to the Chronological Tables, we find a Vipra in the Magadha line, the tenth in descent from Jarasandha, alloted to the eleventh century before the Christian era! Without laying claim to any such antiquity we may at least bespeak our Vipra Deva a place in the *Indu vansa* line of *Magadha*.

So it went on, with the lettering of coin after coin deciphered and translated, and a place found for each in the tables of kings. Then there were also new translations of inscriptions from Karli and Bodh-Gaya to be talked about, before Prinsep's audience was at last vouchsafed his greatest revelation. 'The foregoing', he declared, 'are, after all, but trifling ordeals for the new alphabet, compared with the *experimentum crucis* of the Delhi lat inscription, which the antiquarian listener will not be satisfied until he sees performed in his presence. To this, then, I will now hasten, contenting myself with one or two sentences to demonstrate the perfect applicability of the system, and reserving for a future occasion the full interpretation of this strangely multiplied and important document . . . I cannot select a better example for our first scrutiny than the opening sentence of the inscription.'

The opening sentence of Delhi No. 1 – 𑀤𑁂𑀯𑀸𑀦𑀁𑀧𑀺𑀬 𑀧𑀺𑀬𑀤𑀲𑀺𑀮𑀸𑀚𑀳𑁂𑀯𑀁𑀆𑀳𑀸 – had been observed to repeat itself over and over again at the start of a great many sections or paragraphs of text in the pillar inscriptions and on the Girnar and Dauli rocks. This Prinsep could now read as *Devánamapiya piyadasi lája hevam ahá*. 'Here', he declared, 'we perceive at once that the language is the same as was observed on the Bhilsa [i.e., Sanchi] fragments – not Sanskrit, but the vernacular modification of it, which has been so fortunately preserved for us in the Pali scriptures of Ceylon and Ava. *Devánam piya piyadasi lája* is precisely the Sanskrit, देवानां प्रिय प्रियदर्शि राजा, "The beloved of the gods king Piyadasi" . . . *Hevam ahá*, I recognised at once as an old friend in the Pali version of the Buddhist couplet *Ye dharma* etc., so thoroughly investigated in the Journal for March 1835: *evam aha*, "thus spake".' After conferring with Ratna Paula, his Pali-speaker from Ceylon, Prinsep had concluded that this opening phrase was best represented in English as 'Thus spake King Piyadasi, Beloved of the Gods'.

It was the 'declaratory formula' of a royal edict: 'The simplicity of the form reminds us of the common expression in our own Scriptures – "Thus spake the prophet", or in the proclamation of the Persian monarch – "Thus saith Cyrus, king of Persia". There is none of that redundant and fulsome hyperbole which we find in the Sanskrit grants and edicts of later days.'

From this opening sentence, Prinsep had at first been inclined to believe that what followed in the text would be 'the doctrines of some great reformer, such as Shakya, to whom the epithets *Devanampriya priya-darsi* might be applied'. But the second sentence set the issue at rest once and for all. It read ᘝᐟ ᘒᘀᐟᐣᘀᘓᘊᘂᐟᘒᐣᘁᘈᘂ, *Saddavisati vasa-abhisitena me*. Ratna Paula had no difficulty in interpreting this almost immediately as *satta visati vasse abhisittena me*, 'In the twenty-seventh year of my reign'. So these pillars and rock inscriptions were unquestionably the work of a monarch, and a mighty one at that, since his rule had extended at least from the Himalayan foothills to central India, and from the Arabian Sea to the Bay of Bengal.

There was a huge amount of work to be done before a full and accurate translation of the texts of Delhi No. 1 and its companion inscriptions could be presented before the Society. But even a cursory reading of their contents revealed them to be very different from the usual records of self-glorification to be found on later tablets and plaques – boasts of victories won, enemies vanquished and descents from the sun or the moon. As Piyadasi's commands were unravelled word by word, so Prinsep, William Mill and Ratna Paula had become increasingly aware that they were also unravelling the workings of a most unusual mind, one that had been stilled for more than two thousand years and whose thoughts, carved into polished rock columns and boulders, had stood unread for almost as long. These three had broken that long, dark silence.

'Here in my domain,' ran the first edict of Piyadasi, Beloved of the Gods (as given in a modern translation rendered by the Venerable S. Dhammika of the Buddhist Publication Society in Kandy), 'no living beings are to be slaughtered or offered in sacrifice. Nor should festivals be held, for Beloved of the Gods, King Piyadasi, sees much to object to in such festivals . . .' The second edict spoke of medicines being made available to all, of wells dug and trees planted along roads. Subsequent injunctions spoke of religious tolerance and good government, but government based on the moral precepts of the Law:

Beloved of the Gods, King Piyadasi, does not consider glory and fame to be of great account unless they are achieved through having his subjects respect Dharma and practice Dharma, both now and in the future .. There is no gift like the gift of Dharma, no acquaintance like acquaintance with Dharma, no distribution like distribution of Dharma, and no kinship like kinship with Dharma. And it consists of this: proper behaviour towards servants and employees, respect for mother and father, generosity towards friends, companions, relations, Brahmans and ascetics, and not killing living beings. Therefore a father, a son, a brother, a master, a friend, a companion or a neighbour should say, 'This is good, this should be done.' One benefits in this world and gains great merit in the next by giving the gift of the Dharma.

It was all a very far cry from the duties of the king as set out in the Vedic and Hindu scriptures, where a monarch's first duty was to expand his kingdom and make war against his neighbours

But who was the author of these extraordinary edicts? Who was the great ruler Piyadasi – or, as found in one variation at Girnar, Piyathisa – who regarded himself as Beloved of the Gods? Prinsep professed himself baffled: 'In all the Hindu genealogical tables with which I am acquainted, no prince can be discovered possessing this very remarkable name. If there ever reigned such a monarch in India, his memory must have been swept away with every other record of the Buddhist dynasties we know to have ruled in India unrecorded by fame.' Only one possible candidate presented himself, one who had emerged from George Turnour's recent translations of the Pali chronicles of Ceylon:

In Mr Turnour's epitome of Ceylonese History, then, we are presented once, and once only, with a name of a king, Devenipeatissa, as nearly identical with ours as possible . . . King Deveni Peatissa succeeded his father on the throne of Ceylon in the year of Buddha 236, or BC 307. One of his first acts is thus related by Mr Turnour: 'He induced Dharmasoka, a sovereign of the many kingdoms into which *Dambadiva* (*Jambudwipa*, or India) was divided, and whose capital was *Pattilipatta*, to depute his son Mihindu and his daughter Sangamitta, with several other principal priests, to Anuradhapura for the purpose of introducing the religion of Buddha. They arrived in the year 237, the first of this reign and the eighteenth of that of Dharmasoka'

The edicts were clearly the work of a man profoundly influenced by the Buddhist teachings, so it was perfectly conceivable that the Piyadasi or Piyathisa of the inscriptions was Ceylon's first royal convert, Devenipeatissa. But why should the edicts of a king of Ceylon be scattered across north and central India? Surely Ceylon's Great Chronicle would have had something to say on the matter if his edicts had extended all over India? Neither Prinsep nor his audience were convinced, and so the meeting broke up with the biggest question of all – who was Piyadasi, Beloved of the Gods? – left unanswered.

Like all such great endeavours, the first sudden breakthrough was followed by a period of slower progress as Prinsep, with the help of William Mill and the Pali specialist Ratna Paula, toiled over the meanings of unclear characters, ambiguous words, and phrases that made no sense. It was also a cumulative process, advanced from time to time by new information from other quarters that always seemed to appear quite fortuitously at exactly the right moment to nudge the process of discovery along another step or two or to correct its direction by a degree or so. Not unsurprisingly, the most significant of these nudges came from George Turnour in Columbo.

A year earlier Turnour had written to Prinsep attacking Dr Wilson's dating of events as set out in his *History of Kashmir* and challenging his view that Ashoka Maurya's faith was of 'very little moment'. His translation of the *Mahavamsa* showed how wrong Dr Wilson had been in supposing that monarch to be a mythical figure: Ashoka was not only a real figure in Indian history, but a supremely important one. Just how important, he had now discovered from his reading of a second Pali text, the *Dipawanso*, which was a commentary on the first. The news of this discovery was despatched to James Prinsep within weeks of his momentous lecture of 6 June (thus coinciding more or less with the accession of Queen Victoria).

'Since I came down to Colombo, I have made a most important discovery,' wrote Turnour. While sorting through a collection of

Pali works brought to Ceylon from Siam by a Sinhalese official in 1812 he had found a hitherto unstudied commentary: 'In running over the book cursorily I find the following lines . . . in reference to Dharma Asoka: "Here then we find that Asoka was surnamed Piyadassi; and if you will turn to the fifth Chapter of the *Mahawanso*, especially pages 28 and 29, you will see the circumstances under which the Buddistical edifices were simultaneously erected all over India."'

With this simple statement the identity of Piyadasi, the Beloved of the Gods, was finally revealed: he was none other than Ashoka Maurya, known also as Dharma Ashoka, upholder of the Law, grandson of Chandragupta/Sandrokottos. And, of course, it made perfect sense.

This was almost – but not quite – the last piece of the jigsaw.

In March 1838 a more complete and accurate impression of the Girnar rock inscription became available to James Prinsep. On 14 March he wrote another of those letters to Alexander Cunningham that bubble over with enthusiasm and good cheer. The Girnar inscription differed from the pillar edicts in a number of passages, and in one he had found a line that linked Piyadasi/Ashoka to Egypt and the Ptolemys:

> The passage in the 14th edict is much mutilated, and I long for a more correct copy. It really becomes interesting to find Egypt and Ptolemy known to Asoka! I must give you the real text:

> *Yona raja paran cha tena chaptaro rajanan tulamayo*
> Greek king furthermore by whom the Gypta rajas Ptolemy
> *cha antigina cha maga cha * * **
> and Antigonus and Magus and * * *
> *savata devanampiya dhammanusasti anubatate yata pajati*
> everywhere Beloved of the God's religious precept reaches
> where goes.

Hurrah for inscriptions!

Here was proof of diplomatic links between Ashoka's empire and the West, in the form of Alexander the Great's successors: the Egyptian king Ptolemy was probably Ptolemy II (ruled 285–247 BCE); Antigonus was probably Antigonos Gonatos of Macedonia

(278–239 BCE); and Magus was the King of Cyrene (now Libya, 300–258 BCE). A later reading showed the missing name to be that of Alexander (ruler of Epirus, 272–258 BCE). These four rulers were all alive in 258 BCE. The Girnar rock edict stated that it had been set there by Ashoka's orders 'twelve years after my coronation', which meant that Ashoka must have come to the throne in or very soon after the year 270 BCE (the general consensus today is that he reigned from 268 to 233 BCE).

The very last piece of the jigsaw was more in the nature of confirmation than further discovery. It fell into place with the arrival of a complete copy of the rock edict at Dauli in Orissa. Here Ashoka had added an extra paragraph to explain why he wished his edicts to be engraved at this place in what was then the country of Kalinga. It was in part a call to non-violence, but also a moving personal testimony of remorse and conversion:

> Beloved of the Gods, King Piyadasi, conquered the Kalingas eight years after his coronation. One hundred and fifty thousand were deported, one hundred thousand were killed and many more died. After the Kalingas had been conquered, Beloved of the Gods came to feel a strong inclination towards the Dharma, a love for the Dharma and for instruction in Dharma. Now Beloved of the Gods feels deep remorse for having conquered the Kalingas . . . Now it is conquest by Dharma that Beloved of the Gods considers to be the best conquest and it has been won here, on the borders, even six hundred yojanas [leagues] away, where the Greek king Antiochus rules, beyond there where the four kings named Ptolemy, Antigonos, Magas and Alexander rule, likewise in the south among the Cholas, the Pandyas, and as far as Tamrapani . . . I have had this Dharma edict written so that my sons and great-grandsons may not consider making new conquests, or so that if military conquests are made, that they be done with forbearance and light punishment, or, better still, so that they consider making conquest by Dharma only, for that bears fruit in this world and the next.

Instead of going to war against his rivals in the West, Ashoka had made peace with them. To this day, James Prinsep's unlocking of the Delhi No. 1 script, now known as Ashoka Brahmi, remains unquestionably the greatest single advance in the recovery of India's lost past. The discoveries made in Calcutta and Columbo in that extraordinary summer of 1837 did much more than unlock the words on the pillar and rock inscriptions of Delhi and else-where. They gave early Indian history a solid foundation it had never had before; they transformed a name into a figure of flesh and blood; and they allowed the world to see into the mind of a monarch of the third century BCE – no ordinary monarch, but one whose influence had extended far beyond the boundaries of the empire he had carved out for himself, and continued to be felt for centuries. His pillar and rock edicts have been found as far afield as Kandahar in modern Afghanistan and Jatinga-Rameshwara in modern Kerala – a total of forty-two to date. Only one of these, a rock edict found in Hyderabad in 1915, carries Ashoka's full name, which appears as *Devanam piyasa asokasa*.

When the time came to assess what had been achieved under the auspices of the Asiatic Society of Bengal in the twelve months fol-lowing the deciphering of Delhi No. 1, the editor of the *JASB* was in no doubt as to the scale of these achievements and to whom they were due:

> Advances have been made in restoring the early History of India which throw into the shade the investigations of the great men of the preceding thirty years. In this department the Honourable Mr Turnour of Ceylon, stands pre-eminently con-spicuous, and Mr Hodgson of Nipal, with Mr Cosma de Koros, the learned author of the Thibetan Dictionary and Grammar, have worthily prosecuted the same studies . . . and the results obtained from all these sources have been established by the crowning discovery of all, the key to the ancient inscrip-tions of Asoka in Pali [*sic*], the merit of which rests with our Editor himself . . . Through the Journal attention was first drawn to the coins of past ages, as a means of following back-ward the series of Indian Kings and Dynasties. General Ventura, Mr Masson, Sir A. Burnes, and others, have in consequence devoted themselves to the collection of coins and relics in the countries which were the scene of Grecian enterprise; and

Colonel Stacey, Dr Swiftney, Captain Cunningham, Mr Tregear, and many more have pursued the same line in different parts of India, placing themselves all in communication with our Editor, that their discoveries might through him be combined in one general result.

But this was the voice of an acting editor, not James Prinsep writing about himself: for the breakthroughs of 1837–38 had had one unexpected and fatal consequence. Instead of the pace easing, the opposite had happened. The succession of discoveries initiated by Prinsep had fired imaginations across India and Europe, resulting in an upsurge of enthusiasm among Orientalists and their supporters, all clamouring for further information and bursting with new ideas – and all focused on the person of James Prinsep. Deluged with demands on his attention from every quarter, he did his best to respond while at the same time carrying out his official duties as Assay Master at the Mint. But he had also become caught up in a new challenge that was proving every bit as taxing as the first, the deciphering from coins and inscriptions recovered from India's north-west frontier and beyond of what was then known as the Bactrian alphabet – a script today known as Kharosthi.

The pressure became too much for him: 'The study and exertions required for the satisfaction of these numerous references to his individual skill . . . were too severe for the climate of India, and the Editor's robust constitution sunk at last.'

In September 1838 the headaches and nausea that had dogged James Prinsep for several months suddenly grew much worse, and he suffered what amounted to a mental and physical breakdown. He was advised to take a sea-trip round the Bay of Bengal, which left him feeling no better, whereupon the doctors pronounced that the only hope of recovery lay in his immediate removal to a kinder climate. His replacement as editor recorded in the Preface to Volume VIII of the *JASB* that, 'After fighting fruitlessly against the approaches of disease for a couple of months, he was at last compelled . . . to quit this country suddenly in the ship *Herefordshire* in the early part of the month of November. His friends and brothers are now anxiously expecting to receive from the Cape of Good Hope, the first accounts of the effect of the sea-voyage upon his health.' But it was clear even then that his case was hopeless, for as William Prinsep recorded in his memoir, 'In mind he had been lost to us all, even to his wife his constant nurse.'

James arrived in London in January 1839 in state of complete collapse, and was taken to the house of his sister Sophia at 31 Belgrave Square. Nothing could be done for him. Professor Horace Wilson visited him, and wrote to a mutual friend in Calcutta that 'nature exhausted by incessant toil, was not able, even with the favourable circumstances of healthy constitution, temperature and regular habits, cheerful spirits, and a time of life scarcely in its prime, to rally from the effects of interest too perpetually excited, application never intermitted'. His wife Harriet reportedly never left his side, nursing him until he died, on 22 April 1840 at the age of forty-one, from an 'affection of the brain, which proved to be a softening of the substances'.

The news reached Calcutta in late July, prompting a meeting in the Town Hall to consider how best the city should honour James Prinsep's memory. It was however representatives of the city's Indian population, at a separate meeting of their own, who provided the most fitting tribute, in the form of a landing-stage and shelter to be known as Prinsep's Ghat (see Plate 12). 'The natives', recorded William Prinsep,

> formed a subscription of their own to build a ghat to his memory. A site was given them by the Governor General at the Coolie Ghat just below the Fort and the erection of a very neat Palladian Porch at the head of a flight of steps was entrusted to our friend Fitzgerald, an officer of Engineers. It is an ornament to the river, and mostly used for the landing of troops arriving by sea . . . It has the name of James Prinsep in the architrave in four different languages, English, Bengallee, Hindee and Persian. My last act in India was to add two stone recumbent lions to slope off the stairs, which I got done at Buxar for 400 rupees. It is called Prinsep's Ghat so that our name cannot easily be forgotten in India.

Later strengthening of the embankment at this point of the river led to the removal of the steps, but the porch itself still stands.

William was a little over-optimistic, however: today it is popularly known as Princes Ghat, and is thought to be the place where some great prince once disembarked.

The loss of James Prinsep was a blow from which the Orientalist movement in India did not recover. Already seriously damaged by the victory of the Anglicists in 1835, it now went into a rapid decline. 'During James Prinsep's life-time,' his protégé Alexander Cunningham later wrote, 'the materials collected by these "field archaeologists" and "travelling antiquarians", as he called them, were all made over to him, but since his death, each observer has worked independently in his own line and has published separately the results of his own labours.' The records of the Asiatic Society of Bengal speak for themselves: after reaching a peak during the Prinsep years, the membership fell year by year; instead of one Secretary, his work was now divided among two or three; and, although the *JASB* continued to be published year after year, it was no longer at the forefront of Indian studies. In 1838 what had formerly been the Literary Society of Bombay changed its name to the Bombay Branch of the Royal Asiatic Society, effectively transferring its allegiance away from India to England. The Ceylon Society followed suit.

In Ceylon, too, the moral climate had changed, and the island's state religion was now looked upon by the authorities with growing disfavour. In 1841 the Christian missionary R. Spence Hardy, author of *A Manual of Buddhism*, let it be known that it was 'the bounden duty of the government of the country, from its possession of the Truth, to discountenance the system [of Buddhism] by every legitimate means'. Buddhism had to be confronted in a struggle that could only end 'in the discomfiture of those who have risen against the Lord and his Christ'. In that same year George Turnour's health deteriorated and he took home leave in an attempt to recover it. He returned to Europe, found the chill of the English winter too much for him, and settled in Naples, where he died in April 1843 at the age of forty-three, his second volume of the *Mahavamsa* still uncompleted. Within ten years of his death the religion enshrined by the British administration in the Kandyan Convention of 1815 had been to all intents disestablished, and all formal ties between the government and the Buddhist Sangha had been severed.

Another casualty of these years was Alexander Csoma de Koros. In November 1835 he had moved to Siliguri, close to the semi-independent hill-state of Sikkim, whose Raja had that same year ceded part of his territory to the Government of India – including a village called Dorje Ling, the 'place of the thunderbolt' – to serve as a military sanatorium. Csoma de Koros's plan was to cross Sikkim and enter Tibet, but he lost his nerve. The British political officer at Siliguri, Major Lloyd, reported to his superiors that he had encouraged Csoma de Koros to push on to Lhasa, but found the Hungarian reluctant to do so: 'He always said such an attempt could only be made at the risk of his life.' Brian Hodgson wrote inviting Csoma de Koros to join him in Kathmandu, but the Nepalese Government would not allow it. After two years in Siliguri studying Bengali and Sanskrit, Csoma de Koros returned to Calcutta, where James Prinsep made this 'unpresuming student' very welcome and offered him back his post as librarian at the Asiatic Society of Bengal.

In February 1842 Csoma wrote to the Society's new Secretary, Mr Torrens, to say that he was off on his travels again, to 'make a tour of Central Asia'. His letter read like a will, stating that in the event of his death on the journey he wished to leave all his property to 'this noble establishment'. He then made his way north once more to Siliguri. The stretch of country between Siliguri and Kurseong, immediately below what had now become the British hill-station of Darjeeling, was part of the Terai, the jungle belt notorious through Bihar and Bengal for malaria. Those who had to cross this belt did so at speed and in daylight, never at night, but Csoma failed to observe these precautions and bivouacked over-night in the Terai jungle. A day later he began to climb the track that led up into hill country where he saw scenes that must have brought back memories of his earlier days in the Himalayas: prayer-flags, water-powered prayer-wheels, whitewashed *chorten*, carved *mane*-stones, monasteries peopled by monks with shaven heads and red togas. He reached Darjeeling in two days, on 24 March, and a week later went down with fever.

The Superintendent of the Darjeeling sanatorium was a

redoubtable medical man named Campbell. He had been given advance warning of the Hungarian's visit, and as a keen student of languages had been looking forward to his arrival; it was disturbing to find his distinguished but eccentric visitor prostrate from a malignant fever, 'for the cure of which he would not be persuaded to take any medicines until it was too late to be of any avail . . . He took out of his box a small bit of decayed rhubarb and a phial of tartar emetic, and said, with apparent distrust in their virtues, "As you wish it, I will take some tomorrow, if I am not better."' His personal effects, Dr Campbell noted, were minimal: 'Four boxes of books and paper, the suit of blue clothes which he always wore, and in which he died, a few sheets, and one cooking-pot. His food was confined to tea, of which he was very fond, and plain boiled rice, of which he ate very little. On a mat on the floor, with a box of books on the four sides, he sat, ate, slept, and studied, never undressed at night, and rarely went out during the day.'

During a brief recovery his patient was able to convey to Dr Campbell that 'all his hopes of attaining the object of the long and continuous search were centred on the country of the "Yoogatrs" [Uighurs]. This land he believed to be to the east and north of Lassa . . . To reach it was the goal of his most ardent wishes, and there he fully expected to find the tribes he had hitherto sought in vain.' He died early in the morning of 11 April, comatose and 'without a groan or struggle'. He was fifty-eight. The following day Dr Campbell read the burial service over Alexander Csoma de Koros and saw him interred in the newly-established Christian cemetery, which lies just round the corner from a Tibetan Buddhist monastery.

His asceticism and his long association with Vajrayana Buddhism notwithstanding, Csoma de Koros never accepted the teachings of the Dharma. He considered 'the Tibetan faith' to come 'nearer to the Christian religion than that of any Asiatic nation', but he also regarded much of what he worked on with such single-minded devotion to be 'wild metaphysical speculations'. This did not prevent Japanese Buddhists declaring him a *bodhisattva*, on 22 February 1933, and canonising him as such in the grand hall of Tokyo University. A bronze statue of Alexander Csoma de Koros meditating in the lotus position can be found in the Japanese Imperial Museum.

Of those three hopefuls born at the turn of the century – James Prinsep, George Turnour and Brian Hodgson – the survivor was the one whose health had always seemed the most precarious. Eschewing liquor and meat, cultivating his own vegetables, preferring the company of his fowls to that of his fellow Englishmen, Brian Hodgson became over the years increasingly aloof and hermit-like – and increasingly crusty. He hung on in his mountain kingdom until 1843, continuing to contribute papers to the RAS and the Asiatic Society of Bengal – in total, more than a hundred and seventy – that became increasingly focused on zoology and anthropology.

In 1837, the year of the great breakthrough, Hodgson at his own cost sent eighty-eight Sanskrit texts to the Collège de France, where they were eagerly seized upon by Eugène Burnouf. This was followed soon afterwards by his gift of the third of the three sets of the *Kanjur* that Hodgson had acquired in Kathmandu, which prompted Burnouf to teach himself Tibetan – with the help of Csoma de Koros's *Tibetan Grammar* and *Tibetan–English Dictionary*. Burnouf thus became uniquely placed to study three sets of materials in three different languages – Sanskrit, Pali and Tibetan – pertaining to the origins of Buddhism and the development of Buddhist doctrine.

Following Britain's disastrous adventure into Afghanistan, the First Afghan War of 1838–41, the agreeable but lightweight Lord Auckland was replaced as Governor-General of India by Lord Ellenborough, erratic and overbearing. Since Auckland was thought to have allowed his judgement to be swayed by headstrong 'politicals', Ellenborough was determined to steer clear of them. His instructions to the British Resident in Kathmandu were to cease his meddling in Nepal's internal affairs. But Hodgson, having lived more than two decades in the country, had come to regard himself as a major player in the machinations that surrounded the Nepalese court. Time and again during the Afghan War he had intervened or intrigued to break up the hard-liners seeking a second war against the EICo, and he now found it impossible to stand on the sidelines. Had he gone quietly, an alternative diplomatic post of equal seniority would have been found for him. But he decided to make what his biographer, Sir William Hunter, described as 'a somewhat needlessly emphatic protest against a piece of unfairness in high places', for which his punishment was the insulting offer of the junior post of assistant commissioner at the fledgling hill-station of Simla.

Hodgson resigned. He pensioned off his *bibi*, settled an allowance on their offspring, disbanded his menagerie, and sailed for Europe with all his papers, drawings and manuscripts. The bulk of his natural history collection – more than ten thousand specimens and eighteen hundred sheets of drawings of mammals and birds – went to the British Museum (they are now divided between the Natural History Museum and the London Zoological Society). On his way to England Hodgson stopped off in France, where he met Burnouf and made a further donation to the Collège de France which included sixty paintings and sketches of Kathmandu Valley drawn by his Nepali artist Raj Man Singh (now in the Musée Guimet in Paris; a second set was presented to the RAS: see Plate 16).

But Brian Hodgson's long romance with the East was not yet finished. Unable to settle 'at home', after less than a year he sailed back to India to continue his researches as a private individual. He was forbidden to re-enter Nepal, so as the next best thing he found a home for himself at the nearest Indian equivalent to Kathmandu, the sanatorium of Darjeeling. Here he settled down to the life of a near-recluse, now concentrating his efforts on ethnology. In 1853 he again went to England, found a wife, Anne South, and returned with her to Darjeeling until her poor health finally persuaded him to quit India for good in 1858. The couple settled in Gloucestershire, where Hodgson abandoned his Oriental studies for the life of a country gentleman, riding to hounds until he was sixty-eight. Anne Hodgson died in 1868; he married Susan Townsend in 1870 and died in 1894 (see Plate 15).

Although he was celebrated as a savant in France and Germany, Hodgson's homeland was slow to honour him. The man who has been called 'the father of Indian zoology', the 'founder of the true study of Buddhism', the 'highest living authority on the native races of India', and much else, was not elected a Fellow of the

Royal Society until 1877, while Oxford University waited until his eighty-ninth year before conferring an honorary doctorate upon him. The Victorian Establishment could not forgive Brian Hodgson his action in trading what was seen as rightfully belonging to Britain for the *boutonnière* of a *chevalier* of the Légion d'honneur (1838), the gold medal of the Société Asiatique (1838) and honorary membership of the Institut de France (1844). In so doing he had enabled a Frenchman to claim the laurels that would have sat better on the brow of an Englishman, preferably that of the greatly esteemed Dr Horace Hayman Wilson – whose hoard of 540 Sanskrit manuscripts became the core of the Bodleian Library's Sanskrit collection after his death in 1860.

The outcome of B. H. Hodgson's collaboration with the enemy was the publication in 1844 of Eugène Burnouf's seminal *Introduction à l'histoire du Buddhism Indien*, the first comprehensive account of Indian Buddhist history and Buddhist doctrines. Burnouf always acknowledged his great debt to Hodgson as the man who had provided Buddhist studies with its first 'true and most solid base', and with him Buddhist studies became truly international, no longer confined to the Indian subcontinent.

Prior to Burnouf no one had come near to grasping the essentials of Buddhist philosophy, or applied to it the full rigour of European scientific method. Its moralities could be understood and related to, but poor translations combined with religious preconceptions prevented any real understanding of Buddhism's principal concepts. The Dharma was seen as a set of Moses-like commandments rather than the Buddha's teachings as a whole; *bodhi* was always read as 'wisdom', with Gautama Buddha's 'enlightenment' or 'awakening' at Bodh-Gaya being thought of as some sort of supreme act of will vaguely akin to Christ's crucifixion; and *nirvana* was most commonly interpreted as 'paradise' rather than the 'extinguishing' of self and an end to the otherwise endless cycle of death and rebirth.

Romantics like Schlegel had earlier seen Buddhism (and, indeed, Brahmanism) as a primal *fons et origo* out of which all religions had sprung, a universal truth that answered to their romantic longings. Burnouf's *Introduction à l'histoire du Buddhism Indien* changed all that by presenting Buddhism as it really was: a profoundly unsettling view of the human condition that offered an equally disturbing means of release from that condition. Among those who greeted it as a revelation was Arthur Schopenhauer, who saw it as the vindication of his own views. 'You will arrive at Nirvana,' he wrote shortly after his first reading of Burnouf's work, 'where you will no longer find these four things: birth, old age, sickness, and death . . . Never has myth come closer to the truth, nor will it.'

11

Alexander Cunningham and the Chinese Pilgrims

O NLY ONE man in India felt he deserved to be regarded as James Prinsep's rightful heir. He had after all made his debut at the tender age of twenty with a note on the coins recovered from the Manikyala tope that drew from Prinsep a public commendation: 'We compliment our young friend upon the success with which he has commenced his numismatic studies.' A year later, and entirely on his own initiative, he had begun the dig into the stupa at Sarnath that had produced the stone slab with the Dharma inscription, winning Prinsep's support, and funding for continued excavation. And Lieutenant Alexander Cunningham, like his hero, was one of a close-knit band of brothers, of whom three went out to India as Engineer officers. In 1836 he had secured a plum appointment as one of the aides-de-camp to the incoming Governor-General. As part of Lord Auckland's court, his good nature made him 'a great favourite' with both the Governor-General and his two clever sisters, Emily and Fanny Eden. During two very sociable years in Calcutta he had put his free time to good use in ordering the coinage, and thus the true chronology, of India's most distinguished Hindu dynasty, the Guptas. He had also come into direct contact with James Prinsep, who brought him in to his office to help sort out and classify the large numbers of ancient coins being sent in. 'During a great part of the years 1836 and 1837,' wrote Cunningham a quarter of a century later, 'I was in almost daily intercourse with him. With our mutual tastes and pursuits this soon ripened into the most intimate friendship. I thus had the privilege of sharing in all his discoveries during their progress . . . When I recollect that I was then only a young lad of twenty-three years of age, I feel as much wonder as pride that James Prinsep should have thought me worthy of being made the confidant of all his great discoveries.'

Unfortunately for young Alexander, his military duties kept interfering with his antiquarian pursuits. In October 1837 Lord Auckland and his entourage began an extended tour of the Upper Provinces, concluding with a state visit to the Sikh ruler of the Punjab, Ranjit Singh. Fifteen months later, as the Edens returned to British India, Cunningham was despatched into the mountains of Kashmir to survey the sources of the rivers of the Punjab. He returned to the plains a year later to discover that the new editor of the *JASB*, Mr Courmin, had declined to publish the engravings he had made of the Sarnath tope – and that some forty bas-reliefs and statues of Buddhas recovered during his excavations there and left on site had been thrown into the nearby River Varna by a utilitarian-minded officer of the Public Works Department to serve as a breakwater for the piers of the new Duncan Bridge. On top of that, fifty to sixty cartloads of stones from his excavation of the nearby Chaukhandi mound had been used for the foundations of what was to be Benares's first iron bridge.

In that same year, 1840, Alexander Cunningham married Alice Whish, the daughter of a Bengal civil servant, and took up a temporary appointment as executive engineer to the Nawab of Oude which saw him chiefly occupied in laying out a new road from Lucknow to Calcutta. This did not prevent him writing to the Asiatic Society of Bengal offering to take on more archaeological work in the area. If he were in Patna, he wrote, 'I would have the topes across the Ganges opened in two months'. Nothing came of this, and in the following year active service as a field engineer took the Cunninghams to the newly-established military station of Nowgong, in Central India, which might fairly be described as being in the middle of nowhere. Alexander was then twenty-eight, still a lowly lieutenant on meagre pay, with a wife to support and limited prospects.

Among other Orientalists also ploughing their own lonely

furrows at this time only one was having any public success. This was James Fergusson, who at sixteen or seventeen had joined his family's merchant company in Calcutta. Several years before the great crash of 1830 he had branched out to set up his own indigo company, out of which he had done so well that within the space of nine years he felt able to retire with 'a moderate competency'. But instead of going back to England as a latter-day nabob, Fergusson equipped himself with a *camera lucida* and a party of helpers and in 1835 began an extended tour through India, visiting and recording every known major architectural site he came across (see Plate 18). What started as little more than a wish to see and make accurate drawings of old buildings grew into something much more ambitious. 'At that time,' he later declared, 'thanks to the learning and enthusiasm of Mr James Prinsep, great progress was being made in the decipherment of Indian inscriptions, and the study of the antiques of the country. I determined to try if the architecture could not be brought within the domains of science. For several years I pursued the study almost unremittingly, and bit by bit the mystery unravelled itself.'

Fergusson became a historian of architecture, having conceived the revolutionary notion that India's temples and caves could be dated from their appearance and the means employed in their building. Initially with his *camera lucida* and sketch-books, later by means of photographic prints, he first gathered his data and then analysed it to produce a chronology based on style, decoration and building methods – a prodigious undertaking that made Fergusson India's first expert on architecture and, in time, the Western world's leading authority on the comparative architecture of India, the Middle East and Europe. Much of his early work was concentrated on the predominantly Buddhist rock-temples of western India, the subject of a paper read at a meeting of the Royal Asiatic Society in London in November 1843 and of a subsequent lecture to the Royal Institute of British Architects on 'The Ancient Buddhist Architecture of India'.

His views were well received in England but hotly contested by Alexander Cunningham in India, who subsequently lost no opportunity to challenge Fergusson's dating – not without reason, since Fergusson ignored the evidence of inscriptions, on the grounds that they could have been added long after the caves themselves had been cut out of the rock. Fergusson was particularly suspicious of inscriptions carved in Ashoka or Gupta Brahmi, believing that 'the Buddhists affected an older character as more sacred, as we sometimes use old English letters in modern inscriptions'. What really mattered to Fergusson was appearance, which meant that he arrived at his dating 'almost entirely from a critical survey of the whole series, and a careful comparison of one cave with another, and with the different structural buildings in their neighbourhood'.

This was an inherently flawed approach, not least because there was only one structural building that could be linked to the caves of Western India – the Great Tope at Bhilsa (Sanchi) – and this Fergusson had never seen. As he himself had to admit in his second publication, *Picturesque Illustrations of Ancient Architecture in Hindoostan*, published in 1848, 'There is nothing in India that I now regret more not having been able to visit personally than the group of Buddhist topes and buildings near Bhilsah . . . Though I thought of it, I abandoned the idea, as I had then before me the whole of the western caves, and I felt convinced that they contained, not only the most numerous and complete specimens of Buddhist architecture in India, but also, what was of equal importance to me, the most unaltered.' Ignoring the evidence of the Ashokan inscriptions found on the gateways and railings that James Prinsep had made famous with his breaking of the Ashoka Brahmi script, Fergusson declared that the Great Tope belonged 'to the Gupta dynasty of Canouge, and therefore to the seventh or eighth century'.

Cunningham's hostility may well have been based on more than academic concerns, however, for one outcome of Fergusson's first lecture in 1843 had been a call from Colonel William Sykes, President of the RAS, for the appointment of a qualified person to continue the recording of Indian antiquities begun by Fergusson. This was very much what Alexander Cunningham had himself called for five years earlier in a letter to the Director of the RAS in which he urged the formation of an archaeological survey of India – but he had tried to play the Evangelical card, arguing that such a body would further the Christian cause in India by showing that Brahmanism 'was of comparatively modern origin, and had been constantly receiving additions and alterations; facts which prove that the establishment of the Christian religion in India must ultimately succeed'. This nonsense had not gone down well with the Director of the RAS, none other than Doctor and Professor Horace Hayman Wilson, a staunch proponent of Brahminical learning. It also seems to have turned Colonel Sykes, an influential member of the EICo's Court of Directors, against Cunningham, because in the event two comparative unknowns were appointed Archaeological Enquirers, both junior military officers with a talent for draughtsmanship.

The first was Lieutenant Robert Gill of the Bombay Native Infantry, who was given the special duty of recording the paintings in the caves at Ajanta. This suited Gill very nicely since he was an avid *shikari* as well as an artist. He made his way to Ajanta in 1844, found a base for himself at an old Mughal *sarai* or traveller's post-house in the nearby plains, and settled down to a daily routine of drawing, painting and shooting that continued, incredibly, for the next twenty-seven years – during which time he is reputed to have reduced the local tiger population by at least a hundred and fifty kills. Gill's solitary dedication to his work was in a class of its own but, as it turned out, an almost total waste of time. In 1855 the thirty canvases on which he had made life-size copies in oils of the finest of Ajanta's frescos were sent to England to be exhibited in the Crystal Palace; in 1866 all but five were destroyed in a fire. Undaunted, Gill began his work all over again, armed this time with a camera. Another artist, John Griffiths of the Bombay School of Art, now took over the painting. A decade later Griffiths' paintings were despatched to the Victoria and Albert Museum – and were, in their turn, destroyed by fire.

Gill's fellow Archaeological Enquirer, Captain Markham Kittoe of the Bengal Native Infantry, was equally unlucky. He had first come to the attention of the Secretary of the Asiatic Society of Bengal in 1836, with some rather clumsy sketches of Muslim monuments drawn while on line of march with his regiment. James Prinsep was touched by his enthusiasm, however, and a year later had written to Alexander Cunningham asking him to keep an eye out for 'poor Kittoe'. Cunningham was not impressed, for Kittoe was by his own admission a man of modest attainments: he described himself to Cunningham as 'woefully deficient . . . a self-educated man, and no Classic or Sanskrit scholar'. Furthermore, he had lately been thrown out of his regiment for 'bringing indiscreet charges of oppression against his Commanding Officer, for which there was but little foundation save in his own over-sensitive disposition'. Prinsep found Kittoe a temporary appointment as Secretary of the Coal Committee which involved him in an extensive tour through Orissa in search of coalfields for exploitation. This allowed him to make, at Prinsep's request, a detailed impression of the Ashokan rock inscription at Dauli – which he later claimed to have 'discovered' on his own initiative. After his spell as a coal prospector Kittoe spent two lonely years in the wilds of Chota Nagpur as a road officer in charge of one of the most isolated stretches of the high road from Calcutta to Bombay. He then took some local leave, hoping to restore his fortunes by making his name as an antiquarian explorer. This, he later claimed, was in accord with 'the wishes of my late amiable and learned patron, James Prinsep, who often expressed a wish that I should ramble over the district of Behar'.

His plans set Kittoe and Cunningham on a collision course, since both men had the same purpose in mind, which was to establish and trace the route through India taken by the Chinese Buddhist pilgrim Fa Hian, as set out in Monsieur Jean Pièrre Abel Rémusat's *Foe Koue Ki*.

In his preface to the last volume of the *JASB* he edited, James Prinsep had noted that a 'grand work' on a Chinese Buddhist traveller in India, involving the labour of three successive translators, had been published in Paris at the expense of the French government. 'Alas!' he had lamented. 'When shall we in India have the opportunity of seeing these works at any tolerable period after their publication?' His concern was entirely understandable: a detailed account of a journey made through India in the first decade of the fifth century CE, it was bound to shed a great deal of light on Gupta India and on the status of Buddhism at that time. The translation had been in preparation for years. When ill-health forced its originator Rémusat to abandon his work it was taken over by Heinrich Julius Klaproth, and when he and Rémusat both died (in 1832 and 1835), M. Landresse had finally seen it through to publication.

The first British Orientalist to have access to the completed work was, of course, Wilson, who now dominated Indian studies in England. As well as holding the Sanskrit chair at Oxford, he was Librarian to the EICo and Director of the RAS in London. Despite his labours on the Hindu *Puranas*, he found time to set down his own interpretation of the route taken by the pilgrim Fa Hian on his travels through India in search of early Sanskrit texts.

Fa Hian's outward journey had taken him westwards from northern China across Chinese Tartary and then down through the gorges of the upper Indus into the northern Punjab and Afghanistan – the land of Gandhara, where Fa Hian had found the Dharma to be flourishing to a remarkable degree, with hundreds of monasteries and stupas to be seen in every quarter, extending deep into the mountains to the west and southwards as far as Mathura. From Mathura he had journeyed east through a country still well provided with monasteries until he came to the country of Buddha's birth and teaching. Here the going had not been so easy, and from this point Fa Hian's itinerary became increasingly hard to follow. It seemed that this was no longer a Buddhist country, and the further Fa Hian travelled towards the north-east, the fewer were the *viharas* and the wilder the country. He reached Kapilavastu, the seat of the Sakya clan, and Lumbini, Buddha's birthplace, only to find 'empty desolation'. At Kushinagar, to the south-east, he visited the site of Buddha's *parinirvana*, marked by stupas and monasteries. Then he went south into the country of the Lichchavis to the city of Vaisali, afterwards crossing the Ganges at the confluence of five rivers to reach the city of Pataliputra, in the kingdom of Magadha. This Fa Hian described as the richest city in India, with a magnificent royal palace in its midst, most wonderfully decorated.

From Pataliputra Fa Hian went south to Rajagriha, to find the ancient capital of Buddha's King Bimbisara abandoned and desolate in the midst of a ring of hills, but on all sides stupas and caves closely associated with Buddha and his disciples. After visiting the nearby village where Buddha's chief disciple, Sariputra, had died, Fa Hian continued south to Bodh-Gaya, moving from one sacred site to the next with apparent ease. He then settled in Pataliputra, where he spent three years in a *vihara*, studying and copying manuscripts. His later travels had taken him to the mouth of the Ganges, and then by sea to the country of the lions, Singhala or Ceylon. There he had found himself once more in thriving Buddhist country, where he had seen a pipal grown from a cutting of the original Bodhi-tree, and the Relic of the Tooth. Two years later he had sailed to China by way of Java, eventually arriving back at his point of departure, Nangking, in 414 CE, fourteen years after he first set out.

Having given this summary, together with his own thoughts as to the identification of the places mentioned by Fa Hian, Wilson returned to his Sanskrit translations. He took the view that there was no point in providing an English version of a French translation of a Chinese text, so eleven years passed before such a translation became available: *The Pilgrimage of Fa Hian from the French Edition of the Foe Koue Ki of MM. Rémusat, Klaproth and Landresse*, published in Calcutta by the Baptist Mission Press in 1848.

In the summer of 1843 Alexander Cunningham received a copy of Rémusat's *Foe Koue Ki*, together with M. Reinaud's *Fragments Arabes et Persanes*, containing information on the travels of a second and later Chinese traveller through India, a pilgrim named Huan Tsang. Cunningham was then on his way towards Delhi on military business, but found an opportunity to visit the ruins of Kanauj, the imperial capital of northern India for six centuries, until its destruction by Shahab-ud-din Ghori in 1194. Here he had his first chance to test the accuracy of Fa Hian's itinerary.

Fa Hian's account stated that he had arrived at Kanauj after travelling towards the south-east for seven *yojanas* from Seng-kia-shi, where according to legend Buddha had descended from heaven after spending three months preaching the Law to its celestial inhabitants. Riding out from Kanauj in a north-westerly direction, after forty-five miles Cunningham came to a small village called Samkassam, surrounded on all sides by mounds. Soon afterwards he wrote in triumph to the RAS to say that he had discovered the ruins of the Buddhist 'Samkassa' of the Pali texts and the Hindu 'Sankasya' of the *Ramayana*:

Fa Hian says that Seng-kia-shi was 7 *yeu-yans* from Kanouj, which are equivalent to 28 *kos* [the Indian *kos* being roughly the equivalent of two English miles]. Now the distance of the village of Samkassa from Kanouj is always called 25 *kos kurri* (or long), and 28 *kos narm* (or short) . . . The village of Samkassa consists of only fifty or sixty houses, on a high mound, which has once been a fort: but all around it for a circuit of six miles there is a succession of high ruined mounds of bricks and earth, which is said to be the walls of the old city. My Munshi's expression of wonder, after having visited these ruins, '*Kanauj se bara hy*', 'It is even larger than Kanauj', will convey some notion of their great extent.

Cunningham followed up this little coup by again pleading that someone 'conversant with the sculptured forms and religious practices of the present day, and with the discoveries made by Prinsep and others in Indian Palaeography and Numismatology' should be appointed to 'tread in the footsteps of the Chinese pilgrims Hwan Thsang and Fa Hian'. With a copy of their travels in his hand, such an appointee would now be able to 'distinguish one monument from another, and say with certainty for what purpose each one of the greater stupas was originally designed'. But by the time this second bid from Cunningham reached the RAS in London it was too late, for the EICo had already appointed Markham Kittoe.

Kittoe began his archaeological survey armed with a part-translation into English of Rémusat's *Foe Koue Ki* prepared for him by one of the Asiatic Society of Bengal's co-Secretaries, J. W. Laidley. As soon as this precious document reached him he set off from Calcutta for Bihar, although the Hot Weather had come upon the land and he was woefully unprepared: 'I labour under great disadvantages,' he wrote in his first letter to Laidley, 'viz. want of means and want of an establishment of good craftsmen and a good pundit.' His subsequent letters were filled with further complaints: about the weather – 'I suffered much from the effects of the sun last week'; about shortages of staff – 'being entirely dependent on my own personal exertions in ferreting out curiosities'; and about hostile natives – 'the ignorant bigots fancy that we have some extortion in view and are searching for money'.

Kittoe's first attempt to follow Fa Hian's footsteps through south Bihar was little short of a disaster. Fa Hian had set off on this section of his journey from Pataliputra, so it made sense for Kittoe to do the same and start from Patna. Instead, he sent a 'trustworthy servant' to cover the first leg, from Patna to Rajgir. As a result he wrongly identified the town of Behar (not to be confused with the region and modern state of Bihar) as Fa Hian's first pilgrimage site, 'the little hill of the isolated rock'(later identified by Cunningham as Giriyak, ten miles south of Behar) – and then missed the second point on Fa Hian's itinerary, 'Na-lo' (Nalanda), where Buddha's chief disciple Sariputra had been born and where he had died. Kittoe's trusty servant was ordered to look for Na-lo four miles to the south-west of Behar but reported back that he had found nothing there – although he had observed extensive ruins with 'several high tumuli, also many fine sculptures, numerous large tanks and wells' a few miles further south at a village called Burgaon. This Kittoe dismissed because, according to Fa Hian's itinerary, Na-lo was sited one *yojana* or four *kos* east of Raja-Griha – and Raja-Griha was indisputably the modern village of Rajgir, whose antiquity was well established.

'One *yojun* west of Na-lo', Fa Hian had written, 'brings you to the new town of the royal residence [that is, Raja-griha]. This town was constructed by the king A-tche-chi [Ashoka]: it has two monasteries; on leaving it at the western gate, at three hundred paces you come to a tower, lofty, grand, majestic, and beautiful, which A-tche-chi erected when he obtained some of the relics of Foé [Buddha].' Had Kittoe gone over the ground to the north and east of Rajgir himself, instead of leaving it to his servant, he would have realised both the servant's mistake and the mistake in Fa Hian's text: Rajgir was indeed one *yojana* from Na-lo – but one *yojana* to the south, not the west. Cunningham was the first to realise that Fa Hian's directions were often badly flawed; he later enjoyed the immense satisfaction of correcting Kittoe's error over Na-lo and, in the process, made one of the greatest discoveries of his career – but that was still a long way off.

At Rajgir, Kittoe did much better. It was by now well-established that this had been the old capital of Magadha before Chandragupta made his base at Pataliputra, and that there was an inner, older city encircled by hills as well as a second, outer city built nearby in the plains. From the *Mahavamsa* and the Burmese chronicles it was known that Gautama Buddha had made

Raja-Griha the headquarters of his ministry under the patronage of the ruler of Magadha, King Bimbisara. His first *vihara* was here, built in an orchard donated by the king's court physician; his cousin and enemy Devadatta had set a mad elephant on him in the vicinity; he was said to have taken his midday meal in one cave, and to have meditated in another on the summit of one of the five surrounding hills, a peak known as Griddha-Kuta, the Vulture Peak, where he had also preached a number of his most important teachings, including the Lotus Sutra. Soon after his death, Raja-Griha was the scene of the first Buddhist Council, held by his followers to codify his teachings.

Fa Hian's description of the old city of Raja-Griha now offered Kittoe the first opportunity to locate some of these long-forgotten sites. It began: 'Leaving the [new] city by the south gate, and proceeding south four *li*, one enters a valley and comes to a circular space formed by five hills, which stand all round it, and have the appearance of the suburban wall of a city. Here was the old city of King Bimbisara . . . Inside the city all is emptiness and desolation; no man dwells in it.' Fa Hian had visited both the Pippala, the pipal tree cave 'in which *Foé* regularly sat in meditation after taking his meal', and the Saptaparni hall or cavern – 'the place where, after the nirvana of *Foé*, 500 *Arhats* [enlightened persons] collected the *Sutras*' – at different points on the hill that lay between the old and new cities of Rajgir.

To Kittoe's joy his searches produced a magnificent rock-hewn cave, known locally as the Sone Bhandar or Treasury of Gold, hewn into the south side of this hill (see opposite). 'The cave', he reported, 'has been sadly ill used by a *zemindar* [landowner], who tried to blow it up with powder many years ago, hoping to find hidden treasure.' Even so, one large chamber was intact, with a rectangular door and a square-cut window, containing 'some rude outlines of Buddhas cut into it' and a 'handsome Jain (miniature) temple, much mutilated'. These 'rude outlines' had every appearance of being Jain in origin, but Kittoe nevertheless pronounced it to be the famous Saptaparni cavern, the site of the First Buddhist Council. 'It would be interesting to clear the rubbish here,' he added, but contented himself with sketching the cave and the Jain *chaitya* or miniature stupa it contained.

SON BHUNDAR CAVE.

Kittoe next examined the massive walls, said to be the work of demons, that encircled the old city and ran along the crests of some of the lower hills. He crossed the central valley, noting the several mounds that marked the site of the old city, and then directed his attentions towards the east, where a deep side-valley led up to one of the highest of the five surrounding peaks: 'Learning that two caves existed about seven miles distant at the eastern end of the valley . . . I therefore determined to examine it: having no horse and it being impracticable for my *palkee*, I took guides and proceeded on foot at four p.m. and after two hours of good walking I reached a narrow passage between scarped rocks . . . the distance travelled will have been close upon fifteen *li* or about seven and a half miles as stated by our pilgrim.' Above him Kittoe thought he could make out two caverns and a deep cleft in the rock face. He turned back at this point 'owing to fatigue and blistered feet', convinced that he had found the caves described by Fa Hian in the next section of his travels:

Entering the valley and going beyond the mountains fifteen *li* south-east you come to the peak *Khi-tche* [Gridda-Kuta, the Vulture Peak]. At the distance of three *li*, from the summit of this mountain there is a cave towards the south. *Foé* sat there in meditation. At thirty paces to the north-west there is a stone grotto; *Anan* [Ananda, Buddha's favourite disciple] sat there meditating. There the demon of the heaven *Phi siun* [Mara], changed into a vulture, appeared before the cave and terrified *Anan*. *Foé* by his supernatural power opened the rock, seized

Anan by the arm with his hand, and swayed his fear; the traces where *Foé* cut with his hand exist to this day. It is thus that the hill came to be named the hill of the cave of the vulture.

Buoyed up by these successes, Kittoe then travelled to Bodh-Gaya – where his attempts to follow Fa Hian's movements turned into a nightmare. 'We now come to the most perplexing part of our pilgrim's narrative,' he wrote, 'for not only do his bearings but his distances puzzle us.' These difficulties were compounded by the sheer number of local sacred sites that Fa Hian had apparently visited:

> Continuing twenty *li* to the south, you come to the place where *Phou sa* [*bodhisattva* or Buddha-to-be] spent six years in mortifications: the place is wooded. Thence three *li* to the west, you come to the place where *Foé* descended into the water to bathe; the gods held branches of trees to cover him at his exit from the tank. Two *li* further to the north you come to the place where the young woman offered *Foé* rice and milk. Thence two *li* to the north *Foé*, seated on a stone under a great tree, and looking to the east, ate the rice . . .

So the list of holy places in and around Bodh-Gaya went on, amounting to more than a score, each the site of some miracle or manifestation and marked by a stupa or temple. Failing to understand that Fa Hian had approached Bodh-Gaya not directly from Gaya but from the hills south of Rajgir, Kittoe became totally confused, and finally contented himself with listing what was to be seen in and around the Mahabhodi temple, before calling it a day.

Galled by his failures, Kittoe made a second 'ramble' over the same ground some ten months later. But, inexplicably, he again picked the wrong time of the year – March, when the Hot Weather was just beginning to stoke up – and again he failed to deliver. A promising site for the missed Pippala cave at Rajgir was reported to him, but 'the heat prevented my visiting it because I could not go by night through the thick thorny jungle . . . I had been daily suffering from exposure and was too unwell to prolong my tour, so I returned to Gaya.'

Because poor Kittoe never presented an official report of this second foray, his one significant discovery was subsequently overlooked: his new identification of Fa-Hian's 'Na-lo'. Having realised the unwisdom of letting his servant do his scouting, he had himself gone out to the village of Burgaon, eight miles west of Behar town and three north of Rajgir – and was at once aware that 'this must have been a famous place . . . There are some splendid tanks [reservoirs] some half a mile or more in length . . . there are mounds innumerable and broken idols also . . . there appear to have been five large towers or temples . . . They appear to have had chambers vaulted in a very clever though primitive manner. . . I consider it to be the "Na-lo" of Fa Hian.' He had, unwittingly, left a marker for Cunningham to find – though Cunningham never acknowledged it.

Kittoe had hoped to spend the Cold Weather of 1848–9 locating the remains of Pataliputra in the Patna area, for he now knew from Fa Hian's account that the ancient city had been sited some distance back from the river's edge and therefore might not have been washed away, as everyone supposed. But alas, poor Kittoe! Instead of continuing in the post of Archaeological Enquirer, he was ordered to Benares and there put in charge of the building of the Queen's College, an unattractive edifice in the Gothic style that was intended to replace Jonathan Duncan's original Sanscrit College. Kittoe hated his new task, confiding to Cunningham that he wished it was out of his hands so he could concentrate on what he enjoyed; but it was clear that he had lost the confidence of the authorities. He began to complain of headaches and loss of appetite, and as soon as the building project was completed in February 1853 he went on home leave. Cunningham thereupon lost touch with Kittoe, but heard later from a mutual friend that 'he went straight to his home and died'.

Alexander Cunningham, meanwhile, had been too caught up in the wars to find time for much archaeology. In 1846 he exercised his field engineering skills in the First Sikh War, earning himself a commendation by throwing two bridges of boats across the river Beas at a critical moment in the campaign. He was then employed in political work in the foothills of the Western Himalayas, before being sent into Ladakh as head of a boundary commission to demarcate the frontier between Kashmir and Tibet, which gave him an opportunity of seeing Buddhism in practice. Then came the Second Sikh War, and more action. He was present at the two close-run battles of Chilianwala and Gujerat, was twice mentioned in despatches for his services as the commander of the pontoon train, and emerged from the war as a brevet-major. At the close of hostilities in 1849 he returned as an executive engineer to Gwalior in central India – and here at last found the time to resume his archaeology.

By chance his elder brother, Captain Joseph Cunningham, had two years earlier been appointed Political Agent in nearby Bhopal, which gave Alexander access to the Great Tope at Sanchi and other antiquities in the Bhilsa area. These now became the chief objects of the brothers' off-duty expeditions, which brought to light five distinct groups of topes within a radius of twelve miles, of which the Sanchi group was the best-preserved. Before they could take their work any further, however, Joseph Cunningham was removed from his post for publishing a too-frank account of the late Sikh War, in which he stated that two of the Sikh commanders had been 'bought' with bribes. They had, but the fact was denied by Government, and Captain Cunningham was 'relegated to ordinary duty'. After sixteen years of distinguished political service, this was too much for him to bear: he left Bhopal for the large military station of Umballa, and there died in his bungalow in circumstances that remain shrouded in mystery.

Some months before Joseph Cunningham's departure he had made representations to Government that the sculptured bas-reliefs on the three standing gateways of the Great Tope at Sanchi were too valuable to be left neglected and unrecorded any longer. Whether this was done at his younger brother's behest is unclear, but in response the EICo's Court of Directors asked for an officer with the appropriate skills to be sent to Bhilsa 'on special duty'. Again Alexander Cunningham was overlooked, this time in favour of a Lieutenant Maisey, known to be a skilled artist. Not to be thwarted, when Maisey began his survey at Sanchi in January 1851, Cunningham broke off from a tour of his district next door and joined him, then took over Maisey's survey and effectively made it his own. Maisey was a decent fellow and did not complain, but acknowledged Cunningham's greater experience (and military seniority) and was happy to fall in with his ambitious plans to sink shafts down into the middle of the Great Tope, and into all the lesser stupas on the site as well.

The results were dramatic. On the very first morning of their shared dig, 23 January 1851, the excavations produced two relics, consisting of fragments of bone contained inside a pair of steatite reliquaries – not from the Great Tope itself, which proved to be solid throughout, but from a smaller stupa nearby. What was special about the reliquaries was that they had been placed inside almost identical stone boxes, each of which carried a short inscription written on the lid in Ashoka Brahmi. One bore the characters 𐨙𐨪𐨁𐨤𐨂𐨟, the other 𐨨𐨱𐨪𐨿𐨨𐨆𐨒𐨫.

Cunningham had no difficulty in translating the first as *SARIP-UTASA* or 'of Sariputa' and the second as *MAHA MOGALA-NASA* or 'of Great Mogalana'. On the insides of the lids were also found inscribed in ink the single letters 𐨯 and 𐨨, which Cunningham concluded were the initial letters of the two persons to whom the bones had belonged (see Plate 21).

The names on the lids were of immediate significance to Cunningham, for they were nothing less than those of Gautama Buddha's right- and left-hand disciples, Sariputa and Maha Mogalana. Greatly excited, Cunningham and Maisey now widened their excavations to include the other four sites in the Bhilsa area. Within days a dig at one of the stupas at Satdhara, six miles west of Sanchi, had also produced a pair of almost identical relic chambers and reliquaries, again bearing the names Sariputa and Maha Mogalana, confirming the importance of the area as a centre of Buddhist faith at the time of Ashoka or his immediate heirs.

Further shafts produced more relics and more names of significance. At Sanchi and also at Andher, some nine miles to the south-east, were found relics of Mogaliputra, whom Cunningham described in his report to the RAS as 'the high priest of the Buddhist religion, who conducted the proceedings of the third convocation or religious synod, which was held in 247 BC'. Other names recovered included those of Majhima and Kasapa, identified by Cunningham from a reference in the *Mahavamsa* as missionaries sent into the Himalayan regions. The relics and names of a further ten Buddhist saints were also recovered. 'These discoveries', wrote Cunningham, 'appear to me to be of the greatest importance for the illustration of the early history of India, for they authenticate in the fullest manner the narrative of the most interesting portions of Asoka's reign.' He concluded (correctly) that Sanchi could be identified as the place, named Chetiyagiri in the *Mahavamsa*, where Ashoka had built a monastery for his son Maheinda, the apostle of Buddhism to Ceylon.

Cunningham lost no time in presenting a paper on what is now regarded as the first 'modern' archaeological dig in India (although Marshall and others who went over the same ground in later years were highly critical of Cunningham's early obsession with finding relics, and of his crude methods) to a meeting of the Asiatic Society of Bengal. He had a lot riding on it, so he was understandably furious when his conclusions, as set out in a subsequent article in the *JASB*, were challenged by the man whose opinion counted above all others, Professor H. H. Wilson. On the basis of a reference in the *Mahavamsa* to Mogaliputra presiding over a Buddhist council in Ashoka's time, coupled with the evidence of the Ashoka Brahmi lettering used in the inscriptions, Cunningham had dated the building of the Great Tope to the third century BCE and assigned a later date, the first century CE, for the erection of its four gateways. Wilson dismissed these dates as much too early, taking his cue from Fergusson but also citing the *Mahavamsa*, which seemed to suggest that no topes had been erected before the middle of the second century BCE.

Cunningham was scathing in his reply: 'So . . . in the opinion of one of the most eminent Sanskrit scholars, a tradition is of greater historical value than a self-evident fact, the truth of which has been admitted by every one except Wilson himself . . . The professor has entirely lost sight of the one great fact on which I relied, that the inscriptions on the caskets are engraved in characters of Asoka's age. On this fact alone I argued that the stupas which contained these relic caskets must be as old as the reign of Asoka.' Cunningham was right – the original brick core of the Great Stupa at Sanchi *was* built in Ashoka's time, although enlarged and embellished with carved stone when the gateways were erected, probably in the latter half of the first century BCE – but he had made Wilson look ridiculous, and Wilson was a powerful man with powerful friends.

The issue of the appointment of a new Archaeological Enquirer was now shelved – and Alexander Cunningham was posted away from Bhopal to Multan, where he stayed for three years. The move took him into new territory, but one equally rich in antiquities. A private dig at Mathura uncovered a Buddhist *vihara* that he was able to date to the Kushan ruler Huvishka, and this led to another public spat with Wilson, who dismissed Cunningham's contention that many of the satraps of the Scythians, who had preceded the Kushans, were followers of Buddhism. Soon afterwards Cunningham tried again to interest the Government of India in authorising 'the employment of a competent officer to open the numerous topes and . . . draw up a report on all the Buddhist remains' – adding, quite unnecessarily, that 'the discovery and publication of all the existing remains of architecture and sculpture, with coins and inscriptions, would throw more light on the ancient history of India, both public and domestic, than the printing of all the rubbish contained in the eighteen Puranas'. This last none-too-subtle jibe at Professor Wilson, whose great work on the *Puranas* had just been completed, did nothing to advance Cunningham's cause.

In 1856 Cunningham was promoted colonel and posted to the EICo's newest province, Burma, acquired as part of the outcome of the Second Anglo-Burmese War of 1852 – a shoddy episode of bullying on the part of a British naval commander that led to the swift capitulation of the Court of Ava and the loss of the remainder of its coastal belt, extending some four hundred miles up the Irrawaddy. Cunningham spent two years there as chief engineer, setting up a public works department, and so missed the horrors of the Sepoy Mutiny of 1857 that convulsed northern India and ended Company Rule. In November 1858, the same month in which the first Viceroy, Lord Canning, proclaimed Crown rule and the division of the subcontinent into British India and Native or Princely India, Cunningham took up the post of chief engineer of the North-Western Provinces and Oude (which later became the United Provinces and, now, Uttar Pradesh), based in Allahabad.

12

Cunningham and the
Archaeological Survey

ALEXANDER CUNNINGHAM returned to an India acutely fragmented by the events of 1857 and ruled by a Viceroy seriously
out of step with the public mood in Britain, which was concerned less with addressing the grievances of the native population
than with exacting vengeance for the outrages perpetrated. Lord
Canning, however, kept his nerve and embarked on a policy of reconciliation that went a long way towards healing wounds, although
relations were never restored to the more or less cordial level of pre-
Mutiny days. He was cold and withdrawn to the point of arrogance, but Charles Canning was a statesman and, moreover, cousin
of Stratford Canning, British ambassador in Constantinople, antiquarian and sponsor of Henry Layard's hugely successful excavations in Nimrud and Nineveh in Mesopotamia between 1845 and
1851. Layard's *Nineveh and its Remains*, published in 1849, was the
world's first archaeological best-seller and helped to stimulate
public interest in ancient civilisations. When Cunningham wrote
to him expressing regret at the Government's neglect of India's
antiquities, Canning listened. Hitherto, explained Cunningham,
the EICo had been 'occupied with the extension and consolidation
of empire', but now that the British Crown had replaced the EICo
as the governing power there was an opportunity to make up for
this neglect, beginning with 'a complete and systematic archeolog-
ical investigation of all the existing monuments of ancient India'.

On 30 June 1861 Cunningham retired from the Army with the

rank of major-general, having completed twenty-eight years of unbroken service. But he remained in India, and five months later took up a new appointment as Archaeological Surveyor to the Government of India, charged by Lord Canning with making 'an accurate description of such remains as most deserve notice, with a history of them so far as it may be traceable . . . investigating and placing on record, for the instruction of future generations, any particulars that might be rescued from oblivion, and throwing light upon the early history of England's great dependency'. There was no opposition from England: Cunningham's old nemesis Dr H. H. Wilson had died in office in May 1860, aged seventy-four.

In the West, attitudes towards Buddhism had been transformed since the publication of Eugène Burnouf's *Introduction to the History of Indian Buddhism* in 1844. Within the space of two decades it had emerged from the shadow of a multiplicity of Hindu gods to become an independent philosophy perceived, as the Frenchman Felix Nève put it in 1853, as 'the only moral adversary that western civilisation will find in the Orient'. Arthur Schopenhauer's new vision of compassion as the basis of morality and of the breaking-down of the barriers 'between the ego and the non-ego' suddenly found an audience diverse enough to embrace his countryman Richard Wagner, who for years tried unsuccessfully to compose a work on 'that human being delivered from all his desires, the Buddha himself', and the American essayist Henry Thoreau, whose *Walden* was written in 1854. Indian studies might have been in a state of semi-paralysis in Britain and India, but great strides were being made on the Continent. In Bonn the Norwegian Orientalist Christian Lassen brought out his four-volume *Indische Alterthumskunde* between 1847 and 1861. In 1855 the Dane Viggo Faustball published his translation from the Pali of the *Dharmapada*, a collection of the sayings of Gautama Buddha, which despite first appearing in Latin helped to make his teachings accessible to the ordinary man and woman. Faustball's monumental edition of the *Jataka* morality tales followed some years later.

This same period saw a vital infusion of energy and modern method, with the arrival at Oxford of a brilliant young German scholar named Friedrich Max Müller, an infant prodigy who had known Goethe, discussed philosophy with Schopenhauer, obtained his doctorate in philology with a translation of the Sanskrit classic *Hitopadesa* at the age of twenty, and discovered the 'new world' of the Vedas under Burnouf in Paris. At twenty-two he had decided to translate the collection of early Vedic hymns known as the *Rig-Veda* and moved to London and Oxford to gain access to all the necessary documents – only to find that Professor Wilson was working, exceedingly slowly, on the same material. Max Müller had fallen into line, contenting himself with assisting Wilson as his editor and making Oxford his home. His loyalty won him the curatorship of the Bodleian in 1856.

A year later Max Müller published an article, 'Buddhism and Buddhist Pilgrims', which sparked a controversy about the nature of the Buddhist Nirvana that rumbled on for years. He took the view that it meant 'utter annihilation' and, as such, represented a philosophy of nihilism that Buddha's followers had been unable either to comprehend or accept:

> All this self-sacrificing charity, all this self-sacrificing humility, by which the life of Buddha was distinguished throughout, and which he preached to the multitudes that came to listen to him, had but one object, and that object was final annihilation. It is impossible almost to believe it, and yet when we turn away our eyes from the pleasing picture of that high morality which Buddha preached for the first time to all classes of men, and look into the dark pages of his code of religious metaphysics, we find no other explanation. Fortunately, the millions who embraced the doctrines of Buddhism, and were saved by it from the depths of barbarism, brutality, and selfishness, were unable to fathom the meaning of his metaphysical doctrines. With them the Nirvana to which they aspired became only a relative deliverance from the miseries of human life; nay, it took on the bright colours of a Paradise, to be regained by the pious worshipper of Buddha.

This 'gospel of negation' remained largely unchallenged for a quarter of a century, and proved a source of great comfort to those Christian theologians who took up the struggle against what they perceived to be the growing moral threat of Buddhism.

To Alexander Cunningham, however, the one advance that really mattered during the 1850s was the publication in Paris of Stanislas Julien's translation of Huan Tsang's travels, *Voyages des Pèlerins Bouddhistes*, which appeared in two volumes in 1853 and 1857. This was much more than a repetition, two centuries on, of Fa Hian's journey: Huan Tsang was a more learned scholar, he spent longer in India, and he provided more detail.

Recent critics of Cunningham have attacked his apparent obsession with Buddhist sites, seeing it as part of a growing antipathy among the British in India towards Brahmin culture that was accompanied by an increasingly sympathetic attitude towards Buddhism. It would be more accurate to see his stance as one among several adopted by the ever more fragmented Orientalist movement. There were those who regarded Moslem culture as more manly than the decadent indigenous cultures of the subcontinent; others took the Jonesian view that Hindu Brahminical civilisation, as evidenced by the literature from the golden age of the Guptas, was supreme; while a third group, grown much bolder since the translation of the Ashokan edicts, saw Buddhism as the Protestantism of the subcontinent – a reforming movement that had grown up as a reaction against Brahminism, only to be defeated by Brahminism's subsequent counter-reformation. This last view undoubtedly found support among the Anglican British, since Buddhism was extinct in India and therefore presented no threat. In Cunningham's case, however, his appetite for exploring Buddhist sites had developed long before the Mutiny.

Less than a month after his appointment Alexander Cunningham began the first of his Cold Weather tours, establishing a pattern of surveying and excavating for five months of the year and then writing up his reports during the remaining seven months. Appropriately enough, he started at Bodh-Gaya, about which Huan Tsang had written in great detail. 'He describes minutely all the temples and statues which surrounded the celebrated Pipal tree,' wrote Cunningham in the first of his reports. 'Several of the objects enumerated by the Chinese pilgrim I have been able to identify from their exact correspondence with his description.' Much of Huan Tsang's text was taken up with tales of divine apparitions and miraculous happenings, but it also provided valuable information on the changes of fortune that the site had undergone between the building of the first Buddhist shrine and his own visit in the year 637 CE. Those intervening years had included at least one period of anti-Buddhist iconoclasm, led by a Hindu king of Bengal named Sasanka whose attacks on Buddhist sites in Bihar had taken place only a generation before Huan Tsang's visit and involved the destruction of the stone colonnade that had surrounded the Mahabodhi temple and the uprooting of Bodh-Gaya's most potent symbol, the Bodhi tree:

> Recently King Sasanka of the kingdom of Karnasuvara cut the tree, dug it up to the water springs but still he could not destroy the bottom of the roots. He then burnt and sprinkled the juice of sugar-cane on it wishing to destroy the bottom of the root completely. A few months afterwards King Pu-la-na-fa-mo [Purnavarma] who was said to be a descendant of King Asoka, on hearing that the tree had been cut, cast his body on the ground, invited the monks and for seven days made offerings to the tree and poured the milk of several thousand cows in the large pit. When he had done it for six days and nights the tree grew a little more than 10 feet. Fearing that it might be cut again afterwards, he surrounded it with a stone wall 24 feet high.

The malevolent King Sasanka died a painful death from sores and rotting flesh and was succeeded by King Purnavarma, who restored the site, setting up a new railing and replacing the stone slab known as the Diamond Throne that the Buddha was said to have meditated upon. But the tree's recovery was, of course, a pious fiction; as the *Mahavamsa* makes clear, the destroyed Bo-tree was actually replaced by a cutting taken from the pipal tree growing in Anuradhapura which had been planted centuries earlier by Ashoka's daughter, Sanghamitta. It was also apparent to Cunningham that some time before Huan Tsang's visit the site had been inundated by a flood and buried several feet deep under sand.

From Bodh-Gaya Cunningham moved on to Rajgir, where he lost no time in dismissing Kittoe's identification of the Sone Bhandar cave as the famous Saptaparni Hall, the scene of the First Buddhist Council. It was far too small to have held even fifty

Arhats, let alone five hundred. He thought it much more likely that this was the Pippala cave, where Buddha had come to eat his daily meal at midday and to meditate. The next point of call was the village of Burgaon, just a few miles to the north. Armed with Huan Tsang's directions – seven *yojanas* (or forty-nine miles) from the pipal tree at Bodh-Gaya and about thirty *li* (seven miles) from the new city of Rajagriha – and knowing exactly what Dr Buchanan and Captain Kittoe had already seen on the ground, he had no difficulty identifying the location of what had once been the powerhouse of Mahayana Buddhism: 'The remains of Baragaon consist of numerous masses of brick ruins, amongst which the most conspicuous is a row of lofty conical mounds running north and south. These high mounds are the remains of gigantic temples attached to the famous monastery of Nalanda.'

The quadrangles of the great monastic university itself could be readily traced in a number of square patches of cultivation amid a mass of brick ruins covering an area of some 1,600 feet by 400 feet: 'These open spaces show the positions of the courtyards of the six smaller monasteries which are described by Huan Tsang as being situated within one enclosure forming altogether eight courts. Five of the six monasteries were built by five consecutive princes of the same family, and the sixth by their successor who is called King of Central India. No dates are given but from the total silence of Fa Hian regarding any of the magnificent buildings at Nalanda . . . I infer that they were built after AD 410.' This was bang-on: a subsequent visit and excavation provided physical confirmation in the form of a seal of red clay bearing the stamped inscription '*Nalanada Mahavihara Arya Bhikshu Sanghasya*' – 'Venerable Community of Monks of the Great Vihara of Honoured Nalanda.' As Cunningham had surmised, this famous centre of learning at the birthplace of Buddha's beloved disciple Sariputra had come into being under the patronage of King Kumara-Gupta just a decade or two after Fa Hian's visit to India, and had continued to flourish throughout the era of the Guptas and after. In fact, Huan Tsang had himself spent five years studying here, as had generations of scholars from both India and abroad. 'In the establishment,' Huan Tsang had written, with the familiarity of a privileged alumnus, were some thousands of brethren, all men of great ability and learning, several hundred being highly esteemed and famous; the brethren were very strict in observing the precepts and regulations of their order; they were looked up to as models by all India . . . Of those from abroad who wished to enter the schools of discussion the majority, beaten by the difficulties of the problems, withdrew; and only those who were deeply versed in old and modern learning were admitted, only two or three out of ten succeeding.

It was from Nalanda that many of the esoteric teachings of tantric Buddhism had been carried to western Tibet at the end of the tenth century, leading to the diffusion of Vajrayana Buddhism throughout that country and from thence into Mongolia.

This first tour of Cunningham's produced three more Huan Tsang-related identifications. The most dramatic was the location of the ancient city of Kausambi, mentioned in the *Mahabharata* and the *Puranas*. A cross-referencing of Fa Hian's and Huan Tsang's accounts led Cunningham to the village of Kusam, beside the Jumna river some thirty-five miles upstream of Allahabad. 'My previous enquiries', wrote the General, 'had led me to expect only a ruined mound some 20 or 30 feet in height covered with broken bricks. What was my surprise, therefore, when still some distance from the place on the north-east side, to behold, extending for about 2 miles a long line of lofty earthen mounds as high as most of the trees.' These were the ramparts of the ancient city, a four-mile circuit broken by six depressions that marked the city's former gates. Among the ruins of the city itself he identified the railings of a Buddhist stupa, the inscribed pedestal of a Buddhist statue, and a polished Ashokan column.

The two other identifications were less satisfying, because they merely confirmed those already made by Dr Wilson in Oxford. One, Vaisali, capital city of the Lichchavis, where Gautama Buddha had halted on his journey towards the hills to deliver his last sermon, Wilson had identified as the village of Basarh, thirty miles north of Patna, where Brian Hodgson had found the Ashokan pillar surmounted by a lion and where James Prinsep's correspondent, Mr Stephenson, had found the Buddhist statue with its *Ye dharma* invocation. Huan Tsang had spoken of a city surrounded by a wall and a Buddhist monastery five *li* to its north-west at the place where the Buddha had delivered his sermon. But Vaisali was also associated with a legend told in the *Jatakas* of an earlier incarnation of the Buddha being fed with honey by monkeys. This was commemorated, according to Huan Tsang, by a pond known as the Monkey Tank 'to the south of a stone pillar about 50 feet high surmounted by a lion, at an Asoka tope, to the north-west of the relic tope.' Cunningham had no difficulty matching Huan Tsang's account with what he found on the ground: 'The correspondence between the several objects so minutely detailed by Huan Tsang and the existing remains is complete.' Cunningham's identification was subsequently challenged, but confirmed in 1903 by the discovery here of Gupta seals bearing the name Vaisali.

The final verification of Cunningham's first season was far less conclusive: the scene of Gautama Buddha's death and *parinirvana*, Kushinagar. To get there, Huan Tsang had travelled from Vaisali 'north-west through a great forest, the road being a narrow dangerous path, with wild oxen and wild elephants, and robbers and hunters always in wait to kill travellers, and emerging from the forest he reached the city of Kou-shih-na-ka-lo [Kushinagar]. The city walls were in ruins, and the towns and villages were deserted.' The spot where the Buddha had made his 'ultimate extinguishing' was in a grove of *sal* trees 'three or four *li* to the north-west of the capital, on the other side of the Ajitavati river, and not far from the west bank of the river'. A temple containing a giant image of the recumbent Buddha had been built here and beside it 'a tope, built by Asoka, which though in ruins was still above 200 feet high. In front of the tope was a stone pillar on which were recorded the circumstances of the Buddha's decease.'

Taking his cue from a reference made by Dr Buchanan to a large mound and associated ruins, Dr Wilson had placed Kushinagar at Kasia, an isolated village some thirty-five miles east of the town of Gorakhpur in north-eastern Bihar. Cunningham tentatively went along with this view, while noting that it would only be confirmed when Dr Buchanan's 'extensive mass of ruin' was excavated.

A photograph taken during the following summer at the lakeside retreat of Naini Tal in the foothills of Kumaon shows the

General, aged forty-eight, seated among a group of younger Royal Engineer officers. Bald of pate and decidedly stout about the waist, he wears a moustache and goatee that give him a decidedly Yankee air (see Plate 20).

Cunningham's second survey took him away to the area of the Gangetic plain between Delhi and Oude, where he secured two more Buddhist plums by tracking down the ancient city of Sravasti, capital of Kosala, which had played host to Gautama Buddha and his community every rainy season for twenty-five years, and the associated monastery of Jetavana, which in Huan Tsang's time had boasted a magnificent seven-storeyed pagoda. Here his excavations uncovered an exceptionally magnificent statue, known today as the *Bala Bodhisattva*:

A third mound near the north end of the central line of the enclosure gave promise of a better result than the others, as a previous excavation had disclosed the head and shoulders of a colossal figure, which from its curly hair and long split ears I knew to be that of Buddha . . . After a few hours' work the four walls of the temple were brought to light, and the figure was seen to be leaning against the back wall . . . As the excavation proceeded it was seen that the statue was a standing figure which had broken off a few inches above the ankles by the fall of the temple.

The pedestal of the statue bore an inscription which identified the site conclusively as Sravasti. Taking advantage of the extensive railway system that was fast spreading deep into the North-Western Provinces from Bengal, Cunningham brought the statue down to Calcutta and presented it to the Asiatic Society of Bengal's Museum – an action he later had cause to regret, for when he visited the museum ten years later he found it 'placed in the midst of a herd of stuffed deer and antelopes, which completely hid its inscribed pedestal from view . . . But perhaps the Naturalists, who then monopolised the direction of the Museum, may have considered this arrangement a highly appropriate compliment to Buddha, who in several previous births had been a "King of Deer".'

15. (*left*) Brian Houghton Hodgson in his political officer's uniform, aged seventy-two: an oil painting by Louisa Starr-Canziani exhibited in 1872

16. (*above*) 'The Great Chaitya of Swayambu Nath in Nepal with part of the Vihar': a pencil drawing by Hodgson's draughtsman Man Singh, undated but signed in Devanagari script 'Raj Man Singh, Nepal'

17. (*below*) 'Buddhist temple called Kash Chait': the Bodnath stupa in Kathmandu Valley, with Tibetan traders and their pack-sheep gathered at its foot, from a watercolour drawn in about 1856 by Dr Henry Oldfield, surgeon at the British Residency from 1850 to 1868

18. The exterior of Chaitya Cave 19 at Ajanta, drawn by James Fergusson with the aid of his *camera lucida* during his travels in central India in the late 1830s

19. Section of wall painting from Ajanta drawn in April 1866 by Edward and Arthur West, two of four brothers who worked on the railways of Western India between 1844 and 1875 but spent much of their free time mapping and drawing the rock-cut temples of the region

20. General Alexander Cunningham (centre, balding, with beard) and fellow Sappers on leave in Naini Tal in October 1862 prior to starting his second archaeological season

21. (*below*) The first 'modern' archaeological dig: Lieutenant Frederick Maisey's plan of the excavation of Stupa No. 3 at Sanchi in 1852, where relics of two disciples of Buddha were first recovered

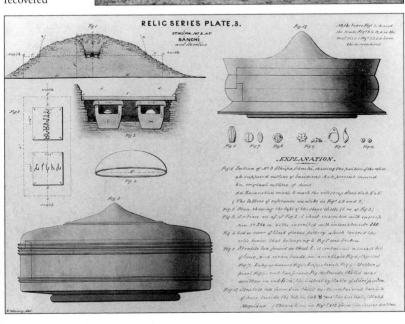

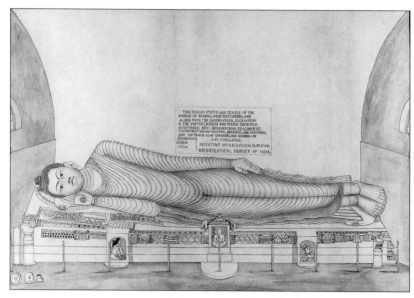

22. (*above*) The Mahaparinirvana or Great Final Extinguishing: a pen-and-ink drawing by Ramnarayan Bhaggat, draughtsman, of the reclining Buddha at Kushinagar (modern-day Kasia), discovered and restored by Cunningham's assistant A. G. Carlleyle in March 1877

23. (*below*) The Mahabodhi temple at Bodh-Gaya, showing its dilapidated condition prior to the restorations undertaken first by the Burmese and then by the Archaeological Survey of India: photographed by Thomas Peppé in 1870

Three Western pioneers in the revival of Buddhism: 24. (*above, left*) Sir Edwin Arnold, Editor of the *Daily Telegraph* and author of *The Light of Asia;* 25. (*above, right*) Madame Blavatsky and Colonel Henry Olcott, co-founders of the Theosophical Society; 26. (*below*) Henry Olcott with Sinhalese monks at Malikanda Temple, Colombo, *c.* 1890

27. Part of the ruins of Mihintale, where Buddhism was first preached in Ceylon: photographed before its clearance by Joseph Lawton in 1870–1. The Etvihara Dagoba (in the background) was built to enshrine a single hair of the Buddha

28. The base of the pillar found at Nigliva, with the all-important Ashokan inscription at its base: photographed by Dr Führer, from his *Monograph on Buddha Sakyamuni's Birthplace in the Nepalese Tarai*, 1897

29. William Peppé shows Dr Führer his excavation of the stupa at Piprahwa, just south of the border with Nepal, in January 1897

30. The five caskets recovered from the Piprahwa stupa, one inscribed to reveal that it contained the ashes of Sakyamuni Gautama interred by the Sakya clan

31. The Ashokan lion capital that now forms the national symbol of the Republic of India, with the base of the column in the foreground: recovered during F. O. Oertel's excavations at Sarnath in the Cold Weather season of 1904–5

The following Cold Weather Cunningham took his men north to the Punjab, locating sites and beginning excavations at the ancient Gandharan cities of Taxila and Sagala. Then, as he prepared to return to the North-Western Provinces to begin a series of more thorough excavations, he learned that his department had became the victim of a round of cost-saving cuts initiated by the new Viceroy, Lord Lawrence. The Archaeological Survey of India was abolished in 'a cold fit of parsimony', and the Cunninghams had no option but to return to England.

The General spent the next four years writing a history of Buddhist India that drew heavily on the evidence of the Chinese travellers and his own archaeological field-work. His intention was to follow this first volume with a history of the Muslim period – but thanks to James Fergusson and some of Cunningham's supporters in England, this second volume was never written.

Fergusson was now a world-renowned authority on the history of architecture, with an impressive list of books to his name. In 1867 he published the first three volumes of his master work, *A History of Architecture in all Countries from the Earliest Times to the Present Day*. Early in that same year he was asked to arrange an exhibition of photographs and plaster casts of Indian sculptures for the Indian Court at the International Exhibition to be held in Paris. He was particularly anxious to include some sculptures believed to have been recovered from the site of Amaravati by Colin Mackenzie in 1817, and his enquiries after their whereabouts led him to a disused coach-house in Hayes Wharf that had once belonged to the EICo. Here, to his astonishment, he discovered not only Mackenzie's sculptures but additional bas-reliefs that had lain abandoned for more than a decade. These had originally been dug up at Amaravati in 1845 by the local Collector, Walter Eliot, and sent down to Madras, where they had been stored out in the open for sixteen years before being shipped to England and the EICo's India House. But the Mutiny intervened, the EICo was wound up, and the stone was simply dumped in the coach-house.

Fergusson now had access to Colonel Mackenzie's original papers and drawings from 1817, and with them and the 160 newly-recovered pieces of stone was able to work out what the original Amaravati stupa had looked like in the days of its glory – greatly assisted by the fact that many of the carved decorations that had once covered the stupa and its surrounding railings themselves carried representations of the stupa. Although similar in general form to the Great Tope at Sanchi, the Amaravati stupa was more evolved. It was twice as large, three times as high, and far more ornate. There were no gateways to match the four magnificent carved entrances at Sanchi, but this was more than made up for by the stonework of the surrounding colonnades (today displayed in the British Museum's magnificent Asahi Shimbun Gallery).

The *Mahavamsa* had described a 'temple of the sands' on the Coromandel coast that briefly housed the Sacred Tooth and other relics of Buddha when they were recovered from a ship that had beached on the nearby coast on its way to Ceylon. Fergusson concluded that this must be it: 'The outer rails, at least, are part of the Temple of the Sands, which, according to the Ceylonese computation, was commenced in the year 322. Judging from its elaboration, it may have taken fifty years to complete. If this be so the date of the completion may be about the year 370 or 380 of our era.'

Fergusson, now seriously out of his depth, gave a lecture at the Royal Asiatic Society entitled 'Tree and Serpent Worship'. As at the Great Tope at Sanchi, the sculptures at Amaravati seemed to be largely devoid of images of the Buddha – and it was this that led Fergusson astray. He noted how depictions of the *chakra* or spoked wheel almost invariably showed it surrounded by worshippers bowing before it, and correctly interpreted it as the symbol of the Dharma (see opposite). But there were just as many depictions of trees being worshipped, to say nothing of many-headed snakes and other articles besides –

> Objects like cushions, which are frequently represented as placed on a throne, and always as objects of worship . . . and below the throne in which these objects are placed are impressions of Buddha's feet . . . both here and at Sanchi, they seem always to have been objects of special adoration and reverence . . . Another peculiarity of these sculptures . . . is the continual presence of a horse – not as a beast of burden but as an animal to be reverenced if not worshipped. Sometimes he is represented as issuing from a portal with an umbrella of state borne over his

head; at others he occupies a place of honour in front of the Dagoba . . . The first impression is that this may have reference to some *Aswamedha* or horse-sacrifice . . . but on the whole, it seems more probable that it is a remnant of the Scythic faith of this people before they migrated into India.

He concluded that the great tope of Amaravati, far from being devoted to the Buddha, was primarily the centre of a snake-worshipping cult.

Cunningham could have made mince-meat of Fergusson, but the heavy sarcasm that is a feature of his early reports was noticeably absent when he responded to Fergusson's claims. 'I can perceive no snake worship in these illustrations,' he declared mildly. 'On the contrary, I find that the Nagas are generally doing homage to Buddha, in perfect accordance with the Buddhist legends.' The Nagas were the snake gods of eastern India, who had been converted by a previous incarnation of Buddha and thereafter gave him their support. They were to be found all over the Amaravati stupa, always depicted standing on their tails and with their many hoods extended – to shelter the unseen presence of the Buddha from sun and rain. As to tree-worship, this was no ordinary tree, but the Bodhi-tree under which Gautama had achieved his Buddha-hood. The early Buddhist concept of the emblematic image that symbolised but did not embody the Buddha had still to be fully understood, but Cunningham had at least made a start. He also contested Fergusson's dating, which he said was out by a couple of centuries – and he was right. The general consensus today is that this undertaking of almost unparalleled artistry and beauty must have been built during the second century CE, just as depictions of the corporeal body of Gautama Buddha were first starting to appear in north India – and indeed, among the few precious surviving Amaravati sculptures are a handful of scenes showing Gautama Buddha in human form.

Cunningham had good reason for letting Fergusson off so lightly: he had become an important ally. In 1870, as a result of representations made to the Secretary of State for India by Fergusson and others, the Archaeological Survey of India was revived and Alexander Cunningham reappointed, with the rather grander title of Director-General. Cunningham was now fifty-six, and he decided he needed some assistants. His budget would not run to qualified Europeans so he appointed two local men with engineering skills, J. D. Beglar and Archibald Carlleyle, of whom little is known other than that Beglar was a Eurasian and Carlleyle a geologist who had originally gone out to India to tutor an Indian prince. As the General grew older and less mobile, they and others increasingly took on more field-work on his behalf.

It was in Bihar again that Cunningham began the first of a new round of archaeological surveys in the Cold Weather months of 1871–2, though the emphasis now was on examining sites as a whole, not simply on driving shafts into the most promising mounds. His 'old friend' Fergusson, as he now called him, had led the way in the 1860s, setting up the Palestine Exploration Fund, which was now conducting excavations in and around Jerusalem following the most modern principles, taking some account of layers of occupation, and using lesser artefacts such as shards of pottery for dating purposes.

Cunningham returned to Burgaon village, the site of Nalanda, only to find to his great irritation that the Assistant Magistrate and Collector of Patna, Mr A. M. Broadley, had just beaten him to it and was employing a huge workforce of local labour to remove the tons of earth covering the largest of the stupas. Mr Broadley was entirely unabashed, justifying his excavation on the grounds that others with less altruistic motives would be doing it if he were not:

Burgaon has been the brick quarry of Bihar for centuries, hence it is that the walls, gates, and houses have disappeared, while the massive tumuli are as yet untouched. To give an idea of the enormous number of bricks taken from the place, I may mention that the zemindar of the village has built two large houses with them, one three storeys high; the principal *ryots* [agriculturalists] of the village have brick houses, more substantial and spacious than those of the landlords of other places; and I trace these large and massive bricks in the modern Jain temple of Burgaon, in the wall which surrounds its garden, and in the mosque and merchants' houses of Silhao. These depredations have not been confined to the bricks; the exquisitely carved lintels and pillars have disappeared to ornament Mahomedan tombs and shrines, and one door of extraordinary beauty now forms the entrance to the *durgah* of Shah Ahmed Charamposh at Bihar [Behar town]. For these reasons I had little hope of success when I began on the 15th October, with the aid of 1000 labourers, to excavate the great central tumulus.

With his army of workers Broadley made fast progress, and within ten days had uncovered a Buddhist *vihara* with an eighty-foot-square pyramid-shaped structure at its heart that rose in a series of terraces each some fourteen feet high. 'The first two terraces of the building are now almost as perfect as when Hoien Thsang saw them fourteen hundred years ago,' he wrote in his description of what was undoubtedly the finest and most complete set of monastic buildings yet uncovered in India:

On the western side of the court was the great entrance door, which was uncovered by me perfect, but was thrown down in my absence by the workmen who imagined I wished to remove the whole edifice. This doorway was of extraordinary beauty, and measured twenty feet across and more than twelve feet high. . . . Beyond this, one enters by another door an inner chamber twenty-two feet square, the walls of which are in their ruined state still fourteen feet high. This was doubtless the *sanctum sanctorum* of the building, and I discovered at its western end a headless Buddha four feet high, placed on a handsome *singhasan* or [lion-]throne of black basalt, divided into five compartments; the first on each side containing single figures, the next lions couchant, and the centre one two devotees in the act of making an offering.

To Cunningham's indignation, Broadley rounded off his dig by re-erecting and embellishing one of the pillars he had uncovered. Cunningham's rebuke was public and brutal: 'Mr Broadley has omitted to mention two facts [in his report], which, I believe, may be ascribed partly to his ignorance and partly to his modesty. To the first I should attribute his having fixed the pillar with its brick pedestal *upside down*, in spite of the two Gupta inscriptions, with their *matras*, or head lines, quite distinct. To the second I would ascribe his neglecting to mention that in his anxiety to leave evidence of his own rule in Bihar, he had the whole of the uninscribed surface of the pillar covered with rudely-cut inscriptions, in which his name figures twice.'

After the setback at Nalanda, Cunningham badly needed a spectacular success to show the worth of his revived department: he found it close at hand, at Rajgir. On his first visit ten years earlier he had dismissed Markham Kittoe's claim to have found the site of Saptaparni Hall in the rock-hewn cave at the foot of the south side of the Vaibhara Hill known as Sone Bhandhar, declaring it to be Buddha's Pippala cave. Now he decided he had been wrong and Kittoe right after all. He had overlooked what Kittoe himself had pointed out in his original report – a line of holes along the front wall of the cave which showed that the cave had at one time been extended by a porch.

But if this was the Saptaparni Hall, where then was the Pippala cave? Both Chinese pilgrims had provided a location. Huan Tsang had written: 'To the west of the north gate of the mountain city was the Pi-po-lo mountain . . . To the west of the hot springs was the Pi-po-lo Cave in which the Buddha often lodged.' Rajgir's hot springs were (and still are) a well-known place of pilgrimage for Hindus, located at the eastern foot of the Vaibhara Hill at a point where a gap in the ring of hills links new Rajgir with ancient Rajgir to the south and forms the old city's north entrance or gateway. It followed that the modern Vaibhara Hill must be Huan

Tsang's Pippala Hill or Hill of the Pipal Tree. Fa Hian's account was even more specific: 'As they kept along the mountain on the south, and went west for three hundred paces, they found a dwelling among the rocks, named the Pippala cave, in which the Buddha regularly sat in meditation after taking his meal. Going on still to the west for five or six *li*, on the north of the hill, in the shade, they found the cavern called Sraptaparna, the place where after the nirvana of Buddha, 500 Arhats collected the Sutras.'

Alexander Cunningham's account of how he located the Pippala cave speaks for itself:

Two points in the description led me to the discovery of the cave I was in search of, which was quite unknown to the people. Close to the hot-springs, on the north-east slope of the Baibhara hill, there is a massive foundation of a stone house, eighty-five feet square, called *Jarasand-ki-baithak*, or 'Jarasandha's throne'. Now, as Jarasanda [a flesh-eating demoness in one of the *Jataka* tales] was an *Asura* [demon], it struck me that the cave should be looked for in the immediate vicinity of the stone foundation. I proceeded from the bed of the stream straight to the *baithak*, a distance of 289 paces, which agrees with the 300 paces noted by Fa Hian. Seated on the *baithak* itself, I looked around, but could see no trace of any cave; and neither the officiating Brahmans at the hot-springs, nor the people of the village, had ever heard of one. After a short time my eye caught a large mass of green immediately behind the stone basement. On pushing aside some of the branches with a stick I found they belonged to trees growing in a hole, and not mere surface brushwood. I then set men to cut down the trees and clear out the hollow. A flight of steps was first uncovered, then a portion of the roof, which was still unbroken; and before the evening we had partially cleared out a large cave, forty feet in length by thirty feet in width. This, then, was the Pippal, or Vaibhara cave of the Chinese pilgrims, in which Buddha had actually dwelt and taken his meals. The identification is fully confirmed by the relative position of the other cave, called Son-Bhandar, which corresponds exactly with the account given by Fa Hien. In a direct line the distance between the two caves is only 3000 feet, but to go from one to the other it is necessary to descend the hill again to the bed of the stream, and then to ascend the stream to the Son–Bhandar cave, which increases the distance to about 4500 feet, or rather more than 5 *li*. The Son–Bhandar cave was therefore beyond all doubt the famous Saptapani cave of the Buddhists, in which the first synod was held in 478 BC, three months after the death of Buddha.

Not all Cunningham's surveys and excavations were triumphs, however. His earlier success in finding the ancient city of Sravasti in 1863 had given him a lead in the search for two other important Buddhist sites, Kapilavastu, where Prince Siddhartha had been raised, and the garden of Lumbini nearby, where he had been born. To reach Kapilavastu from Sravasti, Fa Hian had first travelled twelve *yojanas* to the south-east to reach the town of Too-we (which Cunningham identified as the present village of Tadwa); he and his party had then travelled east for 'less than one *yojana*' to reach the city of Kapilavastu, which he found in ruins: 'Of inhabitants there were only some monks and a score or two of families of the common people. At the spot where stood the old palace of King Suddhodana [the father of Prince Siddhartha] there have been made images of the prince and his mother; and at the places where that son appeared mounted on a white elephant when he entered his mother's womb, and where he turned his carriage round on seeing the sick man after he had gone out of the city by the eastern gate, stupas have been erected.' From Kapilavastu, Fa Hian then went east for fifty *li* to reach the site of the garden of Lumbini, where Queen Maya first bathed in a pond and then 'laid hold of the branch of a tree, and, with her face to the east, gave birth to the heir-apparent'.

By Huan Tsang's time the country of Kapilavastu had become even more of a wilderness. He had approached directly from Sravasti, 'going south-east for above 500 *li*', until he came to the Kapilavastu country. Everything was now in ruins, but the 'solid brick foundations of the palace city within the royal city still remained and were above 15 *li* in circuit'. Huan Tsang also noted two stupas, one at the south gate of the city.

On the basis of this information, Cunningham first plumped

for a small village called Nagarkhas, some ninety miles to the south-west of Sravasti, as the site of Kapilavastu. At the start of the Hot Weather of 1875 he asked his assistant Archibald Carlleyle to take a small reconnaissance party out to the area while he and the rest of the team returned to the Survey's headquarters in Calcutta. Carlleyle had already excelled himself that season, conducting a dig at Kasia which provided dramatic confirmation of Cunningham's (and Wilson's) identification of this as the site of Buddha's *parinirvana*. 'After digging to the depth of about 10 feet,' he wrote in his official report, 'I came upon what appeared to be the upper part of the thigh of a colossal recumbent statue of stone, but which had apparently been repaired with plaster. I then hurried on the excavations, until I had uncovered the entire length of the recumbent statue of Buddha, lying in a ruined chamber which was about 30 feet in length by nearly 12 feet in breadth.' This discovery made it possible for Cunningham to declare that Mr Carlleyle had fixed the identification of Kushinagar 'beyond all doubt . . . It is quite certain that the statue is the same that was seen by the pilgrim [Huan Tsang], as there is an inscription on the pedestal of the mourning figure, beside the couch, of two lines in characters of the Gupta period.' (See Plate 22.)

Carlleyle eventually returned to headquarters with the news that he had found a much more promising site than Cunningham's for Kapilavastu, at a place called Bhuiladih, which name he had somehow convinced himself was a corruption of Kapilavastu. His nonsensical explanation of how he had worked this out went on for pages and appears to have exhausted his chief into submission: Cunningham gave Carlleyle's identification his blessing and left it at that – perhaps because his mind was now increasingly focused on the far more exciting Gandharan sites that were beginning to emerge in the upper Punjab. And, to be fair to Archibald Carlleyle, his mind too may have been focused elsewhere, for as a pioneer palaeontologist he has the distinction of being the first man to recognise a link between stone tools and microliths such as those he had been collecting and the hunting scenes he found painted on the walls of rock shelters at Morhana Pahar – this *before* the discovery of the first examples of prehistoric rock art in Europe, at Altamira in 1879.

The extent of Alexander Cunningham's accomplishments as Director and subsequently Director-General of the Archaeological Survey of India can best be judged by reading the twenty-four annual reports he wrote and presented, of which the first thirteen were very largely based on his personal discoveries. By far the greater part of his work has no direct bearing on this present book, but mention must be made of his discovery of the Bharhut stupa, at the head of the Mahiyar valley two hundred miles north-west of Sanchi, and the subsequent excavations undertaken there with his assistant Mr Beglar in 1874–5 and 1875–6. Cunningham's decision to remove the best of the carved pillars and gateways to Calcutta was condemned in a contemporary newspaper report as carrying 'a certain aroma of Vandalism', but he was quite happy to declare himself 'willing to accept the aroma since I have saved all the more important sculptures. Of those that were left behind every stone that was removable has since been "carted away" by the people for building purposes.'

One consequence of the Bharhut excavations was that Cunningham was approached by a Buddhist priest from Ceylon named Subhiti, who was able to explain many of the scenes represented in the carvings at Bharhut and Sanchi, most of which illustrated tales drawn from the *Jataka*. At the same time it became clear that both Sanchi and Bharhut were part of a network of pilgrimage trails that had at one time extended right across northern India connecting the many thousands of brick stupas built during the reign of King Ashoka.

If Cunningham had a weakness, it was his reluctance to conduct excavations at sites that seemed unlikely to provide spectacular finds; Patna and the origins of Pataliputra are a case in point. As early as 1811, Dr Buchanan had drawn attention to 'a very considerable heap' just south of the modern town 'which with some small eminences in the neighbourhood are called the five hills, and are attributed to the five sons of Pandu'. In 1844 Markham Kittoe had gone over these same five hills, known as the Panch Pahari or Five Brothers, and had stated his belief that these were the stupas and monasteries south of Pataliputra visited by Fa Hian and Huan Tsang. In the season of 1875–6 Cunningham had the opportunity to put Kittoe's theory to the test, but did little more than walk over the area. However, within weeks of his departure from Patna an officer of the PWD engaged in supervising the digging of a large tank or reservoir close to the railway line came across 'the remains of long brick-work running from north-west to south-east' at a depth of some fifteen to twenty feet beneath the swampy surface. The digging was continued and soon came up against a line of wooden palisades preserved in the wet ground. Those who had studied the subject were immediately put in mind of the great wooden palisade of Chandragupta's Pataliputra described by Megasthenes. Unaccountably, General Cunningham never returned to check this out.

Cunningham's reluctance to carry out restoration must also count against him. His excavations at the Mahabodhi temple at Bodh-Gaya, for example, left the newly cleared buildings exposed to the elements. In 1870 the professional photographer Thomas Peppé visited the site, and found it on the verge of collapse. Large masses of the eastern front of the temple were being brought down every rainy season, the porch in the front had 'nearly disappeared and only portions of the arch of its roof adhere to the side walls' (see Plate 23). The Calcutta newspaper *The Englishman* took up his complaints, which in turn led to an appeal from the King of Ava to be allowed to carry out repairs. In 1879 a large party of Burmese builders descended on the site and began an enthusiastic but inept rebuilding programme that did more damage than good, and finally provoked Cunningham to intervene. He inspected the work, and discovered to his dismay that the Burmese were demolishing the many small votive stupas that surrounded the main temple. He and his deputy J. D. M. Beglar then stepped in and began the extensive clearing and restoration that has given the Mahabodhi temple its present appearance. Their work revealed that the original structure had indeed been built at the time of Ashoka but had been replaced by a grander building at the time of Huvishka, one of the so-called Indo-Scythian (Kushan) kings, in the second century BCE.

Alexander Cunningham's accomplishments as a numismatist have barely been touched upon, but some of the best of the British Museum's collection of South and Central Asian coins come from his private collection, bought out of his own pocket. Many more would have been added had not the steamer carrying his baggage back to England on his final retirement in September 1885 foundered off the coast of Ceylon, with the loss of all his belongings, including all his Indian papers. The 'father of Indian archaeology' was appointed a Companion of the Order of the Star of India in 1871, but had to wait for the year of Queen Victoria's jubilee in 1887 for his knighthood. Cunningham was succeeded as Director-General by James Burgess, but after his retirement in 1889 no new appointments were made, so that the Archaeological Survey department he had worked so hard to establish fell into disarray and decline.

13

The Welshman, the Russian Spiritualist, the American Civil War Colonel and the Editor of the Daily Telegraph

IN 1864 a twenty-one-year-old Welshman named Thomas Williams Rhys Davids went out to Ceylon to join the Ceylon Civil Service. His background was unusual in two respects: he was the son of a Welsh Congregationalist Minister, and he had studied Sanskrit in Germany. In Ceylon, as in India, the Sepoy Mutiny had caused both a great deal of heart-searching and a stiffening of resolve, so that Rhys Davids joined a government committed to a policy of Anglicisation. All formal education on the island was now in the hands of Christian educators and only schools teaching the Bible received government funding. Since only those with government-recognised qualifications could get jobs in government, Buddhists were effectively barred from such employment.

As if these impositions were not enough, the Christian missions had also embarked on a campaign aimed at isolating a Buddhist clergy they regarded as self-serving and ignorant. In the same year as Rhys Davids' arrival in Colombo, the two main Christian denominations joined forces to challenge the Buddhist monks to debate the merits of their respective religions in public. These debates became ever more popular, culminating in 1873 in what

became known as the 'Great Debate of Panadura', a two-day dis-
putation at which the Buddhist *bhikkhu* Mohottivatte Gunananda
defended Buddhism to the acclaim of an audience of ten thousand
Sinhalese lay-people.

Intended to demonstrate the superiority of Christianity and to
drive a wedge between the Buddhist clergy and a seemingly in-
different lay community, these debates had the opposite effect.
Widely publicised, they led to a resurgence of interest in Buddhism
on the island, as well as initiating reforms. Two Buddhist secon-
dary schools and a college were founded between 1873 and 1875,
and a new sense of cultural identity began to take shape among the
Sinhalese. A young Buddhist monk named Naranwita Sumanasaru
Unnanse took it upon himself to start single-handedly clearing
the acres of jungle that had swallowed up the ancient city of
Anuradhapura, the capital of King Devanampiya Tissa at the
time of Ashoka, in the plains to the north of Kandy. Word of his
activities eventually reached the Governor, Sir William Gregory,
and led to the appointment of an Archaeological Commissioner and the setting-up of an Archaeological Department (see
Plate 27).

Rhys Davids, meanwhile, learned Sinhalese and Tamil, and
became a magistrate. In a case he was presiding over involving a
Buddhist temple, a Pali document was presented in evidence that
no one present could translate. Rhys Davids' interest was aroused,
and he sought out a monk who could teach him Pali, an old
bhikkhu named Yatramulle Unnanse of whom he later wrote:
'When he first came to me the hand of death was already upon
him. He was sinking into the grave from the effects of a painful
and incurable malady . . . There was a strange light in his eyes and
he was constantly turning away from questions of Pali to questions
of Buddhism . . . There was an indescribable attraction, a high-
mindedness that filled me with reverence.'

A year or two later Rhys Davids became locked in a dispute
over a legal matter with a superior officer. A higher ruling went
against him and as a matter of principle he resigned, returning
to Britain to study law – and taking with him the malaria that
periodically left him prostrate for the rest of his life. He became
increasingly drawn towards a more serious study of Pali, and the

interpretation of Buddhist texts. He looked at the efforts of such earlier Pali scholars as Turnour and concluded that Pali studies in the West needed to be organised, which led to his foundation in 1881 of the Pali Text Society, 'to render accessible to students the rich stores of the earliest Buddhist literature now lying unedited and practically unused in the various manuscripts scattered throughout the universities and public libraries in Europe'.

Rhys Davids was at this time greatly influenced by Max Müller's work at Oxford on comparative religions. Max Müller had been thought too radical to take over the Oxford Chair in Sanskrit – but a new Professorship of Comparative Philology had been created for him, which he held with great distinction until his death. Max Müller was first and foremost a Sanskritist, but in 1872 he gave Oxford's prestigious annual series of Hibbert Lectures, speaking on the subject of the origin and growth of religions. He presented a new interpretation of Buddhism, now arguing that the 'gospel of negation' associated with Buddhism was a later accretion brought on by 'monkish orthodoxy', and that nirvana did not represent a doctrine of utter annihilation. This marked the beginning of a more positive attitude towards Buddhism in the West, one that depended almost wholly on readings of Pali rather than Sanskrit sources, thus on the Theravada rather than the Mahayana tradition of Buddhism. In Britain the main vehicle for this new thinking was Rhys Davids' *Buddhism: being a Sketch of the Life and Teachings of Gautama, the Buddha*, published in 1877 under the unwitting auspices of the Society for Promoting Christian Knowledge.

T. W. Rhys Davids' text presented a vision of Buddhism in which the Pali canon was shown to be the original 'true' Buddhism, later corrupted by Mahayana accretions, rather as the early Christian teaching had been corrupted by Roman Catholicism: 'The development of Buddhist doctrine which has taken place in the Punjab [Gandhara], Nepal and Tibet is exceedingly interesting, and very valuable from the similarity it bears to the development which has taken place in Christianity in the Roman Catholic countries. It has resulted at last in the complete establishment of Lamaism, a religion not only in many points different from, but actually antagonistic to, the primitive system of Buddhism.'

Here was a rationalist explication that Protestant Britain – to say nothing of Protestant Germany and a large section of the United States of America – could understand and identify with. Furthermore, in presenting a scholarly but very human portrait of Gautama Buddha, philosopher and reformer, Rhys Davids was also instrumental in reshaping Western attitudes towards Buddhism in another, quite unexpected way – because it was his *Buddhism* that, with a little help from Max Müller's translation of the *Dhammapada*, provided the source material for Edwin Arnold's *The Light of Asia*. In announcing the formation of the Pali Text Society Rhys Davids had stated that 'the sacred books of the early Buddhists have preserved to us the sole record of the only religious movement in the world's history which bears any close resemblance to Christianity'. Arnold took the same view, calling Buddhism 'in certain aspects an Asiatic Christianity'. His epic poem, published in 1879, became the chief instrument by which Buddhism was brought into the Western mainstream. In the process, it also helped to Westernise Buddhism.

On the face of it, Edwin Arnold was as unlikely a candidate for the man who did most to promote Buddhism in the West in the nineteenth century as could well be imagined, for he was a stalwart of the *Daily Telegraph*, on whose staff he served for twenty-eight years, first as a feature writer and later as its chief editor (see Plate 24). During his sixteen years as the paper's editor, from 1873 to 1889, Arnold gave it a surprisingly radical edge which helped transform it from one of Fleet Street's lesser dailies into *The Times*'s only rival. But Arnold was also, in his own words, 'a witness for religious liberalism'. Before turning to journalism he had briefly worked in India as a teacher, going out in 1857 at the age of twenty-five with his wife and little boy to become the Principal of Deccan College in Poona. There he had learned the local language, Marathi, but also studied Persian and Sanskrit, the last well enough to come up with his own translation of the *Hitopadesa*. His interest in Buddhism was initially aroused by the exploits of General Cunningham and his search for Buddhism's lost sacred places, but it was Rhys Davids' *Buddhism* that provided both inspiration and source material for his poem, which was 'composed during spare moments, being jotted down on anything that was available and then transcribed later'. It is not easy to imagine a newspaper feature writer, let alone the editor of the *Daily Telegraph*, jotting down sections of a fifty-thousand-word blank-verse poem while commuting daily to and from Fleet Street – harder still to imagine a Fleet Street editor being appointed an Officer of the Order of the White Elephant, as Arnold was by the King of Siam in 1879 for 'having made a European Buddhist speak beautifully in the most widespread language of the world'.

The Light of Asia, or the Great Renunciation, Being the Life and Teachings of Gautama, Prince of India and Founder of Buddhism, as told in verse by an Indian Buddhist related the life story of 'that noble hero and reformer, Prince Gautama', whose doctrines were to be judged 'by their influence, not their interpreters, nor by that innocent but lazy and ceremonious church which has arisen on the foundations of the Buddhistic Brotherhood.' It was a work of great lyricism and sensibility, and a splendid example of high Victorian verse in the Tennysonian mode: but it also purveyed a distinctly Protestant vision of Buddhism, and this goes a long way towards explaining the quite astonishing popularity it enjoyed in Victorian households throughout the 1880s and 1890s. Several literary reviewers heralded it as a masterpiece, a reception which cannot have been entirely due to Arnold's status in Fleet Street. *The Spectator*'s reviewer called it 'the only poetic account in a European tongue of an Asiatic faith which is at all adequate', and thought it quite possible that its author might, in two hundred years, 'among the innumerable peoples who profess Buddhism be regarded as a psalmist'.

In the United States the book did even better in the wake of what can only be described as rave reviews from such leading literary eminences as Oliver Wendell Holmes, who thought it worthy to be mentioned in the same breath as the New Testament. More than eighty editions appeared, more than a dozen of them cheap and pirated – the ultimate literary accolade. A dramatisation on Broadway followed and, most curiously, an opera with an Italian libretto, performed in Paris in 1892 to a generous review from George Bernard Shaw.

The Light of Asia also had it critics. In the US its popularity became a source of real concern to some Christians, including Mr Samuel Kellogg, who wrote that 'many who would have been repelled by a formal, drily philosophical treatise upon Buddhism, have been attracted by the undoubted charm of Mr Arnold's verse'. Another troubled American was William Cleaver Wilkinson, whose denunciation entitled *Edwin Arnold as Poetizer and Paganizer* left readers in no doubt as to his position. But dissenting voices and fulminations from the pulpit failed to alter the continuing popularity of Arnold's poem, which helped create an essentially benign image of Buddhism, as exemplified by the Tibetan lama in Rudyard Kipling's novel *Kim*, a lama whose original pilgrimage in India – 'to see the Four Holy Places before I die' – somehow becomes a quest for the very un-Buddhist River of the Arrow. Kipling's old lama derives much spiritual satisfaction from seeing all the Buddhist statues and carvings collected in Lahore Museum, but Kipling also has him express the reformist view – nonsensical to any but fictional lamas – when he explains that he came to India because in his native Tibet 'the Old Law was not being followed; being overlaid, as thou knowest, with devildom, charms, and idolatry . . . and the later ritual with which we of the Reformed Law have cumbered ourselves – that, too, had no worth to these old eyes'.

If Edwin Arnold seems an unlikely propagator of Buddhism, how much more improbable was the combination of an American Civil War colonel-turned-lawyer from Orange, New Jersey – a gentleman of stern Presbyterian upbringing whose family claimed descent from the Pilgrim Fathers – and a Russian noblewoman-turned-clairvoyant? This unlikely pairing came about almost by chance after an English translation of the proceedings of Ceylon's Panadura debate of 1873 was published by the American J. M. Peebles in Battle Creek, Michigan: it caught the eye of Colonel Henry Steel Olcott and drew him towards Buddhism at a time when he was also becoming increasingly entangled in the affairs of the remarkable Madame Helena Petrovna Blavatsky.

Madame Blavatsky claimed to have spent seven years in Tibet in the late 1850s as an initiate of a secret order of *mahatmas* or 'great souls' who called themselves the Great White Brotherhood, a group of spiritual masters supposedly formed originally by the Tibetan reformer Tsongkapa in the fourteenth century. Under the tutelage of a 'Master Morya', who had assumed the body of a dark and handsome Rajput prince, she had studied mystical teachings which she later set out in several volumes of her writings as *The Secret Doctrines* – teachings which the unkind claimed had been lifted from a variety of sources ranging from Max Müller's and Rhys Davids' translations to the English novelist Edward Bulwer Lytton's occult romances. While Madame Blavatsky had indeed travelled far and wide in the years following her flight from a disastrous marriage with the Vice-Governor of Yerevan, there is no evidence to substantiate her claim to have lived in Tibet. Whether she had or not was in any case almost irrelevant, because either Master Morya or his deputy, Master Koot Hoomi, communicated with her regularly and exhaustively by means of telepathy, dreams and automatic writing, to say nothing of 'precipitated letters' that dropped from the ceiling.

At a time when many in the West were suffering a crisis of faith in the wake of the publication of Darwin's *Origin of Species* (1859) and his later *Descent of Man* (1871), Madame Blavatsky began to attract a circle of devotees in America, despite repeated scandals and accusations of fraud. Spiritualism was very much in vogue, and 'forbidden' Tibet was coming to be seen by the romantically-minded as a spiritual paradise untainted by the outside world. Colonel Olcott was an early admirer of Madame Blavatsky, and when the Theosophical Society was formed in New York in November 1875 he became its first President – with Madame Blavatsky as, appropriately enough, its Corresponding Secretary. At first the Theosophical Society's aims were ill-defined and the Masters' messages were chiefly taken up with the Great Mother and Ancient Egyptian occultism, as explained by Serapis of the Luxor Brotherhood, but these soon gave way to the loftier goal of a 'Universal Brotherhood of Humanity, without distinction of race, creed, sex, caste or color'. Its creed drew upon the ancient truths of the mahatmas that underpinned all the religions of the world – and pre-eminent among these was Buddhism: 'incomparably higher, more noble, more philosophical and more scientific than the teaching of any other church or religion'.

One evening in the autumn of 1878 Colonel Olcott received a visitation from a dark stranger dressed in robes and a turban who told him that he had a great work to perform for humanity. Soon afterwards, with creditors knocking on the doors of their adjoining apartments, Madame Blavatsky and Colonel Olcott left New York for India. From their base in Bombay they gradually built up a following of admirers drawn from both the Indian and the Anglo-Indian communities, but at the same time arousing a great deal of hostility. Among those who fell under Madame Blavatsky's formidable spell was a senior member of the Indian Civil Service, Allan Octavian Hume, who went on to play a key role in organising and shaping the National Congress, the chief instrument of Indian nationalism. Another was the editor of the influential newspaper the *Pioneer*, whose proprietor (the present writer's great-grandfather) grew tired of his constant promotion of Madame's 'teacup creed' and sacked him.

In May 1880 this unlikely couple – the one bearded like an ancient prophet, ashen-grey of complexion, austere in appearance and demeanour, the other many times larger than life in both her bloated figure and her personality, at once grotesque and engaging, self-regarding and self-mocking, gipsy and gentlewoman – moved on to Ceylon (see Plate 25). The Sinhalese population received them with open arms, for their reputation as the first sahibs to have publicly expressed their high regard for the ancient religion of the island had preceded them. They underscored this reputation by becoming, on 25 May, the first Russian and the first American to 'take refuge in the Dharma' – they became lay Buddhists by accepting the five Buddhist precepts in a temple at Galle. However dubious this act may now appear, it sent a shock-wave through the island, dismaying the Europeans and giving a huge boost to the morale and self-esteem of the Buddhist community. On landing at the quay at Bombay, Colonel Olcott had knelt down and kissed the ground; here in Ceylon he abandoned his western attire for a dhoti, shawl and sandals (see Plate 26).

The contrasting attitudes of these two 'chums', as they called themselves, can be seen in their very different responses to the Relic of the Tooth at Kandy when it was brought from its golden case for their personal inspection: Madame Blavatsky blurted out that it was as large as an alligator's tooth while Olcott, rather more tactfully, expressed a belief that it obviously dated from one of the Buddha's earlier incarnations, when he had assumed the form of a tiger. Madame Blavatsky soon moved on, directing her energies into building up the Theosophical Society's membership in India from its new headquarters at Adyar near Madras. Colonel Olcott, however, became increasingly involved in the affairs of the Buddhist community in Ceylon and, set up a Buddhist Theosophical Society comprising two divisions, one for clerics and one for lay people. The former had become increasingly isolated from the greater community, to the point where their survival had come to depend on infusions of funds and teachers from Burma. Under Olcott's guidance, the Buddhist Theosophical Society initiated a reforming and unifying process in which ordinary lay men and women were encouraged to become actively involved in the Sangha, the Buddhist community of monks and lay people combined. Declaring that since 'the Christians spend millions to destroy Buddhism; we must spend to defend and propagate it', Olcott set up a Buddhist Defence Committee. He campaigned to raise funds for the formation of Buddhist schools, patterned on the Christian mission schools, which would in time produce an educated élite that no longer looked to England or to Christian teachings for its ideals. He also initiated the formation of Buddhist Sunday Schools and Young Men's Buddhist Association branches to rival those of the Christians and, most remarkable of all, he drew up a *Buddhist Catechism according to the Southern Church* deliberately modelled on the catechisms produced by the missionaries; this was printed originally in Sinhalese but its popularity led to it being published in English and disseminated in Europe and America.

Like the Christian catechisms, Olcott's *Buddhist Catechism* was made up of questions and answers to be learned by heart, and the role it played in the revival of Buddhism in Ceylon, and its reform, was immense. But what is truly extraordinary about this document is that even though it carried the imprimatur of the most respected Sinhalese monk on the island, the Venerable Sri Hikkadowe Sumangala, 'High Priest of Sri Pada and the Western Province and Principal of the Vidyodaya Pirivena', and was approved by him for use in Buddhist schools, the *Buddhist Catechism* reflected Henry Olcott's rationalist views – views that in many instances ran contrary to the Buddhist practices then prevailing on the island.

The *Catechism* asks: 'Did the Buddha hold with idol-worship?'

Answer: 'He did not; he opposed it. The worship of gods, demons, trees, etc. was condemned by the Buddha.' And the summary of Buddhism that the American colonel set down in answer to the question 'What striking contrasts are there between Buddhism and what may be called "religion"?' is a startlingly reformist, almost Presbyterian, interpretation of Theravada Buddhism:

> Answer: Among others, these: It teaches the highest goodness without a creating God; a continuity of life without adhering to the superstitious and selfish doctrine of an eternal, metaphysical soul-substance that goes out of the body; a happiness without an objective heaven; a method of salvation without a vicarious Saviour; redemption by oneself as the Redeemer, and without rites, prayers, penances, priests or intercessory saints; and a *summum bonum*, i.e., Nirvana, attainable in this life and in this world by leading a pure, unselfish life of wisdom and of compassion to all beings.

One of those who attended Colonel Olcott's first public lecture in Ceylon was Don David Hevavitherana, aged sixteen, son of Anglicised Sinhalese parents, who had been educated at an Anglican church school in Colombo and had been present, as a nine-year-old, at the 'Great Debate of Panadura'. His grandfather became the Buddhist Theosophical Society's first President, and in 1884, at the age of twenty, David himself was initiated as a member of the Society.

The following year, however, while accompanying Madame Blavatsky on a tour through India as part of her entourage, he was advised by her to turn away from the occult path she had chosen for herself and instead take up the study of Pali. Meanwhile, a member of the Society for Psychical Research sent out to India to investigate Madame Blavatsky denounced her seances and her letters from the Brotherhood as fraudulent, and in 1885, under pressure from Olcott, she resigned from the Theosophical Society and left India for good.

That same year David Hevavitherana took the vows of a student of Buddhism, and with them the name Anagarika Dharmapala, by which he is today known throughout Buddhist South Asia as its first modern saint. Modern Buddhist biographies of Dharmapala down-play his links with the Theosophists, but there is no doubt that for almost a decade he acted as *chela* or disciple to Olcott's guru or teacher. He was Olcott's interpreter on his travels round Ceylon and India, and accompanied him to Japan in 1889 and to the World Parliament of Religions at the Chicago World's Fair in 1893. These two journeys had profound consequences for the future development of Buddhism both in Asia and in the United States of America. The visit to Japan re-established relations between Japanese Buddhists and the outside world that had been dormant for centuries, and showed Dharmapala that an Asian country could modernise without the intervention of a colonial power. The visit to Chicago convinced him of the need for modernisation and religious reform in Ceylon, where 'gods and priests keep the people in ignorance', while the World's Fair introduced Buddhism to non-Japanese America. Both Dharmapala and Soen Shaku, a Zen master of the Rinzai School in Japan, spoke at the World Parliament of Religions, arousing the interest of, among others, a young German-born publisher named Paul Carus, owner of the Open Court Publishing Company in La Salle, Illinois.

In due course Colonel Olcott's attempts to find common ground between Buddhism on the one hand and Hinduism and Theosophy on the other were rejected by his increasingly militant former disciple, and led Dharmapala to break with the Buddhist Theosophical Society. Nor did Colonel Olcott's struggle to control the increasingly erratic course of the Theosophical Society end with the demise of Madame Blavatsky in London in 1891, for by then another equally forceful and wayward character had come to the fore in the person of Mrs Annie Besant, an Irish protégée of Madame Blavatsky. The rivalry between the Colonel and Mrs Besant took a happier turn when Mrs Besant espoused the nationalist cause in India, to the great concern of the British authorities and the delight of many Indians. But even then dissensions continued to plague the Society, and Colonel Olcott's last years were blighted by a scandal involving the appropriately-named Charles Leadbeater, former Church of England curate and rising star of the Theosophical Society, who spent three years in Ceylon before his sexual predilections were exposed.

Dharmapala attempted a reconciliation in 1905, but it ended in a shouting match after the Colonel called him 'a spoiled child'. Olcott became seriously ill and died at the Theosophical Society's head-quarters at Adyar in 1907. He was cremated with his body draped in Old Glory and the Buddhist flag he and Dharmapala had devised.

In the Cold Weather of 1884–6 Edwin Arnold, by now not merely an Officer of the Order of the White Elephant but also a Knight Commander of the Indian Empire, a Companion of the Star of India and a recipient (Third Class) of the Imperial Order of the Medjidieh, went on a sightseeing tour through India with his second wife. After visiting what were now fast becoming the popular tourist sites of Jaipur, Delhi and Agra, the Arnolds caught the train for Benares – in Arnold's words, the 'Oxford and the Canterbury of India in one'. He admired its 'hallowed architec-ture', but beneath the polite words of his account of the journey was the unmistakable undercurrent of disgust that had by now become the stock response of the Englishman in India to anything associated with Hinduism. He saw Benares as a city of 'ugly sanc-tity' because it had absorbed and obliterated the faith that 'for eight hundred years had a chief seat here'. He moved on to Bodh-Gaya in a happier mood, very aware that he was entering 'the land of the Light of Asia' and expecting to be deeply moved:

> You pass along the banks of the Phalgu to the point where the two streams of the Lilajan and Mohana unite to form that river, traversing a sandy but fertile valley full of sal trees, jujubes, figs and bamboos. The sunny hills look down on the broad shining channel; the peace-ful people sit at their hut doors winding the Tusseh silk cocoons, or draw the palm wine from the toddy trees, or herd upon the plains great droves of milch cattle and black sheep. Underneath the shady topes move the forest-creatures of the Buddha story, in that amity which he created between them and man – the striped squirrel, the doves (pearl colour and blue), the koil, the parroquet, the kingfisher, the quail, and the myna. Especially does the sacred Fig Tree flourish in the neighbourhood – not the *aswattha*, which sends down aerial roots and makes fresh trunks, but the *Peepul*, the sacred Fig, under the shade of which Siddhartha triumphed over doubt.

During Cunningham's tenure of office as Director-General of the Survey of India, the Government of India had come to recognise the succession of Hindu *mahants* living on the site of the Mahabodhi temple as its rightful owners. Their agreement had been sought at all stages of the reconstruction of the main pagoda – and had been freely given. This was the situation when Sir Edwin arrived at Bodh-Gaya in January 1886. As he made his way into the inner sanctum of the Mahabodhi temple to pay his respects to the gilded Buddha from Burma that had been installed on its lion-throne eleven years earlier, however, he was shocked to see a stone lingam, the symbol of Shiva, in the centre of the room. His dismay increased when he found a party of Maratha peasants gathered at the base of the Bodhi tree to present offerings of sacrificial cakes under the direction of the *mahant*.

'I asked the priest if I might have a leaf from the sacred tree,' Arnold later recorded. '"Pluck as many as you like, sahib," was his reply, "it is nought to us." Ashamed of his indifference, I took silently the three or four dark, shining leaves which he pulled from the bough over his head.'

The Government of India might have agreed to protect the site, but Arnold was far from happy at the way it was being looked after:

Painful it certainly is, to one who realises the immense significance of this spot in the history of Asia and of humanity, to wander round the precincts of the holy tree, and to see scores and hundreds of broken sculptures lying about in the jungle or on the brickheaps . . . numberless beautiful broken stones tossed aside, cut into Buddhas and Bodhisats with a skill often quite admirable . . . a whole pile of selected fragments – five or six cartloads – lying in dust and darkness, the very first of which, when examined, bore the Buddhist formula of faith, and the second was an exquisite bas-relief of Buddha illustrating the incident of the mad elephant who worshipped him.

From India the Arnolds travelled on to Ceylon, where Sir Edwin was received by the Buddhist clergy almost as if he were a patron saint. He in turn was able to offer his hosts the leaves he had plucked from the Bodhi tree. 'I found them prized by the

Sinhalese with eager and passionate emotion,' he later wrote. 'The leaf presented by me to the temple at Kandy, for example, was placed in a casket of precious metal and made the centre of a weekly service, and there and then it befell that, talking to the gentle and learned priests at Panadure – particularly to my dear and wise friend, Sri Weligama – I gave utterance to the suggestion that the temple and its appurtenances ought to be, and might be by amicable arrangement with the Hindoo College and by favour of the Queen's government, placed in the hands of a representative committee of the Buddhist nations. I think there never was an idea that grew so fast.'

Some days later Arnold dined with the Governor of Ceylon, Sir Arthur Gordon, who was taking a keen interest in the excavations by then under way at Anuradhapura. The Governor approved his idea, and when Arnold returned to London in the spring he began lobbying for support for his plan to oust the Hindus from the Mahabodhi temple and transfer it to Buddhist control. He wrote to politicians in Britain, to the leaders of every Buddhist sect he could think of – and to the *mahant* at Bodh-Gaya, sending him a copy of his epic poem on the *Bhagavad Gita* to show that he bore his faith no ill-will. Everyone, it seemed, was keen on the idea – except the *mahant*, who, according to Arnold, grew 'more exacting in his expectations, and clung closer to the possession of the temple'. The *mahant* petitioned the civil authorities in Gaya and Patna and they supported his claim of ownership.

After three years of negotiations which led nowhere, Sir Edwin Arnold began a fresh round of appeals, beginning with the Secretary of State for India, whose support he won by the assurance that he might, if he so wished, 'be forever remembered in Asia, like Alexander, or Asoka, or Akbar the Great'. The Viceroy was more cautious, but let it be known that he 'would be inclined to favour any friendly negotiations – so long as no religious ill-feeling was aroused'.

Now Anagarika Dharmapala became involved. In January 1891, five years after Arnold's visit, Dharmapala and a Japanese Theosophist met some Bengali friends and travelled to Bodh-Gaya, where they occupied a guest-house built for visiting pilgrims from Burma, vowing not to leave until Buddhists had taken over the temple site. Dharmapala then added his voice to Arnold's, writing to Buddhists in Ceylon, Burma, Siam and Japan explaining the conditions prevailing at the Mahabodhi temple and appealing for support. However, before the matter had gone much further it was brought to an abrupt end by a visit from the Collector of Gaya, who made it plain that the ownership of the site rested with the *mahant* and ordered the Buddhists to leave.

At a public meeting held in Colombo on 31 May 1891 the Maha Bodhi Society was formed, its prime aim the protection of the Mahabodhi temple at Bodh-Gaya, together with the establishment of a monastery, and a college to be run on the lines of the ancient Buddhist University at Nalanda. The Society was intended as much more than simply a body for the restoration of Buddhist Bodh-Gaya: it was the first international Buddhist organisation, a body that would undertake the 'glorious work of Buddhist revival, after a torpor of seven hundred years, whence dates the destruction of Buddhism in India'. The thirteenth Dalai Lama of Tibet became the Maha Bodhi Society's first President, Colonel Henry Olcott its Director, and Anagarika Dharmapala its Secretary. Sir Edwin Arnold wrote from England to give the Society his full backing, using the columns of the *Daily Telegraph* to argue the Buddhists' case and twice travelling to Japan to lecture on the subject.

After some metaphorical arm-twisting from the Collector of Gaya, the *mahant* at Bodh-Gaya was persuaded to sell to the Maha Bodhi Society a small plot of land about a hundred and fifty yards to the north-west of the Mahabodhi temple. A month after the Colombo meeting Dharmapala took possession on behalf of the Maha Bodhi Society, and hoisted the Buddhist flag. This was followed by the world's first International Buddhist Conference, a very modest affair convened at Bodh-Gaya at the end of October in that same year. By unhappy chance, the conference took place on the eve of a visit to Bodh-Gaya by the Lieutenant-Governor of Bengal, and the first thing that caught his eye when he visited the Mahabodhi temple was a Japanese flag left there by a delegate. This set alarm bells ringing in Government House in Calcutta, and the order went out that the Mahabodhi site was not to be sold to any foreign power or organisation.

In the following year the situation was further complicated by the death of the old *mahant* and his replacement by a younger man whose hostility towards the Buddhists and their aspirations took a more violent form. Matters came to a head in April 1894 when Dharmapala returned to Bihar with a seven-hundred-year-old stone statue of Buddha from Japan that the Buddhists proposed to install inside the Mahabodhi temple. When the *mahant* got to hear of it he sent a private message to Dharmapala in Gaya, threatening to kill any Buddhist who came on to Bodh-Gaya.

Dharmapala's response was to set out for Bodh-Gaya at dawn the following day with his companions and the statue. In the event, they installed the image in the upper floor of the nearby Burmese Pilgrims' Resthouse rather than in the main temple, but no sooner had they done so than a crowd of Hindus ran in brandishing clubs and sticks. The statue was thrown into the courtyard below and Dharmapala was among those injured in the assault. A number of the *mahant*'s followers were charged and convicted – only to have their convictions later overturned on appeal by the Calcutta High Court. The Government of India was sympathetic, but conscious of the fact that it had a vast Hindu constituency and only a very few Buddhists. The inescapable fact was that the *mahant*'s predecessors had been recognised to be in possession of the site at least since the survey of Dr Francis Buchanan in 1811.

The notorious Buddha Gaya Temple Case became a *cause célèbre* among Buddhists the world over and continued to rumble on for decades. Anagarika Dharmapala refused to let the matter drop, but the death of Sir Edwin Arnold in 1904 deprived him of his most influential supporter. Constantly rebuffed by the British authorities he turned to the Indian nationalists, but they had their own agenda to consider. In 1923 an Indian lawyer from South Africa, M. K. Gandhi, agreed there was 'no doubt that the possession of the Temple should vest in the Buddhists' – but added that it would have to wait for the time 'when India comes into her own'. In 1933, as he lay dying, Dharmapala made it known that he would seek rebirth as a Hindu Brahmin in Benares, so that he could return to Bodh-Gaya in a better position to continue his struggle for the return of the Mahabodhi temple to Buddhist control; to date, no such Brahmin has made his presence known or felt.

Today Anagarika Dharmapala is revered in Ceylon as much for

his nationalism as for his Buddhism. Using the Buddhist news-paper *Sinhala Baudhaya* as his mouth-piece, he embarked on a double-pronged campaign that linked Buddhism with nationalism and the revival of Buddhism with the recovery of a sense of national identity. He called on the Sinhalese to recall the traditions of the *Mahavamsa*, to identify themselves with King Dutugamunu, who had liberated the island from Tamil domination in the second century BCE and so 'rescued Buddhism and our nationalism from oblivion'. They too could 'free themselves from foreign influences . . . with the word of the Buddha as their guiding light.' This was inspiring stuff and it made Dharmapala a national and even an international hero, for his example kindled Buddhist revivals in Burma and Siam as well as in Ceylon.

Dharmapala must also be credited with the revival of the prac-tice of meditation, widely seen today as an integral element of Buddhism. Traditionally confined to monks, passed down from master to pupil by personal and private initiation, the practice had died out entirely in Ceylon, Burma and Siam. In a Sinhalese mon-astery in 1890 Dharmapala discovered a treatise which he studied carefully before passing it on to Thomas Rhys Davids, who trans-lated it for the Pali Text Society under the title *The Manual of a Mystic*. From this time onwards meditation was no longer the exclusive preserve of initiates, but became available to lay followers through public instruction.

Nor has Dharmapala's first guru, Colonel Henry Olcott, been entirely forgotten: in 1967, on the sixtieth anniversary of his death, the Government of Sri Lanka issued a commemorative postage stamp bearing the Colonel's face. Yet few Sri Lankans are aware that the man who played the leading role in designing their national flag was a US Army colonel – just as few Indians are aware that the man who first organised an exhibition of *swadeshi* or home-produced goods to show Indians that they had no need of Lancashire cotton-goods or other English-made products was not M. K. Gandhi but this same American colonel.

14

The Search for Buddha's Birthplace

WITH THE break-up of the Archaeological Survey that followed the retirement of General Cunningham's successor in 1889, archaeological exploration and the preservation of India's ancient monuments slipped off the political agenda. Some provincial governments maintained their own departments, others left it to local administrators to do what they thought best. Individual enterprise went unchecked, and there was a return to the days when 'an excavation' meant just that: attacking a stupa with picks and shovels to recover whatever lay buried at its heart, rather than the careful digging of trenches to discover the site's original form and purpose. One such local enthusiast was James Campbell, Commissioner of Customs, Salt, Opium and Akbari in Bombay Presidency in the 1890s, who excavated at several sites in Gujarat. Among his early triumphs was finding a new Ashokan rock edict – it was taken to bits, mislaid and lost – and a relic subsequently identified by the accompanying inscription as a segment of Buddha's alms bowl – it was thrown away. He then moved on to tear apart the 'Girnar mound', a large stupa a few miles south of the famous Girnar rock inscription discovered by James Tod in 1822.

Here, like Cunningham in the past, Mr Campbell was unable to convince the local landowner or his own labour force that he was not after treasure – suspicions confirmed when after three weeks of digging the labourers disturbed a large cobra, for cobras were known to be the guardians of buried treasure. The workmen toiled with renewed vigour, but the cobra refused to vacate the site. A snake-charmer was summoned, but the cobra declined to show itself: 'A few days after the disappearance of the guardian cobra and his refusal to be charmed, the boys' school in Junagadh town became almost empty. Mothers were keeping their boys at home because it was rumoured fifty boys were to be sacrificed to the great cobra to coax him into showing the thirty *lakhs* of treasure of which he was trustee, and which were wanted by the State for railway extensions.' The 'treasure' finally resolved itself into the now familiar reliquary box of stone, which in this case held a round copper casket containing a tiny silver casket, within which was an even tinier gold casket 'bright and untarnished in spite of its 2000 years, and in shape and size like a small chestnut . . . In this tiny bowl were seven tiny articles: four precious stones, two small pieces of wood, and a fragment about the size of one's little finger of what seems to be bone.' It was one more of King Ashoka's reputed 84,000 stupas.

Not all Campbell's contemporaries were so cavalier, and two in particular, though amateurs in the modern sense, were highly professional in their approach to India's archaeology and the study of the past. The older was Vincent Smith, a Trinity College Dublin man, son of a well-known Anglo-Irish numismatist and archaeologist. Smith was a 'Competition-Wallah', one of the post-Mutiny breed of civil servants selected by merit rather than family contacts, and had come first in his year in the annual competitive examinations by which the Indian Civil Service now chose its recruits. He went out to India in 1871 and joined the administration of the North-Western Provinces and Oudh. Having cut his teeth on all the usual up-country district postings as sub-divisional officer and assistant magistrate, he did a couple of tours as a land settlement officer, making his first mark by writing *The Settlement Officer's Manual for the North-Western Provinces*. But despite his ability promotion came slowly, and it was not until 1889, when Smith was forty-five, that he was appointed a District Magistrate and Collector. For well over a decade he had been gathering material for what he planned to be the first comprehensive history of ancient northern India.

Just as Prinsep had been inspired by Jones, and Cunningham by

Prinsep, so Smith was inspired by Cunningham. He used every available opportunity, official and unofficial, to go over the ground Cunningham and his assistants had first walked in the 1860s and 1870s. He read many times over the latest translations of the Indian travels of Fa Hian, Huan Tsang and others. While serving as magistrate of the town of Basti, about a hundred and twenty-five miles north of Benares, he throughly explored the surrounding countryside – and came to the conclusion that many of Cunningham's identifications of Buddhist sites in the plains country south of the Himalayan foothills of Nepal were wrong. In 1885 a Mr Duncan Ricketts, manager of an estate whose lands extended to the Nepalese border, came to him with news of a stone pillar sticking up out of the ground about five miles north of his bungalow, well inside Nepalese territory. It was inadvisable for a British official to trespass across the frontier, so Smith asked for a rubbing to be made of the inscriptions on the pillar. They were identified as 'medieval scribblings', so Vincent Smith left the matter there. It was probably the greatest mistake he ever made.

Working quite independently of Smith at this same period and in the same field was Dr Lawrence Austine Waddell, another of that distinguished band of medical men of Scots parentage and Glaswegian education who did much more in India than practise medicine. Things had changed since the days of John Company, and Dr Waddell was now an officer in a quasi-military body, the Indian Medical Service: he bore military rank, was subject to military constraints, and was expected to answer the bugle's call. He went out to Calcutta in 1880 at the age of twenty-six and spent his first six years as an assistant sanitary commissioner in Bengal before serving in Burma as part of the military force that brought about the deposition of Ava's last king and the acquisition of Upper Burma in 1886. He spent the next seven years as a medical officer in Darjeeling, where he did some useful research into the autotoxicity of venomous snakes, developed an interest in mountaineering and ornithology, and began to study Tibetan Buddhism. From his copious writings it is clear that this last subject both fascinated and shocked him. He had grown up in the household of a Scottish Presbyterian minister, and the tone of such books as *The Buddhism of Tibet, or Lamaism*, published in 1897, shows that he viewed

Vajrayana Buddhism in much the same light as his co-religionists viewed Catholicism. During this same period of duty in Darjeeling Dr Waddell also began to develop what Anglo-Indians liked to call a *shauq*, or obsessive interest, which in this case took the form of trying to trace the footsteps of Fa Hian and Huan Tsang.

Like Vincent Smith, Dr Waddell pored over Cunningham's Archaeological Survey Reports and came to the same conclusion: that Cunningham had got a lot wrong, particularly in his siting of the places associated with Gautama Buddha's birth and death. 'For many years past,' Waddell later wrote, 'I had been devoting a portion of my holidays to a search for this celebrated ancient site – Kapilavastu – as well as for that of the Buddha's death – Kusinagara – ever since I had realised that General Cunningham's identification of the villages of Bhuila and Kesia with those sites was clearly altogether false . . . Pursuing my search for these two famous lost sites, and attempting to trace the itineraries thither of the Chinese pilgrims, I cross-quartered the greater part of the country in question which lay within British territory, traversing in this search some thousands of miles, of which several hundreds had to be done on foot.'

Waddell and Smith faced the same difficulties. In the first place, the landscape of the jungly Terai country had changed since Gautama Buddha's time: 'This tract of plains was so much cut up by the ever-shifting channels of the mighty rivers which debouch from the Himalayas, that it was almost impossible, in the absence of characteristic inscriptions and without digging, to identify conclusively any of the ruins.' There was also the problem of finding time. In Waddell's case, while his employers were prepared to allow their officers to serve in a medical capacity on bona fide expeditions – as Austine Waddell twice did in Sikkim – they did not look kindly on them simply going off to dig holes in the ground.

Waddell's first search was a failure. Armed with a pilgrim's guide supplied to him by a Tibetan lama in Darjeeling, he journeyed some distance up the Brahmaputra River into Assam looking for the site of Gautama Buddha's *parinirvana* before concluding that the information in the guide was 'very erroneous'. He had better luck in the following year, 1891, when he explored the hills near Monghyr in East Bihar and successfully located one of the lesser

Buddhist sites visited and described by Huan Tsang, a retreat where Gautama Buddha had spent the rainy reason in the sixteenth year of his ministry. During the laying of a nearby railway line the hillside had been extensively quarried by British contractors – one of whom had carried off a cartload of stone statues, since lost – but Waddell discovered the footprint of the Buddha in the rock Huan Tsang had seen and described, proving that Cunningham had been wrong and he was right.

In 1892, when he found himself in Patna with two free days at his disposal and a sketch-map in his hand, Waddell did even better. Cunningham's failure to find anything of significance here had helped to perpetuate the belief that Pataliputra must have been swept away centuries before by the changing course of the river. Dr Waddell thought otherwise, and came to Patna armed with a simple chart on which he had drawn the locations, as suggested by their directions, of all the monuments Fa Hian and Huan Tsang had visited during their respective visits to Pataliputra. Taken individually the directions made little sense, but when put together and cross-referenced they showed quite clearly that 'the chief monuments and palaces lay to the south of the old city which itself fringed the right bank of the Ganges'.

The chart led Waddell over the railway line that marked the southern limits of Patna City, to the series of mounds known as Panch Pahari or the Five Brothers, briefly investigated by both Kittoe and Cunningham. 'I was surprised to find', he afterwards wrote, 'most of the leading landmarks of Asoka's palaces, monasteries, and other monuments when re-examined so very obvious that I was able in the short space of one day to identify many of them beyond all doubt.'

The first mound he came across was about a mile to the north of the main group and known locally as Bhikna Pahari or the Hill of the Monk. According to his chart this was where King Ashoka had built a large artificial hill between the city of Pataliputra and his palace to honour his younger brother Mahendra, who had become an ascetic and made his home in one of the caves on the Vulture's Peak at Rajgir. Poking around, Waddell was pleased to note that the base of this mound was made up of huge blocks of stone. He then walked south over the open fields to reach the main group,

Panch Pahari. 'It will be remembered', Waddell continued, 'that the most southerly of all the monuments of the ancient city was the group of the five great stupas of Asoka, the ruins of which were described in the seventh century [by Huan Tsang] as being like "little hills"; and I found that they by their position, form, and traditions were without doubt the ruins of these very identical five stupas.' The entire area was littered with broken slabs 'lying about, under trees, or at wells, or plastered into the walls of buildings'.

The next day Waddell examined the area to west of the Bhikna Pahari mound, in and around the modern village of Kumrahar, which by his reckoning marked the site of Ashoka's palace. Here he found 'various fragments of sculptures and other confirmatory details', and learned from the villagers that whenever they sunk wells they struck massive wooden beams at a depth of about twenty feet beneath the present surface of the ground. This sounded very like the row of wooden palisades uncovered a mile or so to the north and west in 1875 by the PWD during the digging of a reservoir, and suggested that more portions of Megasthenes' wooden walls lay underground waiting to be discovered. If such was indeed the case, it meant that large parts of ancient Pataliputra 'had not been washed away by the Ganges or other river, as generally supposed, and that many structural remains of Asoka's city still existed'. But it would require extensive manpower and digging to uncover them.

Waddell immediately wrote a report of his discoveries to the Government of Bengal and asked to be allowed to dig a number of trial trenches. Permission was given and funds allotted, but first Waddell fell ill and had to take sick-leave, and then in April 1895 he was caught up in another military campaign and found himself marching deep into the furthest recesses of India's north-west frontier as part of the relieving force sent to rescue the beleaguered garrison at Chitral. This was followed by promotion to Surgeon-Major and a new appointment as Professor of Chemistry and Pathology at Calcutta's Medical College. It was his teaching duties that now kept him from proceeding with the Patna dig and forced him to hand over to a local officer of the PWD, Mr C. A. Mills, who in May 1896 supervised the digging of exploratory trenches at a number of sites in accordance with Dr Waddell's instructions.

On 22 May Waddell received a telegram from Mills asking him to come at once: 'Have found stone carvings, beams, one coin supposed to be Chinese, images, foundations of buildings, moulded bricks, stone pebbles, etc. Please come by Saturday's mail if possible.'

Waddell duly caught the Saturday Mail from Howrah and arrived in Patna to discover among the finds 'a magnificent colossal capital of a distinctly Greek type', recovered from the site which he believed to be the precincts of Ashoka's palace. A number of carved stone colonnades and pillars were also found that were similar in form to the Sanchi colonnades but of a simpler and earlier style – in fact, more like the Ashokan pillars recovered by Cunningham and Beglar during their excavations at Bodh-Gaya. A month later Waddell made a second flying visit to examine another important discovery, a broken pillar lying at the centre of a court bordered by rows of brick cells. Although it bore no inscription, it was unmistakably 'a gigantic pillar of Asoka, one of those polished stone monoliths which the emperor set up and inscribed with his edicts when no rocks were near, and of which two existed in his capital at the time it was visited by the Chinese pilgrims'. Huan Tsang had described how the fanatical King Sasanka of Bengal had smashed the stone footprints of Buddha revered at this site, so it was highly probable that this was the associated pillar, of which Huan Tsang had written: 'Near the temple of the footprint stone . . . was a stone pillar above 30 feet high with an inscription much injured.' But before any further excavation could take place the Rains began and brought digging to a halt.

In the meantime other developments that had been taking place in the Terai country in northern Bihar soon drew the attentions not only of Austine Waddell and Vincent Smith but of many other interested parties.

In March 1893 a Major Jaskaran Singh, an officer in the service of the Government of Nepal, out hunting in the jungle close to the Indian border at Nigliva, exactly due north of Benares, came to hear of a stone pillar known to the local Tharu jungle-dwellers as Bhimasena-ki-nigali or Bhimsen's Smoking Pipe. He asked to see it and was taken to a large man-made tank or reservoir beside which was lying a broken pillar of polished stone. He cleared away the jungle and found the base of the pillar, upon which were inscribed four lines of ancient writing (see Plate 28).

For centuries this strip of forest running east and west along the foothills of the Himalayas had been a no-man's-land, inhabited only by a small number of aboriginal jungle dwellers who had developed an immunity to the pestilential vapours that lurked there, the notorious 'Tarai fever'. However, although it was accompanied by side-effects that included 'singing in the ears, noises in the head, deafness, headache, flushed face, bloodshot eyes, dimness of sight and eruptions on the skin', the quinine commercially manufactured from the cincona bark now being grown in plantations in India and Ceylon provided a reasonably effective preventative, permitting the exploitation of the hitherto closed Terai belt. South of the border the Government of India had facilitated the commercial exploitation of the Terai for its valuable timber, granting licences for the opening-up of the land to a number of large estates, many owned by Europeans and local *zamindars*. North of the border no such exploitation took place, except that the Terai became the exclusive hunting preserve of the rulers of Nepal, a stretch of jungle teeming with big game in the form of tiger, rhinoceros, elephant and water-buffalo.

Major Jaskaran Singh's discovery led to an appeal from the Government of Nepal to the Government of India for help in deciphering the text on the pillar, and thus events were unwittingly set in train of which the consequences are alive to this day. The request was passed to the Government of the North-Western Provinces and Oude, whose territories bordered the area of the Terai where the pillar lay, and in December a Dr Alois Führer, Archaeological Surveyor for that province, set out from his headquarters at Lucknow on the branch line of the Bengal and North-Western Railway to Uska Bazaar, just short of the border with Nepal. Two days' march through the jungle brought Dr Führer to Nigliva, the place where the Nepali major had seen the pillar. Dr Führer found the fallen pillar and its base without difficulty – and recognised the inscription as Ashoka Brahmi. He took two rubbings, surveyed the immediate area – noting one large mound nearby and several smaller ones – and returned to Lucknow.

Soon afterwards Dr Waddell wrote to Dr Führer asking for

details of the inscription, but received no reply. For reasons that will become clear, we know very little about Dr Führer except that he had been appointed to his post in 1885 and was an alumnus of the University of Vienna where his former mentor, Georg Bühler, was now Professor of Indian Philology and Archaeology; Bühler himself had been Professor of Oriental Languages at Bombay's prestigious Elphinstone College in the 1860s and had established himself as a leading Sanskritist, second only to Oxford's Max Müller. So it was perfectly reasonable for Führer to have sent his rubbings to Professor Bühler in Vienna for translation – but more than a year passed before Professor Bühler's translation of the Nigliva inscription was published, in the European journal *The Academy* in April 1895. In the meantime, Waddell again wrote to Führer and again received no reply.

When in April 1896 Dr Waddell finally got to see Professor Bühler's translation and Dr Führer's subsequent report, he was delighted. The undamaged section of the pillar inscription read: 'When the god-beloved king Piyadasi had been anointed 14 years, he increased the stupa of Buddha Konakamana for the second time; and when he had been anointed **** years, he himself came and worshipped it, caused to obtain ****.' From Dr Führer's notes he learned that the pillar had stood close to a complex of brick ruins dominated by one large stupa rising some thirty feet out of the jungle, and surrounded by a raised processional path some fourteen feet high. But what Dr Führer had either failed to notice, or failed to mention, was that the 'Konakamana' of the Ashokan inscription was the Pali equivalent of the Sanskrit name of one of the early Buddhas, Kanakamuni. The significance of this was that both Fa Hian and Huan Tsang had visited Buddha Kanakamuni's stupa – and both had placed it close to Kapilavastu, Buddha's ancestral home, which in turn was close to Lumbini, his actual birthplace.

Huan Tsang had provided the most detailed description. To get to Kanakamuni's stupa from Kapilavastu he had first travelled south for fifty *li*, or about 10 miles, to 'an old city' and then 'above thirty *li*', just over six miles, north-east (see Map A), which suggested to Dr Waddell that Buddha Kanakamuni's stupa must be between five and seven miles south-east of Kapilavastu. Huan Tsang had seen three topes among the ruins, one of which was said to hold Buddha

Kanakamuni's relics. Before this third stupa was 'a stone pillar above 20 feet high, with a lion on the top, and a record of this Buddha's decease on the sides. This pillar had also been set up by Asoka.'

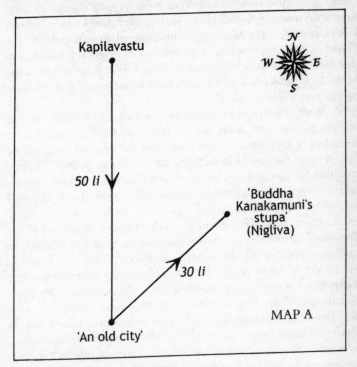

Kapilavastu

50 li

'Buddha
Kanakamuni's
stupa'
(Nigliva)

30 li

MAP A

'An old city'

If the Ashokan pillar found by Major Singh at Nigliva did indeed mark the site of the stupa of Buddha Kanakamuni, and if Huan Tsang's directions were correct, then the ruins of the city of Kapilavastu, as well as the place where Buddha was born, had to lie within a few miles of that spot – almost certainly to the north-west. What made Dr Waddell even more sure of himself was that the Chinese pilgrims' accounts tallied more or less with the information contained in his Tibetan pilgrimage guide, which placed Kapilavastu eight to nine days' walk east of Srivasti, and Lumbini half a day to the south of Kapilavastu and then half a day east.

As soon as he had worked this out, Dr Waddell wrote to the Secretary of the Asiatic Society of Bengal expressing polite surprise that no one seemed to have noticed that the Ashokan pillar found at Nigliva had 'an importance far beyond that of its own mere inscription, for it supplies a clue to the hitherto undiscovered birth-place of Sakya Muni . . . This pillar of Konakamana in the Nepalese *tarai*, appears still to be fixed in its original position; and that most trustworthy topographer, Hiuen Tsiang, records that the "city" of Kapilavastu lay within seven miles or so to the north-west of this very identical pillar.'

To Waddell's irritation, his letter was returned to him with an accompanying note from the Secretary informing him that he would have to wait for a response until the next meeting of the Society – at the end of June. So he decided to go public: 'Finding that that Society showed so little interest in this important matter and in order to arouse public interest in so romantic a subject, I threw my memorandum into popular form as an article to the Calcutta *Englishman* entitled, "Where is the Birthplace of the Buddha?" ' Now he was even more specific, declaring that all the evidence pointed to the same conclusion: 'That the long-lost birthplace of Sakya Muni, with its magnificent monuments, certainly lies at a spot in the Nepalese Tarai, about seven miles to the north-west of the Nepalese village of Nigliva . . . [and] . . . That the Lumbini or Lumbana grove (the actual birthplace) will be found three or four miles to the north of the village of Nigliva.' Declaring that they now stood 'on the verge of one of the most important Indian archaeological finds of the century', Waddell urged the Government of India to 'take early steps to procure the sanction of the Nepalese Government to its full exploration'.

Waddell's article was immediately reproduced by all the other English-language newspapers in India and aroused a great deal of public interest. The outcome was an offer from the government of Bengal to bear the expenses of a six-week exploration of the site, provided the Government of Nepal was agreeable and provided Dr Waddell's employers would grant him six weeks' leave. The Nepalese had no objections, but the Director of the Medical College in Calcutta did: Waddell was denied his six weeks' leave, and before he could arrange a later date he learned that the

Government of India had already given permission for Dr A. Führer to take over the explorations.

It was generally agreed that, quinine or no quinine, camping in the Terai was too dangerous for Europeans before the end of November, and in the last week of November 1896 three parties advanced on the border area, one from the Nepal side and two from India. Dr Führer returned from Lucknow to Nigliva, now fully alerted to the significance of the inscription on its broken column. He was met by a squad of Nepali sappers, sent to assist him on the instructions of the local regional governor, General Khadga Shamsher Jang Rana. However, unknown to him, General Khadga Rana had also decided to investigate a second pillar: the standing column spotted by the estate manager Mr Duncan Ricketts in 1885, the rubbing from which Vincent Smith had examined. This lay just over ten miles south-east of Nigliva, near a village called Rumindei. The General went there, not on Dr Führer's instructions – as he later implied – but in response to a letter from Dr Waddell, passed on to him by the British Resident in Kathmandu. At Rumindei General Khadga Rana was joined by Mr Ricketts, who had ridden over from his bungalow five miles to the south. Together they watched the general's Nepali sappers dig down on all sides of the column until they reached its base at a depth of twelve feet.

In the meantime, Dr Führer had been handed a note asking him to join General Khadga Rana at Rumindei. He hurried over. According to his official report, what he saw there was 'a slightly mutilated pillar, rising about 10 feet above ground'. The report then continued: 'On digging away the accumulated debris, it proved to be an Asoka monolith, 24 ft 4 in high, standing upon a masonry platform, and to bear about 9 ft 8 in from its base a well-preserved inscription of the Maurya period in five lines. The inscription fixes with absolute certainty the situation of the garden of Lumbini, where according to the Buddhist belief Prince Siddhartha was born (see overleaf).'

Vincent Smith was at this time based sixty miles away at Gorakhpur. His official duties as City Judge prevented him from getting away, but he later wrote his own report on what was found at Rumindei – and who found it:

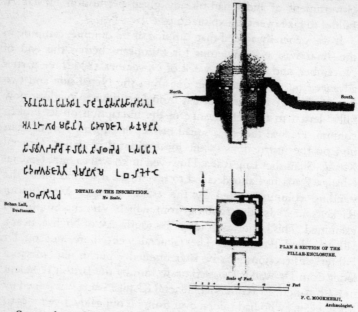

DETAIL OF THE INSCRIPTION.
No Scale.

Bohan Lall,
Draftsman.

PLAN & SECTION OF THE
PILLAR-ENCLOSURE.

Scale of Feet.

P. C. MOOKHERJI,
Archæologist,

Some three feet below the surface of the ground was found the inscription of Asoka. Mr Ricketts had the good fortune to be present while the inscription was being unearthed. *Dr Führer arrived a little later.* The pillar, which is of polished sandstone, is split vertically down the middle, probably by lightning, and the top is broken off . . . The inscription is in four and a half lines of beautifully incised and well-preserved characters, averaging about 30 millimetres, or little over an inch in height . . . The main purport of the record is that King Piyadasi, beloved of the Devas, when anointed twenty years, came to this spot, and worshipped, saying: 'Here was Buddha Sakyamuni born', and caused a stone pillar to be erected testifying: 'Here in the Lummini village was the Honourable One born.'

Thus have been set at rest all doubts as to the exact site of the traditional birth-place of Gautama Buddha in the 'Lumbini garden'.

Further confirmation that this was indeed the site of Prince Siddhartha's birthplace was found five months later when two of Mr

Smith's ICS subordinates from Gorakhpur visited the site and found within a Hindu shrine a stone bas-relief showing Queen Maya giving birth (see illustration above). 'The Brahman in charge', wrote Smith, 'was very unwilling to permit the image to be seen, but some persuasion and rupees overcame his scruples. The image is of nearly life-size, and the infant is represented, according to the legend, as emerging from the right side of his mother, and being received by attendants . . . Several examples of sculptured representations of the birth of Gautama are known in collections from Gandhara, but I do not know of any example in India proper.'

The first to realise the full significance of the pillar at Rumindei was Dr Führer, who as Vincent Smith's account shows had appeared on the site only after the excavations had been under way for some time. He stayed long enough to take two impressions of the Ashokan inscription and to note that the Lumbini pillar, as we may now safely call it, was close to four stupa mounds. He then returned to his own camp at Nigliva to pursue what was the main objective of his trip – to find Kapilavastu, which according to Dr Waddell's interpretation of Huan Tsang was 'about seven miles to the north-west of the Nepalese village of Nigliva'. He duly began to explore the jungle in that direction, and at a distance of about six miles from Nigliva found himself on the edge of a thick forest and what appeared to be extensive ruins, continuing for several miles to the north and south. He had found Kapilavastu – and it was exactly where Dr Waddell had said it would be.

At some point over the next few days Dr Führer completed a first rudimentary translation of the Lumbini inscription – enough to realise the enormous significance of the sentence *hida-Budhe-jate Sakyamuni-ti*, 'Here was Buddha Sakyamuni born', and of the phrase *Lumminigame* – 'Lummini village'. He at once arranged for his rubbings of the Lumbini inscription to be posted to Professor Bühler in Vienna, and he then set about considering the implications of this discovery.

On 23 December the Allahabad *Pioneer* ran an exclusive that was carried five days later by *The Times* in London and scores of other national newspapers, reporting two great linked discoveries: the birthplace of the Buddha at Lumbini, and the ruins of the city of Kapilavastu, where the young Prince Siddhartha had grown up. The news had been conveyed in a telegram by the discoverer himself, Dr Alois Führer, Archaeological Surveyor of the North-Western Provinces and Oude, deputed to the Nepalese Durbar. It was Dr Führer who had discovered the first pillar at Nigliva, in 1895 while on secondment to the Government of Nepal, and it was he who had subsequently discovered the Lumbini pillar on 1 December. And it was only by locating the Lumbini pillar and reading its text that he had then been able to discover Kapilavastu, as Dr Führer himself explained in detail:

The discovery of the Asoka Edict Pillar in the Lumbini Grove at Rumindei enabled me to fix also, with absolute certainty, the site of Kapilavastu and of the sanctuaries in its neighbourhood. Thanks to the exact notes left by the two Chinese travellers I discovered its extensive ruins about eighteen miles north-west of the Lumbini pillar, and about six miles north-west of the Nigali Sagar [the tank beside the smashed column at Nigliva] . . . The whole site is at present as dreary and desolate as when seen by Fa-hien and Huien-Tsang; yet every sacred spot mentioned by the two pilgrims can be easily mentioned.

To have given the real source of the information that had led him to Kapilavastu would have meant giving another man some of the credit for this great double discovery, and this Dr Führer was not prepared to do. For of course it was not the discovery of the Buddha's birthplace at Lumbini that had enabled him to find Kapilavastu, but Dr Waddell's identification of the Nigliva pillar as the site of the Buddha Kanakamuni stupa. If Dr Führer had indeed followed 'the exact notes of the two Chinese travellers' to get to Kapilavastu from Lumbini, he would have found himself some twenty to twenty-five miles to the south: to get to Lumbini, Huan Tsang had left Kapilavastu by its south gate and first proceeded thirty-two *li* to the south-east to visit a spring or well called the Arrow Spring. He had then walked from the Arrow Spring eighty or ninety *li* to the north-east, to the Lumbini grove, an itinerary which put the site of Kapilavastu approximately sixteen to eighteen miles south-west of Lumbini (see Map B overleaf).

Dr Waddell had, of course, made his prediction for the site of Kapilavastu *before* the identification of the Lumbini pillar from the reading of its Ashokan edict. Had he made it afterwards, he would certainly have had to amend his conclusions, because Huan Tsang's directions for reaching Kapilavastu from Lumbini contradicted those he had given earlier for getting to Kapilvastu from the Buddha Kanakamuni stupa at Nigliva. Put these two sets of directions together on a map showing the two established locations – Lumbini, and Buddha Kanakumi's stupa at Nigliva – and Kapilavastu appears in two widely separated places (see Map C overleaf):

In February 1897 Dr Führer received the unqualified blessings of his patron Professor Bühler in a laudatory article, published in the Royal Asiatic Society's *Journal*, which proclaimed his discoveries 'the most important which have been made for many years'.

There was little Dr Waddell could do. He wrote a restrained letter of protest to the RAS criticising Führer's 'characteristic forgetfulness' in suppressing all reference to his (Waddell's) share in the discovery. Had Führer then apologised and admitted the oversight

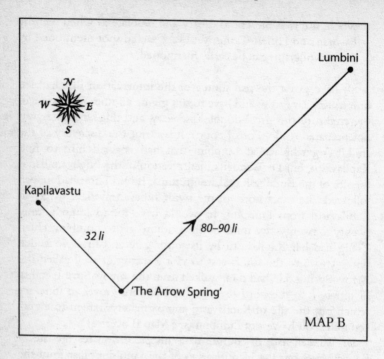

MAP B

all might have been well, but his response was to write an ill-judged letter in which he called Dr Waddell 'egoistical' and flatly denied having made use of his work. He had never received any letters from him – and in any case, Dr Waddell had said that Lumbini would be found four miles north of Nigliva, whereas he had found it thirteen miles to the east-south-east. Neither assertion was true. In a second and much stronger letter Dr Waddell demonstrated that this was not the first time the Archaeological Surveyor of the North-Western Provinces and Oude had taken all the credit for himself in announcing a discovery, but the third. At this point, in December 1897, the Council of the RAS stepped in and declared the discussion closed: the issue, of course, was anything but.

The finding of the three Buddhist sites just inside the Nepalese border had caused a stir among Duncan Ricketts' fellow estate managers on the Indian side of the border. One of them was William Peppé, who with his brother George managed a large

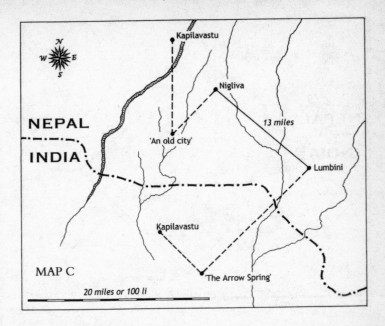

tract of land known as the Birdpur Grant that extended right up to the Nepalese border immediately to the south of the area where Major Singh had found the Nigliva pillar fragments in 1893, and where Dr Führer had more recently found Kapilavastu. The Peppés' bungalow at Birdpur was six miles south of the border, seventeen miles south of Nigliva and twelve miles south-west of Lumbini. Soon after the discoveries over the border had been announced William Peppé began to take an interest in the mounds or *kots*, as they were known locally, that littered the northern area of the Birdpur estate close to the border. They were particularly prominent in and around the village of Piprahwa, just half a mile short of the border (see Map D overleaf).

Peppé decided to take a look at one *kot* 'more prominent than the rest' and got his workmen to dig a trench cutting right across the mound, which exposed a sizeable structure made up of large bricks measuring 16 by 10 by 3 inches (see Plate 29). Satisfied that it was a Buddhist stupa, he stopped his digging and contacted Vincent Smith in Gorakhpur. At the start of the next Cold

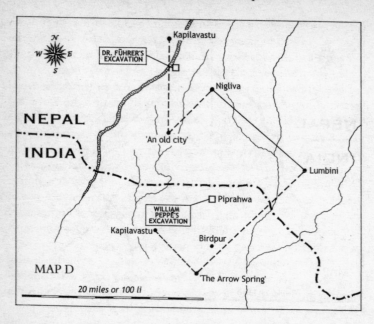

Weather, October 1897, Smith visited the Piprahwa site and pronounced the bricks to be very ancient indeed. Some decades earlier Cunningham had noticed that the bricks of ancient monuments tended to become smaller with each passing century, and from this had drawn up a chart: this suggested that bricks of the large size used on the stupa at Piprahwa dated from the pre-Ashokan period. Following Smith's advice, William Peppé resumed his dig as soon as the Christmas festivities of 1897 were over. A square shaft was sunk from the top of the stupa at the centre, and Peppé took measurements at every stage while his wife made drawings. At a depth of ten feet they found a small soapstone vase, smashed and full of clay but with some beads, crystals and small gold ornaments inside. This was disappointing, but Smith had urged them to continue until they reached ground level, so the work resumed: 'After digging through eighteen feet of solid brickwork set in clay, a huge slab of stone was disclosed, lying due magnetic north and south . . . the cover of a massive sandstone coffer measuring 4 ft 4 ins by 2 ft 8 ins by 2ft 2 ins in a state of perfect preservation . . . hollowed, at the cost of vast labour and expense, from a solid block of rock.' This coffer was weighed on the estate's weighing machine and found to be 1,537 pounds, its cover being an additional 408 pounds.

The lid had been broken into four pieces by the pressure of the bricks above it, but had fitted so perfectly into a groove cut along the outer edges of the top of the coffer that it had not fallen in. The pieces were carefully prised up and the coffer opened, to reveal three small vases of soapstone between six and seven inches high, a little soapstone box and a crystal bowl three and a half inches high, all in perfect condition. Opened, these revealed 'pieces of bone, which are quite recognizable as such, and might have been picked up a few days ago'. Along with the fragments of bone were many tiny gold ornaments including a number of images stamped on gold leaf: human figures, a lion, an elephant, a swastika, stars, and flowers. The smallest of the urns carried a long inscription on its lid which William Peppé photographed, while his wife made scale drawings of all the ornaments (see Plate 30).

The Peppés' photos, drawings and plans were sent to Smith, who passed them on to Thomas Rhys Davids, now Secretary of the RAS, who translated the inscription as follows: 'This shrine for relics of the Buddha, the August One, is that of the Sakyas, the brethren of the Distinguished One, in association with their sisters, and with their children and their wives.' If his reading was correct, then only one conclusion could be drawn: that the Sakya clan had raised this stupa soon after the death of their illustrious kinsman, the Sage of the Sakyas, to contain their share of his relics – and where would this stupa have been raised if not in the Sakyas' capital, Kapilavastu? Or, as Smith put it: 'One point comes prominently in view from the inscription – that the Sakyas, to whom the Buddha belonged, must have had the stupa in their country.'

It was Vincent Smith's contention that the stupa was indeed pre-Ashokan, perhaps one of the original eight said to have contained the ashes and bone fragments of Gautama Buddha shared out after his cremation. It was also possible that, out of deference to the Sakya family, it had been spared by King Ashoka at the time of his redistribution of Buddha's relics from the original eight stupas into the supposed eighty-four thousand. Piprahwa was just over ten miles south-west of Lumbini. Add Piprahwa to the map showing the known sites of Lumbini and Nigliva and Huan Tsang's two sets of directions, and it will be seen that it is reasonably close to where Huan Tsang had placed Kapilavastu in the second of his route directions (see Map D on page 274).

The earlier pilgrim, Fa Hian, had simply stated that Lumbini was fifty *li* east of Kapilavastu – which could apply to both Piprahwa and the site six miles north-west of Nigliva where Dr Führer had found *his* Kapilavastu. But which was the real Kapilavastu – the extensive ruins that looked so very promising and matched Huan Tsang's first route directions, or the Piprahwa site, with its hard evidence of an inscription set down by the Sakya rulers themselves and which matched Huan Tsang's second set of directions?

In December 1897, at about the same time as Mr Peppé and his labourers were cutting the first trench across the Piprahwa *kot*, Dr Führer, fortified with six hundred rupees for his expenses collected for him by Professor Bühler in Vienna, renewed excavations at *his* Kapilavastu. He had selected the most promising area, at a site named Sagarhawa which had a large tank at its centre, and there he had set his force of Nepali sappers to work. They soon uncovered a large central stupa and *vihara*, to which were linked seventeen smaller stupas on square bases. He at once concluded that these lesser structures were the memorials of eighteen members of the Sakya clan who, according to Buddhist texts, had been massacred on the orders of King Vidudabha of Kosala, in revenge for a slight which had taken place during Gautama Buddha's lifetime. A wildly exaggerated version of this massacre was known to Huan Tsang, who in his account of his visit to Kapilavastu noted that 'to the north-east of the capital were several hundred thousand topes where the Sakyas were put to death', their skeletons afterwards being collected and buried.

Following Dr Waddell's charges, the Indian newspapers had carried full accounts of Dr Führer's several alleged attempts to take credit for the work of others. These would certainly have been drawn to the attention of Dr Führer's employers: only some outstanding coup – such as clear and dramatic confirmation of his discovery of Kapilavastu – could save his career. So the pressure was now on, redoubled by William Peppé's discovery of the Sakya relics at Piprahwa just after Christmas. If Führer could find clear evidence to link the seventeen small stupas he had uncovered to the massacred Sakyas, he would have exactly what he needed. He therefore set his sappers to uncover that evidence, and they worked so assiduously that they virtually levelled the site. On 28 January 1898 Vincent Smith and William Peppé appeared, unannounced, at Dr Führer's excavation. 'I remember that Dr Führer specially drew our attention to the recurrence of square stupas as a remarkable novelty,' wrote Mr Smith. What Smith did not add – and never put down in any official paper – was that they also caught Führer in the act of salting his square stupas with clay tokens inscribed with fake pre-Ashokan characters.

All Smith would say publicly was that 'the inscriptions of the Sakyas alleged to have been found in the small stupas at Sagarhawa are impudent forgeries', and that much of Dr Führer's subsequent report had been invented. Dr Waddell, however, went over the ground of the excavations carried out by Dr Führer at Nigliva, and was unable find any sign of the hundred-foot-diameter stupa and its raised processional path described by the German in his first report: 'Every word of it is false. The stone railing, the fallen columns, and the broken sculptures had no existence except in Dr Führer's fertile imagination.'

There can be no doubt that Smith and Waddell both had axes to grind, but a subsequent investigation by Dr Führer's successor, Babu Purna Chandra Mukherji, confirmed that Führer's excavations at Nigliva and Sagarhawa had been badly botched and his claims bogus: 'The large number of the stupas which he identified as the "Massacre of the Sakyas" were no sooner traced than destroyed in the hope of finding relics . . . His alleged discovery of several inscriptions in "pre-Asoka" characters has been proved to be not based on facts. Altogether his results were very unsatisfactory and not less conflicting.'

Equally, there can be no doubt that Dr Führer had been out of his depth. Hindsight suggests that his inept excavations were a desperate attempt to come up with the goods, and that when they failed he resorted to trickery – only to be caught in the act by the most important judge in north Bihar and by one of only two or perhaps three men in the entire subcontinent who would have known that what he claimed to have found were indeed fake artefacts.

There could be only one outcome: Dr Führer's resignation, and his swift disappearance from the Indian scene. So complete was this disappearance that it has proved impossible to find any further trace of Dr Alois Führer. As so often in the case of scandals involving European officials in India, the matter was hushed up, and so effectively that exact details of how the fraudulent pre-Ashokan inscriptions were made remain obscure. No mention of the scandal appeared in the journals of either the RAS or the Asiatic Society of Bengal, and at the latter's next AGM, in February 1899, not a word on the matter passed the lips of its President. The year before he had gone into great detail about all the exciting discoveries taking place in the Nepal Terai, but now he had absolutely nothing to add. Perhaps it was as well, because the Society had just gained a most distinguished new member in the person of the new Viceroy, Lord Curzon – the first such Viceroy or Governor-General for many years to associate himself directly with the Asiatic Society of Bengal.

Dr Führer's personal tragedy – the loss of his reputation and the collapse of a promising career as an archaeologist – was followed almost immediately by a much greater one: the disappearance of his patron, the renowned Sanskritist Professor Georg Bühler, presumed drowned in Lake Constance. On his way from Vienna to join his family in Zurich he had halted at the lakeside, hired a small boat and gone out alone onto the water, apparently to enjoy the moonlight – and was never seen again. Why the Professor should have chosen to go boating in the night was never explained.

Dr Führer's departure and Professor Bühler's death left unresolved the issue of which site was Kapilavastu. In that same year, 1898, Vincent Smith received his much-hoped-for promotion to Chief Secretary of the North-Western Provinces and Oude – only to resign within two years to become a full-time historian. In 1901 he published *Asoka the Buddhist Emperor of India*, followed three years later by the book he had worked on for two decades, *The Early History of India*, which grew in time into the *Oxford History of India*. As for Dr Waddell, his hopes of finding time to return to the Nepal border to carry on where Dr Führer and Mr Peppé had left off were dashed when in September 1900 he received orders to join the expeditionary force being assembled to put down the

Boxer Rebellion in China. He was subsequently despatched to the North-West Frontier to take part in a campaign against the Mahsuds in Waziristan, and this was followed a year later by yet another frontier campaign, which saw him enter Swat as a member of the Malakand Field Force.

The great stone coffer and its caskets found by William Peppé at Piprahwa went to the Indian Museum in Calcutta. At the request of King Chulalankara, the relics themselves found a new home in Siam.

In March 1973, while conducting extensive excavations at Piprahwa, on the Indian side of the border, K. M. Srivastava of the Archaeological Survey of India uncovered forty terracotta seals of the Kushan period bearing the inscription *Kapilava stu bhikshu-sangha*, 'community of Buddhist monks of Kapilavastu'. As far as India was concerned, this effectively resolved the dispute that had rumbled on ever since December 1896. The Nepalese authorities, however, continue to maintain that Kapilavastu lies on *their* side of the border – and they may well be right. In April 2001 Robin Corningham of the University of Bradford announced that a UNESCO-sponsored archaeological expedition under the leadership of Basanta Bidari, Nepal's chief archaeologist at Lumbini, had uncovered painted greyware ceramics contemporary with Gautama Buddha at their most favoured site – Tilaurakot, a village lying three miles north of the border with India and more or less equidistant between Smith and Waddell's Kapilavastu and Dr Führer's.

It could be that all parties are right, and that the remains of the ancient Kapilavastu of Gautama Buddha's time – its city, suburbs, palaces, temples, shrines and *viharas* – are scattered over an area wide enough to satisfy all the claims made for it from Fa Hian onwards.

Epilogue: The Sacredness of India

THE CONTRADICTIONS of British rule in India, its best and worst features, are perfectly summed up in the Viceroyalty of Lord Curzon. 'The sacredness of India haunts me like a passion,' he once declared – but then went on to add, 'It is only when you get to see what India really is, that she is the strength and greatness of England; it is only then that you realise that every nerve, every sinew a man may bring should be used to draw ever tighter the cords that bind us to India.'

Shortly after his installation at Government House in Calcutta in January 1899 Lord Curzon made a speech to the Asiatic Society of Bengal that can now be seen as second in significance only to Sir William Jones's famous discourse of 1784. No Viceroy or Governor-General had a greater sense of history – and of his own place in it – than George Nathaniel Curzon, nor had any come to India better prepared. Although no grandchild of the Enlightenment, Lord Curzon was a product of that 'free-thinking place' Balliol College, Oxford, and the brightest pupil of its reforming Master, Benjamin Jowett. He saw himself as the natural heir to such men as Warren Hastings, Wellesley and Canning, proconsuls who had 'reared the central edifice, lofty and strong, of British dominion in the East' but who had also seen it as their first duty to protect the interests of the Indian people. That duty, he told the assembled members of the Asiatic Society of Bengal, included the preservation of India's culture and the conservation of its historical remains – and it was a duty that had been sadly neglected by his predecessors: 'There have been moments when it has been argued that the state had exhausted its duty, or that it possessed no duty at all. There have been persons who thought that, when all the chief monuments were indexed and classified, one might sit with folded arms and allow them slowly to crumble into ruin. There have been others who argued that railways and irrigation did not leave a modest half lakh of rupees per annum for the requisite establishment to supervise the most glorious galaxy in the world.'

Those attitudes were now set to change, and if any dared oppose him, he would brush them to one side:

If there be any one who says to me that there is no duty devolving upon a Christian government to preserve the monuments of a pagan art, or the sanctuaries of an alien faith, I cannot pause to argue with such a man. Art and beauty, and the reverence that is owing to all that has evoked human genius or has inspired human faith, are independent of creeds, and, in so far as they touch the sphere of religion, are embraced by the common religion of all mankind . . . What is beautiful, what is historic, what tears the mask off the face of the past, and helps us to read its riddles, and to look it in the eyes – these, and not the dogmas of a combative theology, are the principle criteria to which we must look.

Like Jones's call a century earlier, Curzon's address fell largely on deaf ears. This was the high noon of the British Raj, and Anglo-India saw no reason to pander to Indian culture. As for the native Indian community, its intellectuals did not trust a ruler who was, by his own confession, 'an imperialist heart and soul', and who had come to India intent, as he jokingly put it, on assisting the struggling Indian National Congress to a 'peaceful demise'. And for all his noble ideals, by the end of the six years of his Viceroyalty Curzon had managed to antagonise practically every person and every body he came across. Nevertheless, what should be remembered here is his revival of the all but defunct Archaeological Survey under the direction of a properly qualified Director-General. With characteristic passion he fought for a proper allocation of funds, arguing that 'were Germany the ruling power in India I do not hesitate to say that she would be spending many lakhs a year'. And when funds were finally sanctioned but proved inadequate for the enlarged role he had devised for the Archaeological Survey, Curzon simply ignored his Council and authorised more spending. A century earlier Lord Wellesley had adopted this attitude, and now Lord Curzon set the same course – with equally ruinous consequences to himself.

Curzon's plans were approved by the Secretary of State for India in 1901 and in the following year twenty-six-year-old John Marshall, who had trained at the British School of Archaeology in Athens and worked as an assistant to Arthur Evans on the Minoan excavations in Crete, went out to take up the post, accompanied by his new bride Florence. Curzon's brief to him was comprehensive: 'To dig and discover, to classify, reproduce and describe, to copy and decipher, and to cherish and conserve.' Because of the state of disrepair into which so many of India's most prominent monuments had fallen, much of Marshall's time was taken up with conservation, most famously the restoration of the Taj Mahal, the present appearance of which, with its carefully landscaped gardens and its red sandstone surrounds, owes a great deal to the close interest taken in the work there by the Viceroy, who afterwards wrote with justifiable pride that 'if I had never done anything else in India, I have written my name here, and the letters are a living joy'.

During Curzon's tenancy the Archaeological Survey also made important finds, and part of the Curzon legacy is that it continued to do great things under Marshall, and has gone on doing so under his successors up to the present day. Marshall himself is best remembered for his archaeological work at Taxila from 1912 intermittently until 1936, at Sanchi, where he excavated and restored between the years 1914 and 1919, and at Mohenjo-Daro and Harappa, where in the 1920s the systematic excavations of his able assistants D.R. Sahni and R.D. Banerji brought to light the pre-Aryan Indus Civilisation.

The Sanchi that we see today is chiefly Marshall's work. He excavated, cleared and restored the fifty-one buildings on its hilltop. He established its chronology with precision, showing that the original Ashokan stupa with its wooden surround had been enlarged by the Sunga successors to the Mauryas in the first century BCE, with stone replacing perishable wood and brick. This was when the Great Stupa's encircling railing and its four magnificent gateways had been cut, paid for by wealthy traders rather than kings.

In what had become the two provinces of Bihar and the United Provinces, Marshall's assistants employed the new technique of dating by pottery shards to establish when the two regions' many Buddhist *viharas* had been inhabited and the stupas built. The greatest period of building and occupation had been during the Kushan and Gupta eras, between the first and sixth centuries CE, with another burst of activity under the Palas of Bengal between the eighth and eleventh centuries. However, the finest of the stupas dated from the time of the Sungas in the second and first centuries BCE, a period which had seen many of the earlier Ashokan stupas rebuilt and enlarged – the Sakya stupa at Piprahwa being one of the very few left untouched. More Ashokan polished pillars were recovered: one at Sanchi, two at Rampura, the fragments of two more in Jaipur State, and the most magnificent one of all at Sarnath.

Attempts to resolve long-running disputes over the identities of some of the lost Buddhist sites met with limited success. From a large *vihara* at Kasia numerous clay seals were recovered bearing the inscription 'Convent of the mahaparinirvana', proving conclusively that this was indeed Kushinagar, which meant that Cunningham had been right and Waddell and Smith wrong. The many reported Buddhist sites at Rajgir proved more difficult to pin down. After Cunningham a succession of Orientalists combed the hills armed with their copies of Fa Hian's and Huan Tsang's travels – James Fergusson, James Burgess, George Grierson, Vincent Smith, Dr Austine Waddell, Aurel Stein, Sylvain Levy, Sir John Marshall and D. N. Sen, to name only a few of the better-qualified – but none was able to establish conclusively which cave had played what role in Gautama Buddha's lifetime. However, John Marshall's excavations in 1905–6 did uncover a terrace in front of a line of six caves on the northern scarp of the ridge of the Vaibhara Hill which has since been regarded as the most likely site for the First Buddhist Council. He also uncovered the foundations of an early *vihara* at the southern foot of Chhatha-giri Hill that is almost certainly the site of the mango-garden of Jivaka, the court physician who donated land for Gautama Buddha's first monastery.

Pataliputra proved equally elusive. At Kumrahar village, where Waddell had dug by proxy, the remains of a Mauryan hall were uncovered, together with evidence of a great fire, but the general results were disappointing. At nearby Nalanda it was a better story. Here the vast and magnificent complex of stupas, *viharas* and colleges of learning as it appears today is chiefly the work of D. B. Spooner and other assistants of Marshall. Their excavations revealed that it had only gone into serious decline with the death of the last Pala ruler of East Bihar, Govindapaladeva, whose dynasty was itself the last to support the Buddhist religious institutions in India. Soon afterwards the great university had been torched in the frenzy of iconoclasm that accompanied the capture of the nearby stronghold of Behar by Qutb-ud-din's general, Muhammad Khilji, in 1193.

Those same iconoclasts also destroyed Buddhist Sarnath. Here the excavations were initially conducted by F. O. Oertel, Executive Engineer of Benares Division. In 1904 Mr Oertel reported to Marshall that during road-building operations his workmen had uncovered a well-preserved Buddha image at Sarnath. With the Director-General's consent, he conducted a series of digs on the site for three months every Cold Weather, concentrating on the area of the great stupa destroyed by Jagat Singh some hundred and twenty years earlier. These excavations uncovered a large temple which gradually revealed itself to be the centre of the original complex: the spot where Gautama Buddha had preached his first sermon and thus begun to turn the Wheel of the Law, the Dharma. At its heart Oertel uncovered a square shrine made largely of brick but with a mingling of stonework dating from the Gupta period. What was most strange, however, was that part of its foundation consisted of a square monolithic railing some five feet in height that was entirely devoid of ornament, each side being made up of four uprights linked by three lozenge-shaped cross-bars, all cut from a single block of polished sandstone. After much puzzling Marshall realised this must be the *harmika* or square crown that had once topped the original Dharmarajika stupa raised here by Ashoka. This was confirmed by the discovery, just twenty-five feet west of the main shrine, of the remains of a shattered Ashokan column lying where it had been overthrown by vandals – and beside it, its massive seven-foot-high capital (see Plate 31). This was the finest single piece of art-work to be recovered during Marshall's career. 'The capital', he wrote,

> is of the Persepolitan bell-shaped type, surmounted by four magnificent polished stone lions sitting back to back with a wheel between them – symbolizing the law of the Buddha which was first promulgated at Sarnath. Beneath the lions is a drum ornamented with four animals in relief, viz. a lion, an elephant, a bull and a horse, separated from each other by four wheels. The four crowning lions and the reliefs below are wonderfully vigorous and true to nature, and are treated with that simplicity and reserve which is the keynote of all great masterpieces of plastic art. India certainly has produced no other sculpture to equal it.

The column upon which the lion capital once stood had been severed at floor level, and when this floor was raised, seven lines of Ashoka Brahmi characters were found inscribed on its base. This surviving edict enjoined the monks and nuns to avoid creating schisms within the Sangha, its third line declaring that by command of his sacred majesty 'no one shall cause division in the order'. Other inscriptions on the broken portion of the column dated from the Kushan and early Gupta eras, matching the periods when the site had been greatly enlarged and its stupas rebuilt.

After Mr Oertel's transfer in 1906, John Marshall took over the excavations himself, clearing and restoring the area to its present appearance. To house the hundreds of pieces of sculpture and inscriptions uncovered he designed and built a simple museum, modelled on the general form of a Buddhist monastery, which contains three masterpieces of early Buddhist sculpture. The first is the lion capital, unquestionably the finest example of Mauryan art yet uncovered. Fittingly, it was this capital that was chosen as the symbol of the Indian Union at India's Independence in 1947. At the same time, the thirty-two-spoked Dharmachakra or Wheel of

Law the four lions had originally been supporting became the central image on India's new tricolour.

In Marshall's museum at Sarnath the lion capital is flanked by a monumental ten-foot standing *Bodhisattva* in red sandstone that was originally shaded by an equally massive stone sunshade. On the base of the statue is an inscription showing it to have been donated by a monk named Bala in the third year of the reign of King Kanishka of Gandhara, which dates it to around 130 CE. Kanishka came to be revered by Buddhists as a great champion of Buddhism, second only to Ashoka, and it was in his time that images of Buddha first began to appear in northern India – in seeming defiance of the Buddha's commands to seek refuge in the Dharma alone and to look to no one but oneself for liberation.

The third masterpiece dates from the fifth century CE, carved from a block of the same tan-coloured Chunar sandstone that supplied the Ashokan columns, and is perhaps the most exquisite creation of Gupta art. It shows Gautama Buddha in high relief, seated cross-legged in the lotus posture of meditation on a throne, his head encircled by a decorated nimbus surmounted by two flying *apsaras* or celestial nymphs. With his hands he makes the gesture known as *pravartana-mudra* which signifies preaching: he is propounding the Dharmachakrapravartana, the Turning of the Wheel of Law. His features have been only slightly damaged, unlike those of most Buddhist statues, and convey an awesome dignity and calm, the eyes cast downward and inward.

Vincent Smith wrote in his *Oxford History of India* in 1920 that the Muslim invasions 'were fatal to the existence of Buddhism as an organised religion in northern India'. But further researches had now established that Buddhism was already a spent force in India even before the first Muslim raids. As Tibetan and Sinhalese sources had alleged, persecution by Brahmin–dominated rulers played a significant part, but the root causes of Buddhism's fatal decline on the subcontinent were more complex. The widespread adoption of Hindu tantric practices from Bengal had fatally weakened the Sangha from within, but the real hammer-blow was the transformation of Brahminism in the eighth and ninth centuries into the Hinduism we see in India today. The rise of populist devotional cults made Hinduism immediately accessible to ordinary people, while at the same time reformers such as the South Indian revivalist Sankaracharya and his disciple Bhatacharya had been able to capture the moral high ground Buddhism had hitherto held by adopting its doctrines – a process that also saw Gautama Buddha brought into the Hindu fold by the simple expedient of making him one of the many avatars of Vishnu, by then the most powerful deity in the Hindu pantheon.

The excavations of Marshall and Spooner at Taxila and elsewhere in Curzon's newly-created North-West Frontier Province produced a wealth of wonderfully fluid Buddhist sculptures from the first to fourth centuries CE that in the view of Marshall, Waddell, Smith and others showed clear evidence of Hellenistic influence, and were therefore termed 'Graeco-Buddhist' – an interpretation condemned in later years as betraying a pro-European bias. Now the pendulum has swung back, and it is generally agreed that the Kushans, lacking any monumental artistic heritage of their own, adopted and then developed the Greek traditions of their Bactrian predecessors – just as they adopted and developed Buddhism in Gandhara before exporting it, together with their trade goods, along the Silk Route.

With the explorations of the Hungarian-turned-Briton Aurel Stein and his Swedish, French and German rivals – Sven Hedin, Paul Pelliot and Albert von le Coq – from 1900 onwards, the Buddhist treasures of the Silk Road began to emerge, culminating in 1907 in Stein's most fortuitous discovery (as it was seen then) or criminal looting (as the Chinese see it now) of the famous library cave at Dunhuang with its hoard of five hundred cubic feet of manuscripts and scroll paintings, a hoard that included the oldest printed book in the world – the ninth-century Diamond Sutra (now in the British Library, along with the pick of Stein's collection).

This peaceful penetration of Chinese Turkestan was in contrast to the invasion of Tibet by a military force, in the guise of a diplomatic mission, that shot its way through to Lhasa in 1904, an act of extraordinary folly on Lord Curzon's part prompted by his fear that Russia was about to establish a foothold in the country. Politically the Younghusband Mission achieved very little, other than a fatal acknowledgement of China's suzerainty over Tibet. Although the Simla Conference of 1913–14 later recognised

Tibet's independence, it was never ratified by the Chinese government: the damage had been done, with far-reaching consequences for Tibetan independence.

A more positive by-product of the invasion was the partial opening of Tibet to the Western world. The chief medical officer on the mission was Dr Austine Waddell, who was given a special commission to collect as much cultural data as he could. Much of what he brought back – in the form of religious artefacts, including statues cast in copper and bronze, richly decorated ritual instruments, wood-block-printed books, and the painted hangings known as *thankas* – was looted, taken from the monasteries and forts that lined the mission's route to Lhasa, to be later distributed among the museums and libraries of Calcutta, London, Oxford and Cambridge.

Dr Waddell went to Tibet sharing the general opinion of his British colleagues that Tibetan lamas were a degenerate and ignorant lot, and their Lamaism 'a priestly mixture of Shivaite mysticism, magic and Indo-Tibetan demonolatry, overlaid by a thin varnish of Mahayana Buddhism . . . beneath which the sinister growth of poly-demonish superstition darkly appears'. On his return from Lhasa he resigned from the IMS and sailed for England with his treasures to write *Lhasa and its Mysteries*, the best of the many books to come out of this shameful episode. He went on to become the first Professor of Tibetan at a British university, at University College, London. His hostility towards Tibetan Vajrayana softened only slightly over the years. Sharing Rhys Davids' reformist view that Buddhism, just like early Christianity, had become corrupted, Waddell hoped that, with British help, it might one day reclaim itself to become 'a new star in the East which may for long, perhaps for centuries, diffuse its mild radiance over this charming land and interesting people. In the University, which must ere long be established under British direction at Lhasa, a chief place will surely be assigned to studies of the origin of the religion of the country.' There is indeed a university at Lhasa today, but a Chinese-run one.

In the West the processes initiated separately by Edwin Arnold, Thomas Rhys Davids, Henry Olcott and Anagarika Dharmapala continued to unfold. All four played a part in the conversion of the

French socialist and pioneer feminist Alexandra David-Neel, who in 1891 joined Dharmapala in Ceylon and in that same year helped set up the first European branch of the Maha Bodhi Society in Leipzig, attracting the support of a number of German scholars and students of Schopenhauer, most notably Karl Seidenstücker, Karl Neumann and Paul Dahlke, all of whom studied Pali in Ceylon before returning to Germany to found their own Buddhist organisations. The first European woman to be received in audience by both the Dalai Lama and the Panchen Lama, David-Neel nevertheless espoused a modernised Theravada-based Buddhism, a teaching she later set out in her popular account of Buddhist practices, *The Buddhism of the Buddha and Buddhist Modernism* – written as a direct riposte to Daisetzu Suzuki's *Outlines of Mahayana Buddhism*, published in America in 1907.

Whether Thomas Rhys Davids actually considered himself a practising Buddhist is debatable, although he followed Buddhist precepts. 'Buddhist or not Buddhist,' he said of himself, 'I have examined every one of the great religious systems of the world, and in none of them have I found anything to surpass, in beauty and comprehensiveness, the Noble Eightfold Path of the Buddha. I am content to shape my life according to that Path.' If not Rhys Davids, who then was the first Westerner in modern times to profess Buddhism? It may have been the German-American publisher Paul Carus, who was certainly among the first to support Buddhism in the West. The year after Anagarika Dharmapala's initial visit to the United States, Rhys Davids gave a series of lectures at Cornell University which Paul Carus either attended in person or read. His response was to bring out a book entitled *The Gospel of Buddha*, which opens with a very un-Buddhist evangelical call to rejoice at the glad tidings – for 'Buddhu, our Lord, has found the root of all evil. He has shown the way of salvation.' This was fiercely attacked by Christians, which led Carus to write a sequel entitled *Buddhism and its Critics*. In 1897 he invited Anagarika Dharmapala to return to the United States, and it was with his support that Dharmapala founded the first American branch of the Maha Bhodi Society. In the following year Carus invited the young Japanese Buddhist Daisetzu Suzuki to join his publishing house. This in turn led to Dr Suzuki's many works on

Zen and Mahayana becoming popular in the United States, so laying the groundwork for the later spread of Zen and Mahayana Buddhism in America.

This initial flowering of Buddhism in the West suffered after the outbreak of the Great War in 1914, and subsequent events in Germany all but destroyed the various Buddhist schools there. In the United States of America, the work of the Zen masters who had followed in the footsteps of Daisetzu Suzuki was discredited by Japan's attack on Pearl Harbor and the war in the Pacific.

In 1951 troops of the Chinese People's Liberation Army invaded Tibet in order to bring about its 'reintegration into the motherland'. The repressions that followed culminated in the infamous Cultural Revolution of 1966–67, which saw the destruction of virtually every Buddhist edifice and religious art-work in Tibet. Hundreds of thousands of Tibetans perished in the process and millions chose to become refugees for the sake of their faith, crossing the Himalayan barrier to find religious freedom in India, Nepal, Bhutan and Sikkim.

Intended in part to liberate Tibetans from their religion, this gross act of human and cultural genocide – before which the combined brutalities of the Portuguese, Dutch, French and British colonisers of South and South-East Asia pale into insignificance – has had quite the opposite effect. Contact with the outside world has brought about a modernising process within the scattered Tibetan communities that has benefited the majority, particularly in terms of education. Far from declining, religious learning has flourished – not the crude instruction by rote that had come to dominate many of Tibet's monasteries, but genuinely informed teaching. Religious masters once widely separated by geographical barriers and sectarian differences have been brought together under the aegis of the fourteenth Dalai Lama in his headquarters at Dharamsala, in the foothills of the Himalayas north of Delhi. A wealth of knowledge salvaged from the libraries of remote monasteries before they were blown to pieces has become widely accessible. The old tradition of secret one-to-one initiation into the inner mysteries of Vajrayana has given way to the master class, where the guru instructs not one but a roomful of *chelas*.

The impact of the Tibetan diaspora has been felt far beyond the refugee centres of India and Nepal. Perhaps already primed by a sympathy towards Buddhism as a religion of peace – to say nothing of feelings of guilt over its silent acquiescence in China's rape of Tibet – the West opened its doors to Tibetan refugees. And along with the Tibetans has come an abundance of learning and culture. Nowhere has this infusion been more fruitful than in the United States of America, where Buddhism had fallen on hard times and in the 1960s was chiefly represented by the twin phenomena of Hippie Zen and the best-selling books of Cyril Henry Hoskins. This failed correspondence clerk from Devon claimed his mind had been taken over by a Tibetan physician named T. Lobsang Rampa, causing him to write *The Third Eye*, an account of life in Tibet in the first decades of the twentieth century that became a best-seller in twelve countries within a year of its publication in Britain in 1956 (and is still widely available). Centres of Buddhist Studies were founded at a number of American universities, and through the efforts of the Library of Congress thousands of hitherto unknown Tibet texts were published in India; copies were subsequently distributed to academic libraries throughout the States, and the texts are now accessible through the internet. Numerous publishing houses have sprung up to serve and further the growing popular interest in Buddhism in North America and beyond.

Buddhism has also returned to the land of its founder. After the Second World War, the coming of independence to India and Burma in 1947 saw a resurgence of Buddhism in both countries. In India Buddhism had been almost entirely confined to the regions of Ladakh and Alchi known as 'Little Tibet' and the area around Chittagong in East Bengal, to which large numbers of Buddhist Mughs had fled from Arakan in the 1790s. However, in 1912 a bright young Indian 'untouchable' named Bhimrao Ambedkar, born into one of the many social groups considered to be outside the Hindu caste system, arrived to study at New York's Columbia University on a scholarship. After completing further studies in England, he returned to India to practise law and work for the emancipation of the untouchable castes. In 1947 Dr Ambedkar was appointed Minister of Law and, as Chairman of the Constitution Drafting Committee, played the key role in the drafting of the Indian Constitution. Opposed by the Brahmin-dominated Congress government on the issue of the abolition of caste, in 1951 he resigned to implement a scheme for the mass conversion of untouchables from Hinduism to Buddhism; and in October 1956 he and many of his followers converted at a cere-mony at Nagpur. Indian Buddhists are now a force to be reckoned with; the threat of further mass conversion has become a powerful weapon in the struggle for equal rights in India.

Tensions between the two religions are once more a minor but noticeable feature of the modern Indian scene. Their most recent manifestation is a proposal by the government of Uttar Pradesh (formerly the United Provinces) to build a dam just south of the Nepal border that would have the effect of flooding Lumbini – an act seen by Nepalis as a deliberate attempt to inundate the site of Gautama Buddha's birthplace and so give greater prominence to Piprahwa, on the Indian side of the border. On the other hand, the passing of the Bodh-Gaya Temple Act in 1949 saw the formation of a committee of nine members to manage and control the Mahabodhi temple at Bodh-Gaya, the committee being made up of four Buddhists and four Hindus, together with the District Magistrate of Gaya. After fighting a rearguard battle through the courts, the *mahant* of Bodh-Gaya finally conceded defeat, and on Buddha Purnima Day, 23 May 1953, the Mahabodhi temple was finally handed over to the Bodh-Gaya Temple Management Committee.

Thanks to the efforts of men like Jones, Buchanan, Prinsep, Cunningham and Marshall, as well as of those who have followed them, the great Buddhist monuments of Ajanta, Sanchi and Sarnath are now visited and admired by hundreds of thousands of visitors each year. Many Indian nationals seem unimpressed – perhaps India has so much antiquity that they have become blasé, or perhaps they have yet to understand the richness of their heri-tage. But the pilgrimage trails that Fa Hian and Huan Tsang trod so long ago are now followed by thousands of new pilgrims, some of them tourists but many more of them Buddhists, drawn from all over the world. They include grey-robed monks and nuns from Japan and Korea, ochre-robed monks and nuns from Sri Lanka, yellow-robed monks and nuns from Burma, Siam,

Thailand, Cambodia and Taiwan, and yellow-and-red-robed monks and nuns from Tibet, Nepal, Bhutan and Ladakh. And among them there are a steadily increasing number of Westerners, whose robes reflect the Buddhism of their choice.

With their coming, the primal landscape of Bihar, Uttar Pradesh and the Terai has begun to change, particularly at Bodh-Gaya, where around the ancient temple and its Bodhi-tree a town has grown up in which every branch of the international Sangha now has its golden-roofed temple and its pilgrim guest-house.

Among Bodh-Gaya's many annual visitors is the Dalai Lama, who comes to teach the Dharma here every Cold Weather. Under his aegis the landscape of Bodh-Gaya is set to change dramatically again, for on the western edge of the town a forty-five acre park is to become the biggest statement of confidence in Buddhism since King Ashoka embarked on the construction of his 84,000 stupas. A bronze statue is being erected here that will be many times larger than any built before. It will rise five hundred feet into the sky, forty-five storeys high, and the space within will be as great as that of the largest cathedral in Europe. It will be a statue of Buddha Maitreya, the Buddha to come, seated on a stone throne, with his right hand held open in the gesture of giving and the thumb and first finger of the left joined in the gesture of teaching. It will cost in excess of two hundred million dollars, and the project's originators justify the expenditure on the grounds that the statue will inspire peace and the happiness of all sentient beings. The Maitreya will face north, towards the Land of Snows, as if to signal to Tibet's present occupiers that his time will come.

A little knowing, little have I told
Touching the Teacher and the Ways of Peace
Forty-five rains thereafter showed he those
In many lands and many tongues, and gave
Our Asia Light, that still is beautiful,
Conquering the world with spirit of strong grace:
All which is written in the holy Books,
And where he passed, and what proud Emperors
Carved his sweet words upon the rocks and caves:
And how – in fulness of the times – it fell
The Buddha died, the great Tathagato,
Even as a man 'mongst men, fulfilling all:
And how a thousand thousand lakhs since then
Have trod the Path which leads whither he went
Unto Nirvana, where the Silence lives.

The concluding lines of *The Light of Asia*,
by Sir Edwin Arnold, 1879

Acknowledgements

This book could not have been written without the generosity and good advice of many people. In particular, I would like to thank John Keay, whose book on the achievements of the British in India, *India Discovered*, published in 1981, first cleared away the undergrowth and gave me a path to follow; William Dalrymple, who revealed to me some choice plums that a lesser man would have hidden away for himself; John Falconer, Curator of Photographs, Oriental and India Office Collection (OIOC) at the British Library, who always found time for me; Michael Pollock, Librarian of the Royal Asiatic Society, whose patience was inexhaustible; Ivan Prinsep, who gave me the key to his ancestral *toshakana*; Dr Om Prakash Kejariwal, Director of the Nehru Memorial Library, New Delhi, for advice and for allowing me free use of his own researches into the Asiatic Society of Bengal and the Prinsep family in India; Dr Jennifer Howes, Curator, Prints Drawings and Photographs, OIOC, for allowing me to draw on her unpublished article on the Mackenzie Drawings in the British Library (see them yourself via the British Library Home Page); Sue Farrington for her ideas; Patrick Conner of the Martyn Gregory art gallery in Bury Street for tracking down for me two hitherto unpublished portraits of James Prinsep; and Diana Reynolds for most generously allowing me to reproduce one of them.

I should also like to thank the following for their unstinting help in their official and/or private capacities: Professor Richard

Bowring, Master of Selwyn College, Cambridge; Dr T. K. Biswas, Director of the Bharat Kala Bhawan, Varansi; Theon Wilkinson, Hon. Secretary, British Association for Cemeteries in South Asia; Jerry Losty, Curator of Prints, Drawings, Photographs and Works of Art, OIOC; David Blakey, Curator of European Manuscripts, OIOC; Kate Pickard, Archivist, Herbarium and Library, Royal Botanic Garden, Kew; George New-Burden, Archivist at the *Daily Telegraph*; Maggie Magnuson, Librarian, Royal Engineers Museum, Chatham; the Librarian and staff at the Library of the School of Oriental and African Studies; the Director and staff at the National Army Museum; the Director and staff at the OIOC, London Library; Camellia Panjabi, late VP Marketing for the Taj Group of Hotels; Sunita Nair, late Editor of the *Taj Magazine*; and Narayan Singh and staff of the Taj Ganges, Varanasi.

Lastly, a very special thanks to Liz for travelling with me; Vivien for keeping faith with me; Caroline, Grant and John for bringing me back out of the cold; Roger Hudson for (again) reading and bringing sense to my manuscript; Douglas Matthews for (again) his indexing and his invaluable services as a long-stop; and, finally, Liz Robinson, for (again) performing wonders with her editor's pencil.

Glossary

Note: P = Pali; S = Sanskrit; T = Tibetan

acarya (S/P):	teacher; see also *guru*
Adi Buddha (S):	the primal Buddha
Ananda (S):	joy; Gautama Buddha's half-brother or cousin and chief attendant
anatman (P), *anatta* (S):	without soul, spirit or self, the ultimate condition of extinction: the doctrine preached by Gautama Buddha
apsara (S):	celestial nymph
arahant (P), *arhat* (S):	enlightened person who has attained nirvana, thus a Buddhist saint; used to describe Gautama Buddha's disciples
ashtapatha (S):	the Eightfold Path: right views, right resolve; right speech; right conduct; right livelihood; right effort; right recollection; and right meditation
asura (S):	enemy of the gods, demon
atman (S):	soul, spirit, universal consciousness
Asoka, Ashoka:	Emperor of India *c.* 268–233 BCE, third ruler in the Maurya dynasty, patron of Buddhism and promoter of *Dharma*; named on his edicts as Devanampiya Piyadassi, 'The beloved of the Gods and Gracious of Mien'
ashram (S):	hermitage
Avalokiteshvara (S):	one who looks down, the most popular of the *bodhisattvas* in Mahayana Buddhism; in T. *Chenresig*
avatara (S):	descent, incarnation or manifestation on earth of a Buddha or transcendent being
Bhagavad Gita (S):	Song of God, poem in praise of Krishna universally acknowledged as a poetic masterpiece, originally considered as part of the *Mahabharatha* epic but now

297

	accepted as a later addition from the first or second century CE
bhavana (S):	cultivation, thus meditation
bhikkhu (P), *bhiksu* (S):	beggar, thus Buddhist monk
Bimbisara:	King of Maghada in Gautama Buddha's time and an early convert
bodhi (S/P):	enlightenment, in Japanese *satori*, also called *samma sambhodi*; thus *bhodi*-tree, the pipal tree under which Gautama Buddha achieved enlightenment
bodhicitta (S):	awakening mind, thus the aspiration to seek Buddhahood and to act altruistically
Bodhidharma (S):	Buddhist saint, born in Ceylon, went to China in fifth century, practitioner of *zazen*
bodhisatta (P), *bodhisattva* (S):	awakened being, one who is on the way to attaining enlightenment and full Buddhahood but remains in the world to ease the suffering of others
Brahma (S):	the supreme being and, in the Hindu pantheon, creator of the universe
Brahmana or Brahmin (S):	Brahmin, man of the highest, priestly caste in Hindu society, already reborn and therefore superior to others; thus Brahmanism, the form of organised religion that first took shape in the Vedic era
Brahmi:	name given to the script used in much of India at the time of Emperor Ashoka, written in *Prakrit* language
Buddha (P/S):	awakened, thus the enlightened one who has attained *nirvana*; title for *Gautama* Buddha, the historical founder of Buddhism, one of an infinite number of Buddhas who preach the *Dharma*
ch'an (Chinese):	meditation, giving rise to *zen*
chaitya (S):	domed memorial without relics; see also *stupa*
chaitya-griha (S):	sanctuary containing a *chaitya*
chakra (S):	wheel, thus the symbol of Buddha's teaching; in tantric teaching a centre of spiritual energy, but see also *Dharmachakra*
chela (Hindi):	disciple of a *guru*
chhatra (S):	umbrella on top of a *stupa*, symbol of royalty, thus early symbol of Buddha
chos (T):	Tibetan term for the *Dharma*
chorten (T):	Tibetan term for *stupa*
Chenresig (T):	protector of Tibet; see also *Avalokiteshvara*
dagoba (P):	relic mound in Ceylon, from *datugarbha* (S), 'womb of objects', later giving rise to the Portuguese 'pagoda'; see also *stupa*
Dalai Lama (T):	'Great Ocean Lama', title of the head of the Gelugpa school of Tibetan Buddhism, derived from Mongolia but used in Tibet since sixteenth century; see *lama*

Glossary

dakini (S):	female sky spirit, angel
deva (S):	gods
Devadatta:	cousin of *Gautama Buddha*, and his chief enemy
devi (S):	goddess
Dhamma (P), *Dharma* (S):	'that which is right', thus ordained duties; in Buddhism, the eternal law of the universe as discovered and preached by Gautama Buddha; the theory and practice of the Buddhist doctrine, one of the Three Jewels of Buddhism; also, element of consciousness, ultimate reality
Dhammapada (P):	collected sayings of Gautama Buddha
Dharmachakra (S):	the Wheel of the Law, symbolised as a wheel
dhyana (S):	religious contemplation or meditation, thus *dhyana-yoga*, meditational exercises; origin of the Chinese *ch'an* and the Japanese *zen*
Eight Precepts:	vows taken by Buddhist laity and nuns in *Theravada* Buddhism
Five Precepts:	Buddhist undertakings not to kill, steal, lie, be unchaste or take intoxicants
Four Noble Truths:	doctrine expounded at the Buddha's first sermon: that life is suffering; that suffering has a cause; that suffering can be eliminated; and that there is a path to that elimination – the way of leading to cessation
Four Signs:	four signs of mortality shown to the young Prince Gautama by his charioteer Chandaka: an old man, a sick man, a dead man and a monk
Gotama (P), *Gautama* (S):	personal name of Prince Gautama, son of Raja Suddhodana of the Sakya clan, ruler of Kapilavastu, and his wife Maya; born in the palace garden of Lumbini in about the year 563 BCE; named *Siddhartha*; acquired the honorifics *Sakyamuni* and *Tathagata* after achieving enlightenment at Bodh-Gaya at the age of thirty-five when he achieved complete *bodhi* and became *Buddha*
ghat (H):	steps beside a river, crossing point
gita (S):	song or hymn, thus *Bhagavad Gita*
guru (S):	spiritual teacher, thus Guru Rinpoche, the Tibetan name for the Indian teacher who by tradition brought the *Dharma* to Tibet
Hinayana (S):	the Lesser Vehicle or Path, the term used by *Mahayana* Buddhists to describe the first and more exclusive form of established Buddhism, which survives as *Theravada*
Hitopadesa (S):	Book of Sound Counsel, collection of fables stressing morality and Buddhist virtues
Jainism:	religious movement founded by Vardhamana Mahavira, also known as Jina or 'Victor', who lived in Maghada c. 540–468 BCE. His life followed a pattern very similar to

that of Gautama Buddha's and he taught a philosophy superficially similar to Buddhism, but with a different concept of the soul and the means to enlightenment

Jambudwipa (S): land of sweet fruit, one of the seven continents of Hindu cosmology, with Bharata or India occupying its southern quarter

Jataka (P/S): birth stories, compendium of 547 allegorical tales that relate the former lives of the Buddha on this earth

Kanjur (T): translation of the commandments of the Buddha, the Tibetan canon of Buddhist literature, made up of the *vinaya*, *Mahayana sutras* and *tantras*

Kalidasa: Ancient India's preatest poet and playwright, who by tradition lived at the court of the legendary Raja Vikramaditya but probably flourished during the Gupta period. Author of the poems *Raghu-vamsa* and *Megha-duta* and the play *Shakuntala*

kamma (P), *karma* (S): act, resulting effects of previous actions or thoughts; thus the doctrine of *karma* governs the lives of humans and other beings

kot (Nepali): fort

lama (T): religious teacher in Tibet; see also *guru*

Madhyama prathipad (S): the Middle Way, preached by the Buddha in his first sermon at Sarnath: 'Follow neither the satisfaction of your cravings, nor extreme mortification. Lead a moral well-ordered life.'

Mahabharata (S): Sanskrit epic of the war between the Pandavas and Kauravas, assembled over a long period before the fifth century BCE

mahant (H): Hindu chief priest

Mahavira: see Jainism

Mahayana (S): Great Vehicle or Path, an important school of inclusive Buddhism which first took shape in the first and second centuries CE in northern India, embracing new ideas that emphasised compassion, the role of *bodhisattvas*, the teachings of the *sutras* and employment of *tantras*

Mahinda, Mahenda: son of Ashoka, became a Buddhist priest and went to Ceylon, founded monastery of Anuradhapura, died *c.* 222 BCE

Maitreya (S): Loving One, last of the five great *bodhisattvas* and the Future Buddha (T. *Jampo*) to come

mantra (S): mystical incantations of sacred formulae, in Buddhism confined to *tantra*; see also *Om Mane Padme Hom*

Mara: the great tempter, the personification of evil who attempts to distract the Buddha while in meditation

mudra (S): symbolic hand gestures in Buddhism and in Buddhist iconography

Glossary

mujahidin (Arabic):	holy warrior, thus one who takes up arms for Islam
munshi (H):	teacher, thus translator
nat (B):	Burmese Buddhist deity
nibbana (P), *nirvana* (S):	Niban: extinguishing, cessation of craving, suffering and delusion; thus ultimate enlightenment, the Buddhist goal
Om Mane Padme Hom (S/T):	Tibetan *mantra* invoking *Chenresig*, employing a mix of Sanskrit and Tibetan
padmasana (S):	lotus position, the seated posture in which Buddhas and other deities are most often shown in Buddhist and Jain iconography
Pali (S/P):	text, thus Buddhist scripture, now used as the name for the language derived from Sanskrit in which which the *Pali Canon* is written
Pali Canon:	books composed in *Pali* comprising the *Tripitaka*, set down in Ceylon in about 20 BCE from extensive oral traditions handed down by generations of *bhikkhus*, amounting to 136 volumes
pandit (H):	religious teacher, learned man of Brahmin caste
parinibbana (P), *parinirvana* (S):	ultimate extinguishing, term used to describe the death of Gautama Buddha; see also *nibbana*
pipal:	*Ficus religiosa*, also known as the Bo or *Bodhi* tree, under which Gautama Buddha attained enlightenment
Prakrit:	a group of languages derived from Sanskrit, including *Pali*
puja (H):	Hindu worship; in Buddhism devotion or homage
Puranas:	ancient Sanskrit scriptures assembled over many centuries but reworked between the second and fifth centuries CE to conform with Brahmin orthodoxy
saddhu (H):	one who has renounced the world to seek God
Sakya (P), *Shakya* (S):	Lion People, ruling clan into which Gautama Buddha was born
Sakyamuni (S):	Sage of the Sakyas, title of *Gautama Buddha*
samma sambhodi (S):	full enlightenment; see *bodhi*
samsara (S):	universal cycle of birth, death and rebirth, escaped only by achieving *nirvana*
sangha (P/S):	assembly; thus the community of Buddhist monks and nuns, one of the three elements of the *Triratna*
sannyasi (S):	one who has renounced life; thus, a sage
Sanskrit:	Indo-European language in which the earliest religious texts of Vedic Hinduism were written, giving rise to many of the languages of South-East Asia, including *Prakrit* and *Pali*
shakti:	form of religious empowerment associated with the Hindu goddess Kali involving ritual sexual intercourse

Glossary

Sariputta:	senior disciple of Buddha who was born and died at Nalanda
Siddhattha (P), *Siddhartha* (S):	'One who has achieved his purpose'; title of *Gautama Buddha*
shramana (S):	striver, thus ascetic, not necessarily Buddhist except in China; origin of 'shaman'
stupa (S):	domed monument or tumulus containing relics such as ashes of Buddhist saints; termed 'tope' by British antiquarians, from the Pali *thupo*, in Sri Lanka *dagoba*
sutra (S), *sutta* (P):	thread used to tie beads, thus Buddhist scripture as derived from Gautama Buddha's teachings, usually dealing with doctrine
Tathagata (S/P):	One who walks in the right path or follows the way of his predecessors; title of *Gautama Buddha*, much favoured by Chinese Buddhists
tantra (S):	meditation rituals employing esoteric texts as the means to accelerate liberation, the basis of *Vajrayana* Buddhism
Theravada (P)	Doctrine or Path of the Elders, the form of Buddhism preserved in Ceylon/Sri Lanka, based on the teaching of the *Pali Canon*, which spread to Thailand, Burma and elsewhere in south-east Asia
tope, thupo (P):	see *stupa, dagoba*
Tripitaka (S):	Three Baskets, the earliest collection of Buddhist texts, relating to Buddha's teachings, monasticism and scholasticism, also known as the *Pali Canon*
Triratna (S):	Three Precious Jewels – Buddha, Dharma and Sangha – together comprising Buddhism
Vajrayana (S):	Diamond Vehicle or Path, Indestructible Vehicle, the aspect of *Mahayana* as found in Tibetan Buddhism, emphasising the role of *tantra* and meditative techniques as the means of achieving enlightenment
Vedas (S):	earliest texts of Hinduism, therefore most sacred, probably assembled before 600 BCE
vihara (S/P):	secluded dwelling, thus Buddhist monastery or religious complex
vinaya (S/P):	discipline, thus the rule of the Buddhist Order as set down in scripture
yaksha (S):	pre-Buddhist fertility figure associated with abundance, found in Buddhist iconography
yakshi (S):	female version of *yaksha*
yogi (S):	one who practices intensive meditative exercises
zazen (Chinese):	more properly, *ch'an*, school of Buddhist meditation introduced into China by *Bodhidharma* and from thence to Japan; see also *dhyana, zen*:
zen (Japanese):	school of Buddhist meditation in Japan, based on sudden enlightenment; see also *dhyana, zazen*

Bibliography

As this is a book intended for the general reader I have eschewed notes and references in the text. My apologies to scholars where the sources of quotations are unclear, but a little effort should locate them in the following list. Major sources of information were *Asiatick Researches*, the *Journal of the Asiatic Society of Bengal* and the *Journal of the Royal Asiatic Society*: every issue between 1788 and 1848 was consulted, as were copies of the *Journal of the Royal Asiatic Society* up to 1907. The Archaeological Surveys of India vols I–XXII, 1871–85, and the Annual Reports of the Archaeological Survey of India, 1903–20, were also consulted. Again, my apologies for not going into great detail, which would have required the listing of several hundred articles.

Unpublished sources

Hamilton Papers, relating to Dr Francis Buchanan (later Hamilton) Oriental and India Office Collection at the British Library (hereafter OIOC), MSS Eur. K. 156–75; maps and drawings from the Hamilton papers, MSS Eu.D. 95

Joinville, Joseph Eudelin de, MSS. 'Quelques Notions Sur L'Isle de Ceylan' (listed under 'Jonville'), OIOC Eur. D. 60

Kejariwal, Om Prakash, 'The Prinseps of India, a Personal Quest'

Mackenzie Collection, OIOC

Prinsep, Sir Henry Thoby, 'Three Generations in India 1771–1904', OIOC MSS Eur. C. 97

Prinsep, James, 'Early letters from India', OIOC MSS D. 1160/6; 'Late letters from India', Nehru Memorial Library, New Delhi

Prinsep, William, 'The Journal of William Prinsep', OIOC MSS D. 1160/1–3 6

Published primary sources

Arnold, Edwin, *The Light of Asia or The Great Renunciation*, 1884

——*India Revisited*, 1888

Astley, Thomas, *A New Collection of Voyages and Travels*, 1745

Broadley, A. M., *Ruins of the Nalanda Monasteries at Burgaon*, 1872

Becher, Augusta, *Reminiscences in India and Europe 1830–88* (ed. H. G. Rawlinson), 1930

Buchanan, Francis, *Journal of Francis Buchanan (afterwards Hamilton) kept during the Survey of the Districts of Patna and Gaya in 1811–12* (ed. H. V. Jackson), 1925

Carus, Paul, *The Gospel of Buddha*, 1894

——*Buddhism and its Christian Critics*, 1897

Cunningham, Sir Alexander, *The Bhilsa Topes; or Buddhist Monuments of Central India*, 1854

——*The Ancient Geography of India: 1. The Buddhist Period*, 1871

——*Inscriptions of Asoka*, 1877

——*The Stupa of Bharut; a Buddhist Monument*, 1879

——*Book of Indian Eras*, 1883

——*Coins of Ancient India from the earliest times*, 1891

——*Mahabodhi, or the Great Buddhist temple at Bodh-Gaya*, 1892

——*Archaeological Surveys of India*, Vols I–XXIII, 1871–85

Davy, John, *An Account of the Interior of Ceylon*, 1821

Dhammika, S., *The Edicts of King Ashoka: An English Rendering*, 1994

Eden, Emily, *Up the Country*, 1866

——*Letters from India*, 1872

Elphinstone, Mountstuart, *An Account of the Kingdom of Caubul*, 1815

Fergusson, James, *Illustrations of the Rock-Cut Temples of India*, 1845

——*Picturesque Illustrations of Ancient Architecture in Hindostan*, 1848

——*Tree and Serpent Worship*, 1878

Fergusson, James, and Gill, Robert, *Rock-Cut Temples of Western India*, 1864

Fergusson, James, and Burgess, J., *Cave Temples of India*, 1880

Forbes, Major, *Eleven Years in Ceylon*, 1840

Führer, Dr A., *Report of the Archaeological Survey of the NWP & Oude*, 1897–8

——*Monograph on Buddha Sakyamuni's Birthplace*, 1897

Grant, Charles, *Observations on the State of Society among the Asiatic Subjects of Great Britain*, 1797

Kircher, Athanasius, *China Documentis Illustrata*, 1686

Kirkpatrick, Colonel William, *An Account of the Kingdom of Nepal*, 1811

Hodgson, B. H., *Miscellaneous Essays relating to Indian Subjects*, 1880

Hunter, Sir W. W., *Life of Brian Houghton Hodgson*, 1896

Knox, Robert, *An Historical Relation of the Island of Ceylon*, 1691

Hodson, V. C. R., *List of the Officers of the Bengal Army*, reprint 1927–8

Jacquemont, Victor, *Letters from India*, 1834

Jones, Sir William, *Letters* (ed. G. Cannon), 1970

Legge, James, *A Record of Buddhist Kingdoms*, 1886

McCrindle, E. M. (ed.), *Ancient India as Described by Megasthenes and Arrian*, 1877

Macauley, Thomas, *Minute of Education*, 1835

Maisey, General Frederick, *Sanchi and its Remains*, 1892

Marshall, Sir John, *The Monuments of Sanchi*, 1931

——*A Guide to Taxila*, 1936

——*Buddhist Art of Gandhara*, 1960

Mill, James, *History of British India*, 1818

Mukherji, Purna Chandra, *Report on a Tour of Exploration of the Antiquities of the Tarai*, 1901

Parkes, Fanny, *Wanderings of a Pilgrim in Search of the Picturesque*, 1850

Polo, Marco, *Description of the World* (trans. Teresa Waugh), 1989

Postans, Mrs Marianne, *Western India in 1838*, 1839

Prinsep, James, *Essays on Indian Antiquities* (ed. E. Thomas), 1858

Rémusat, Abel, *The Pilgrimage of Fa Hian from the French Edition of the Foe Koue Ki of MM Rémusat, Klaproth and Landresse*, 1848

Roberts, Mrs Emma, *Sketches and Characteristics of Upper Hindoostan*, 1837

Rhys Davids, T. W., *Buddhism, its History and Literature*, 1896

——*Buddhist India*, 1902

Sangermano, F. V., *A Description of the Burmese Empire* (trans. W. Tandy), 1893

Sewell, Robert, *Report on the Amaravati Tope*, 1890

Symes, Lt. Col. M., *An Account of an Embassy to the Kingdom of Ava in the year 1795*, 1800

Tod, James, *Travels in Western India*, 1839

Turnour, George, *Mahavamsa or The Great Chronicle*, 1836

Tennant, Sir James, *Ceylon* (3rd edn), 1859

Waddell, Dr Austine, *The Buddhism of Tibet or Lamaism*, 1897

——*Discovery of the Exact Site of Asoka's Classic Capital of Pataliputra*, 1892

——*Report on the Ruins at Pataliputra (Patna)*, 1903

——*Lhasa and its Mysteries*, 1906

Watters, Thomas, *On Yan Chwang's Travels in India*, Vols I and II, 1904 and 1905

Wilson, H. H., *History of Kashmir*, 1836

——*Ariana Antiqua*, 1841

Upham, Edward, *History and Doctrine of Buddhism*, 1829

——*The Mahavamsi and the Sacred Books of Ceylon*, 1833

Valentia, Viscount, *Voyages and Travels*, 1809

Periodicals

Ceylon Almanac, 1833

Asiatick Researches, 1788–1839

Journal of the Asiatic Society of Bengal, 1831–44

Transactions and Journal of the Royal Asiatic Society, 1829–48 and 1876–1907

Transactions of the Bombay Literary Society, 1819–1840

Royal Engineers Journal, 1894

Secondary sources

Abbott, Gerry, *The Traveller's History of Burma*, 1998

Agarwal, C. V., *The Buddhist and Theosophical Movements 1873–2001*, 2001

Allen, Charles, *A Mountain in Tibet*, 1980

Bibliography

Almond, Philip, *The British Discovery of Buddhism*, 1988

Arberry, A. J., *Asiatic Jones*, 1946

Archaeological Survey of India, *Ajanta*, 1996

——*Sarnath*, 1992

——*Rajgir* (undated)

Archer, Mildred, *Natural History Drawings in the India Office Library*, 1962

——*British Drawings in the India Office Library*, 1968

——*Company Drawings in the India Office Library*, 1972

——*India and British Portraiture 1770–1825*, 1979

——*The Marquess Wellesley Collection*, 1983

——*The British as Collectors and Patrons in India 1760–1830*, 1987

Barrett, Tim, *Singular Listlessness; a Short History of Chinese and British Scholars*, 1989

Barua, Dipak, *Buddha Gaya Temple: Its History*, 1981

Batchelor, Stephen, *The Awakening of the West: the Encounter of Buddhism and Western Culture* (1994)

Bayly, Chris, *The Raj: India and the British 1600–1947*, 1990

Bert, Heinz, & Gombrich, Richard (eds), *The World of Buddhism*, 1984

Beckingham, C. F., *A History of the Royal Asiatic Society 1823–1973*, The Royal Asiatic Society: Its History and Treasures, Simmons and Digby, 1979

Bond, George, *The Buddhist Revival in Sri Lanka*, 1992

Boxer, Charles, *The Portuguese Seaborne Empire 1415–1825*, 1969

Buckland, C. E., *Dictionary of Indian Biography*, 1906

Burnham, Lord, *Peterborough Court: the Story of the Daily Telegraph*, 1955

Butler, Iris, *The Eldest Brother: The Marquess Wellesley 1760–1842*, 1973

Cannon, Garland, *Oriental Jones: A Biography of Sir William Jones*, 1964

——*The Letters of Sir William Jones* (ed.), 1970

Collis, Maurice, *The Land of the Great Image: Being Experiences of Friar Manrique in Arakan*, 1945

Cumming, J. (ed.), *Revealing India's Past*, 1934

Dehejia, Vidya, *Indian Art*, 2000

Dawson, C., *The Mongol Mission*, 1955

Desmond, Ray, *The European Discovery of the Indian Flora*, 1992

Dictionary of National Biography

Dodwell, H. (ed.), *The Cambridge History of India*, Vol. V, 1919

Duka, Theodore, *The Life and Writings of Alexander Csoma de Koros*, 1885

Eck, Diana, *Banaras: City of Light*, 1983

Foster, B. and M., *Forbidden Journey: the Life of Alexandra David-Neel*, 1987

Frere, J. H., *The Site of Kapilavastu*, 1925

Gilmour, David, *Curzon*, 1994

Gooneratne, Brendon and Yasmine, *This Inscrutable Englishman: Sir John D'Oyly*, 1999

Hobsbawm, Eric, *On History*, 1997

Head, Raymond, *Catalogue of Paintings, Drawings, Engravings and Busts in the Collection of the Royal Asiatic Society*, 1991

Hudson, Roger (ed.), *The Raj: An Eye-Witness History*, 1999

Hunter, Sir William, *Life of Brian Houghton Hodgson*, 1896

Imam, A., *Sir Alexander Cunningham and the Beginnings of Indian Archaeology*, 1966

Bibliography

Irwin, John, *The Sanchi Torso*, 1972

James, Lawrence, *Raj: the Making and Unmaking of British India*, 2000

Jones, Sir William, *Letters* (ed. G. Cannon), 1972

Keay, John, *When Men and Mountains Meet*, 1977

——*India Discovered*, 1981

——*The Honourable Company: A History of the East India Company*, 1991

——*The Great Arc*, 2000

——*India: A History*, 2000

Kejariwal, Om Prakash, *The Asiatic Society of Bengal and the Discovery of India's Past 1784–1838*, 1988

Klostermaier, Klaus, *Buddhism: A Short Introduction*, 1999

Knappert, Jan, *Indian Mythology*, 1991

Kopf, David, *British Orientalism and the Bengal Renaissance, 1773–1835*, 1969

Kulkarni, V. B., *British Statesmen in India*, 1961

Lawson, Philip, *The East India Company: A History*, 1987

Legge, James, *A Record of Buddhistic Kingdoms*, 1886

Lopez, Donald, *Prisoners of Shangri-La: Tibetan Buddhism and the West*, 1998

——*Curators of the Buddha: the study of Buddhism under Colonialism*, 1995

McCrindle, J. W., *Ancient India*, 1951

Maitriya Project International, *The Maitreya Project*, 1999

Majumdar, R. C., *Classical Accounts of India*, 1960

Majupria, Trilok, *Religious and Useful Plants of Nepal and India*, 1988

Marshall, Peter, *The Impeachment of Warren Hastings*, 1965

Marshall, Peter (ed.), *The British Discovery of Hinduism in the Eighteenth Century*, 1970

Marshall, Peter, and Williams, Glyndyr, T*he Great Map of Mankind: British Perceptions of the World in the Age of Enlightenment*, 1982

Mendis, G., and Mills, L., *Ceylon Under the British*, 1944

Moyle, Martin, and Zasthpir, Lynn, *The Great Education Debate*, 1994

Mitter, Partha, *Much Maligned Monsters*, 1977

Mitra, Swati (ed.), *Walking with the Buddha: Buddhist Pilgrimages in India*, 1999

Mudeford, Peter, *Birds of a Different Plumage: A Study of British–Indian Relations*, 1974

Mukherjee, S. N., *Sir William Jones, a study in Eighteenth-Century British Attitudes to India*, 1968

Nair, P. T., *James Prinsep, Life and Work, Vol I. Background and Benares*, 1999

Narain, V. A., *Jonathan Duncan and Varanasi*, 1959

Peiris, William, *The Western Contribution to Buddhism*, 1989

Porter, Roy, *Enlightenment: Britain and the Creation of the Modern World*, 2000

Powell, G., *The Kandyan Wars*, 1973

Prothero, S., *The White Buddhist: The Asian Odyssey of Henry Steel Olcott*, 1996

Roy, Sourendranath, *The Story of Indian Archaeology*, 1961

Said, Edward, *Orientalism: Western Conceptions of the Orient*, 1978

Saunders, K. T., *The Story of Buddhism*, 1916

Shastri, S. M., *Cunningham's Ancient Geography of India*, 1924

Schwab, Raymond, *The Oriental Renaissance: Europe's Rediscovery of India and the East*, 1984

Sherring, Revd R., *The Sacred City of the Hindus*, 1898

Bibliography

de Smet, Marc, *In the Footsteps of the Buddha*, 2000

Smith, Vincent (ed. Percival Spear), *The Oxford History of India*, 1957

Spear, Percival, *A History of India*, 1983

Stokes, Eric, *The English Utilitarians and India*, 1959

Srivastiva, K. M., *The Discovery of Kapilavastu*, 1986

Thakur, Upenda, *Buddhist cities in Early India*, 1996

Thapar, Romilla, *A History of India*, 1966

Washington, Pete, *Madame Blavatsky's Baboon*, 1997

Welbon, Guy, *The Buddhist Nirvana and its Western Interpreters*, 1968

Wilkinson, Theon, *Two Monsoons*, 1976

Williams, Rushbrook, *Murray's Handbook for Travellers* (21st edn), 1975

Watters, Thomas, *On Yuan Chwang's Travels in India AD 629–645*, 1904

Wright, Brooks, *Interpreter of Buddhism to the West: Sir Thomas Arnold*, 1957

Index

Index

Index

association with, 278; *Journal (JASB)*,
135, 152, 193
Asoka *see* Ashoka Maurya
Astley, Thomas, 34
Atkinson, Dr (of Calcutta Mint), 141,
144–5
Auckland, George Eden, 1st Earl of, 196,
200–1
Aurangabad, 129, 133
Aurangzeb, Mughal Emperor, 2, 58;
mosque, Benares, 144
Ava *see* Burma

Bactria, 23
Bactrian alphabet *see* Kharosthi
Bagnold, Lieutenant John, 125, 127
Bagram, Afghanistan, 4
Baker, Captain Godfrey, 120
Bakhra Pillar *see* Basarh
Bala Bodhisattva, 226
Bala (monk), 286
Bamian: Buddhist colossi destroyed, 2, 4;
Burnes sends report of, 157
Bandya, Amrita Nanda, 107, 173
Banerji, R.D., 282
Banks, Sir Joseph, 14, 19–20
Baragaon, 223
Barlaam, 26, 29
Barlow, Sir George, 89
Basanta Pal, King of Gaur, 94
Basarh, Tirhut District: Bhim Sen's Lat
(Bakhra Pillar), 169–71, 224
Basilides, 25
Batacharji, Ramajai, 18, 87
Batavian Society, 50
Beglar, J.D.M., 230, 236–7, 262
Benares: Wilkins moves to, 56, 58; ceded to
East India Company, 58; described, 58;
burial in, 93–4; James Prinsep's life and
work in, 141–6; Mint, 141, 145; Arnold
visits, 250; *see also* Queen's College
Bentham, Jeremy, 74
Bentinck, Lord William Cavendish, 145,
148, 165–6
Besant, Annie, 249
Bhagavad Gita, 48, 59, 135
Bharhut stupa, 236
Bhatacharya, 287
Bhikna Pahari, Bihar, 260–1
Bhils (people), 129–30
Bhilsa (Vidisha), 124–5, 127–8, 176, 203
Bhimaka, King, 99
Bhimasena-ki-nigali, 262–3
Bhopal, Nawab of, 126

Bhubaneswar, 122
Bhuiladih, 235
Bidari, Basanta, 279
Bihar: conditions, 8–9, 293; Buchanan
surveys, 90–9; Cunningham's
archaeological surveys in, 230–2; *see also*
Gaya
Bimbisara, King of Magahada, 99, 174,
176, 206, 210
Bindusara, King, 1
Bird, Dr James, 135
Birdpur Grant, the, 273–4
Blavatsky, Helena Petrovna, 5, 244–9; *The
Secret Doctrines*, 245
Boddam (Bihar official), 98
Bodh-Gaya, Bihar: Buchanan visits, 21,
91–8; inscriptions, 60, 172, 184;
Wilkins investigates, 60; Mackenzie
visits, 120; Burney finds inscribed slab
at, 157–8; Mahabodhi tower built, 176;
Buddha's awakening at, 198; Fa Hian
visits, 206, 212; Kittoe visits, 212;
Cunningham visits, 221–3, 237, 262;
Hindu destruction at, 222; Burmese
restoration at, 237; Arnold visits, 250–1;
Buddhist-Hindu differences over
Mahabodhi temple, 251–4, 292; pagoda
reconstructed, 251; Temple Act (1949),
292; international visitors to, 293;
proposed bronze statue, 293
Bodhi-charya, 156
Borobudur *see* Chandi Borobudur
Brahma (Hindu god), 84
Brahmins (Brahmans): Megasthenes
encounters, 24; exclusiveness, 25, 47;
Marco Polo praises, 28; Wilkins taught
by, 47–8, 68; and Buddhism, 79, 81–2,
155, 286; *see also* Hinduism
Broadley, A.M., 230–2
Brothers, Richard, 62
Buchanan, Dr Francis: journeys and
surveys in India, 10–11, 16–17, 19–21,
90, 254; background and career, 11–12;
in Burma, 12–16; in Nepal, 17–18,
87–8; as Supervisor of Institution for
Promoting the Natural History of
India, 19; Wellesley praises, 20; and
Buddhism in Ceylon, 79, 82–3, 173;
discoveries in Bihar, 90–9; leaves India,
99–100; collection and papers
appropriated, 100; name change (to
Hamilton) and life in retirement, 100–1;
Upham cites, 138; on Bodh-Gaya
inscription, 172; at Rajagriha, 223;

Index

Index

Index

Index

Index

Index

Index